The Tanner Lectures on Human Values

THE TANNER LECTURES
ON HUMAN VALUES

IV

1983

Kingman Brewster, Thomas C. Schelling, Freeman Dyson
R. C. Lewontin, Alan A. Stone
Leszek Kolakowski

Sterling M. McMurrin, *Editor*

UNIVERSITY OF UTAH PRESS — Salt Lake City
CAMBRIDGE UNIVERSITY PRESS — Cambridge, London, Melbourne, Sydney

CAMBRIDGE UNIVERSITY PRESS
Cambridge, New York, Melbourne, Madrid, Cape Town,
Singapore, São Paulo, Delhi, Tokyo, Mexico City

Cambridge University Press
The Edinburgh Building, Cambridge CB2 8RU, UK

Published in the United States of America by Cambridge University Press, New York

www.cambridge.org
Information on this title: www.cambridge.org/9780521176453

First published by the Tanner Lectures on Human Values 1983
First paperback edition by Cambridge University Press 2011

A catalogue record for this publication is available from the British Library

ISBN 978-0-521-25749-7 Hardback
ISBN 978-0-521-17645-3 Paperback

THE TANNER LECTURES ON HUMAN VALUES

Appointment as a Tanner lecturer is a recognition of uncommon capabilities and outstanding scholarly or leadership achievement in the field of human values. The lecturers may be drawn from philosophy, religion, the humanities and sciences, the creative arts and learned professions, or from leadership in public or private affairs. The lectureships are international and intercultural and transcend ethnic, national, religious, or ideological distinctions.

The purpose of the Tanner Lectures is to advance and reflect upon the scholarly and scientific learning relating to human values and valuation. This purpose embraces the entire range of values pertinent to the human condition, interest, behavior, and aspiration.

The Tanner Lectures were formally founded on July 1, 1978, at Clare Hall, Cambridge University. They were established by the American scholar, industrialist, and philanthropist, Obert Clark Tanner. In creating the lectureships, Professor Tanner said, "I hope these lectures will contribute to the intellectual and moral life of mankind. I see them simply as a search for a better understanding of human behavior and human values. This understanding may be pursued for its own intrinsic worth, but it may also eventually have practical consequences for the quality of personal and social life."

Permanent Tanner lectureships, with lectures given annually, are established at six institutions: Clare Hall, Cambridge University; Harvard University; Brasenose College, Oxford University; Stanford University; the University of Michigan; and the University of Utah. Each year lectureships may be granted to not more than four additional colleges or universities for one year only. The institutions are selected by the Trustees in consultation with an Advisory Commission.

The sponsoring institutions have full autonomy in the appointment of their lecturers. A major purpose of the lecture program is the publication and wide distribution of the Lectures in an annual volume.

The Tanner Lectures on Human Values is a nonprofit corporation administered at the University of Utah under the direction of a self-perpetuating, international Board of Trustees and with the advice and counsel of an   dvisory Commission. The Trustees meet annually to enact policies that will ensure the quality of the lectureships.

The entire lecture program, including the costs of administration, is fully and generously funded in perpetuity by an endowment of the University of Utah by Professor Tanner and Mrs. Grace Adams Tanner.

Obert C. Tanner was born in Farmington, Utah, in 1904. He was educated at the University of Utah, Harvard University, and Stanford University. He has served on the faculty of Stanford University and is presently Emeritus Professor of Philosophy at the University of Utah. He is the founder and chairman of the O. C. Tanner Company, manufacturing jewelers.

STERLING M. MCMURRIN
University of Utah

CONTENTS

The Tanner Lectures on Human Values   v

The Founding Trustees   vii

The Advisory Commission   viii

Preface to Volume IV   xi

Kingman Brewster   The Voluntary Society   1

Thomas C. Schelling   Ethics, Law, and the Exercise
                         of Self-Command   43

Freeman Dyson   Bombs and Poetry   81

   I. Fighting for Freedom with the Technologies
      of Death   84

   II. The Quest for Concept   104

   III. Tragedy and Comedy in Modern Dress   124

R. C. Lewontin   Biological Determinism   147

Alan A. Stone   Psychiatry and Morality   185

Leszek Kolakowski   The Death of Utopia Reconsidered . .   227

The Tanner Lecturers   249

Index of Names   251

PREFACE TO VOLUME IV

Volume IV of the Tanner Lectures on Human Values comprises the lectures delivered during the academic year 1981–82, except for the lecture at Harvard University by Professor Murray Gell-Mann of the California Institute of Technology. Professor Gell-Mann's paper will be published in Volume V with the lectures for the academic year 1982–83.

Permanent annual Tanner lectureships are established at Clare Hall, Cambridge University; Harvard University; Brasenose College, Oxford University; Stanford University; the University of Michigan; and the University of Utah. The policies of the Trustees provide for additional lectures to be given on a one-year-only basis at other universities. In accordance with this arrangement, Tanner Lectures have been given at the Hebrew University of Jerusalem, the Australian National University at Canberra, and the Jawaharlal Nehru University in New Delhi. A lectureship has been established for 1983–84 at the University of Helsinki.

The Voluntary Society

KINGMAN BREWSTER

THE TANNER LECTURES ON HUMAN VALUES

Delivered at
Clare Hall, Cambridge University

October 29 and 30, 1981

KINGMAN BREWSTER took his undergraduate degree at Yale in 1941. After service as a naval aviator during the Second World War, he studied law at Harvard. Following a year in the European Headquarters of the Marshall Plan and a year at the Massachusetts Institute of Technology, he served for ten years on the faculty of the Harvard Law School. He left Harvard to become Provost at Yale in 1960, and became President of Yale in 1963. He resigned as President in the spring of 1977 to become American Ambassador to the Court of St. James's where he served until 1981. He is currently writing a book which develops some of the themes in his Tanner Lectures and is serving as Counsel to the New York law firm of Winthrop, Stimson, Putnam and Roberts.

I

The honor of a Tanner lectureship tempts all the instincts of pretentiousness. It is particularly seductive to one who, in his two most recent tours of servitude, has been expected to masquerade rhetoric as wisdom. Universities are now responsible for the secular liturgy of our societies. The President, or in your case the Vice Chancellor, is clothed in the pomp of high priest. As for an Ambassador, he had better not venture outside his tied residence without a small card in his left pocket inscribed with banalities suitable for laying wreaths, opening exhibitions, or responding to toasts.

Both of my recent professions were highly verbal. But they did not demand the specific gravity of definitive knowledge of any field. They dwelt, rather, in the region which has been called the horse platitudes.

Actually, at the risk of being a traitor to my former callings, I would also note another attribute of both the academic and the diplomatic professions. That is timidity. How perverse. The one clothed in the privileges of academic freedom, the other protected by the insulation of diplomatic immunity. One might think that, thus fortified against normal citizen risks and responsibilities, both professions would be marked by outspoken boldness. Not at all. The timidity of the scholar is best caught by a remark made to me by a friend and colleague when I became Provost of Yale in 1960. He said, "Kingman, you will find that your faculties are divided into two classes. One very large, the other very small indeed. The small minority are productive. The vast majority are, by their own urgent admission, perfectionists."

There is also another dimension to academic timidity, that is specialism. Particularly in American academic life, you do not find the humanist, particularly the historian, even the economist

[3]

or student of society, certainly not the academic jurisprude, venturing in learned print beyond his narrow specialty. He would run the risk of being called a mere publicist. Scholarly publication is dominated by those who can claim to know more than anyone else about some tightly confined corner of the cosmos.

The timidity of the diplomat derives simply from his bureaucratic dependence. He is a staff member far from home. In the very short term, let alone the long run, events may prove him wrong. Even if "in his heart he knows he's right" the authorities back home may disagree, and disagreement may fester into disapproval. His career is at risk. So diplomatic reporting is always couched in the third person. "It is suggested that . . ." "Foreign office officials indicate that . . ." "Some concern has been expressed that unless . . ." Rarely "I believe," never "I am convinced."

So three cheers for Professor Tanner. There is no way one can respond to his charge to talk about "human values" without breaking out of the ruts of disciplinary specialization. There is no way a lecturer who would be true to the mandate of these lectures can avoid affirming his own convictions.

You, Lord Ashby, so admirably vindicated Professor Tanner's hope in your lectures at the University of Utah in 1979,[1] that it is perilous indeed to try to follow in your footsteps. But it is fun to try.

I assume, Mr. President, that it is the lecturer's privilege to give whatever meaning to his ambiguous title he wishes. When I chose "The Voluntary Society" as the banner under which I preferred to march through these lectures I did have something in mind! The purpose of the State should be to permit life to be as voluntary as possible for its citizens.

The voluntary life has many components. Freedom of choice; but also, the right to be committed to a calling or a cause. Free-

---

[1] Eric Ashby, "The Search for an Environmental Ethic," delivered at the University of Utah, April 4, 1979, and published in *The Tanner Lectures on Human Values*, Volume I, 1980.

dom from coercion; but also, the right to be secure in person and property. For almost all it presupposes minimal assurance of health, welfare, and decency. But it also may, in some measure, require risk, or at least freedom from boredom. In most cases it connotes the ability to develop special relationships with family and friends, yet it also means some measure of private autonomy. It is more than welfare. It is more than the protection of law. But it includes and gives high priority to both.

I use the broad and admittedly ambiguous notion of a Voluntary Society in order not to be restricted to a single concept of the voluntary life. I also use it because it suggests to me both the scope and limits of the proper task of the State. I say scope because the State must enhance both the capacities and the opportunities of the citizen. I say limits, because in our countries the State should not make the choice for the citizen about how to use his capacities, how to select among his opportunities.

This sounds obvious to the point of banality to the Anglo-American ear. But that is only because for a long time now you have not, and, from our founding, we Americans have not, looked to the state to provide, let alone impose, life's purpose and direction for the citizen. Both of us have rejected an "Escape from Freedom" to borrow the title of the American edition of Eric Fromm's classic work.[2] To be sure, even in our two countries, despite Karl Popper's warning,[3] the Open Society still has its enemies. But I am assuming with modest confidence that our peoples as a whole will not find the voluntary life in blind conformity to some creed or catechism handed down from above by either secular or religious authority.

This sense that purpose must be individual is a tradition we share. And as one looks around the world at nations large and small who seek, or who in this century have sought, to organize

---

[2] *Escape from Freedom* (New York: Farrar and Rinehart, 1941).

[3] *The Open Society and Its Enemies*, 5th ed., rev. (Princeton: Princeton University Press, 1966).

all of life around some secular or religious God and his dictates, this Anglo-American tradition is, to say the least, "distinctive." We both insist that life can be truly voluntary only if there is a chance to exercise individual choice.

However, for life to be voluntary, as Ralf Dahrendorf has pointed out, "ligatures" are as important to what he calls "Life Chance" as choice is.[4] If there is no commitment to some-one, some group, some community beyond the self, choice alone will not make life voluntary. In the magnificent questions found in the wisdom of the Talmud:

> If I am not for myself
> who shall be for me?
> But, if I am for myself alone,
> what am I?

In our pursuit of a voluntary society it might be said that each of our countries has emphasized the relative importance of choice and of ligatures according to our own history, and also according to our own physical and economic circumstances. We Americans have tended to emphasize mobility, often at the expense of ligatures. You, perhaps, have relied upon ligatures to keep life voluntary, often at the expense of mobility. (You and I will both take satisfaction and relief from the assurance that this minor observation is the first and last one I plan to make about your society.) The balance of these lectures is addressed to a distinctively American problem: how does a society which has relied upon mobility to keep life voluntary react when the promise of mobility begins to fade? (I would leave it to others more intimately experienced to address themselves to the equally interesting query of how a society which has relied upon ligatures to keep life voluntary should react when the ligaments of family, community, craft, and calling begin to lose their ability to bind.)

---

[4] *Life Chances: Approaches to Social and Political Theory* (London: Weidenfeld & Nicolson, 1979).

I intend to talk about the Voluntary Society in purely American terms, although many of my notions occurred to me as a result of the salubrious circumstance of removal to these islands for my happy Ambassadorial years. I became much more aware than I had been of the distinctive, if not unique, characteristics of the American experience, particularly the American approach to achievement of a voluntary society.

The first lecture will elaborate these characteristics. It will also discuss the challenge posed for them by the realities of the present world. The second lecture will suggest some ways by which American society might be kept voluntary in spite of these challenges.

We Americans are a nation of skeptics, even cynics, about established authority. We were born that way. We declared our independence largely on the grounds of the right of Englishmen not to be pushed around by absentee authority. In the former colony of New York we were even on the verge of rejecting the common law because of the discretion it accorded appointed judicial officers, too reminiscent of Crown appointees. We were even tempted by the seeming clarity of the civil law tradition of our French allies. Happily, that temptation did not last long.

The edifice of democratic government in the newly United States was not shaped by prolonged and gradual whittling away at supreme central authority as were those of our British and Continental forbears. We, in our newly won freedom from colonial fealty, were most reluctant, most gingerly in our creation of any central authority at all. The United States Constitution reeks with distrust of government. First it insists that the delegation of power by the states to the federal government is limited, and those powers not expressly given are reserved to the states. There was and is an acceptance of the fact that there are some things the federal government just cannot do, no matter how much public support there may be for them. The United States Constitution is not a *self*-denying ordinance. It embodies a limited grant of power and other powers are denied, not by the central self, but by the several states and ultimately the people. It is woven around a determination to avoid the creation of a new absentee political landlord who might arrogate to himself more powers than intended by those who created him.

This conviction — that power should be absolutely limited, not just made accountable — differentiates our constitution from those of our ancestors, who might well claim that "parliamentary supremacy" is more truly "democratic" than the American model with its constitutional checks on the popular will.

The spirit of distrust inspired not only the dispersal of political power among the several states, but also insisted upon the trifurcation of power among the executive, legislative, and judicial branches of the central government.

Not only to the parliamentary eye but to some American commentators today this separation of powers is a prescription for governmental paralysis. It was, and, with some exceptions, still is. However, it is a price we seem willing to pay for assurance that discretionary power shall not be unleashed and that even an overwhelming majority shall not find it easy to succumb to the tempting convenience of tyranny.

The arbiters of conflicting jurisdictions, state and federal, the monitors of the exercise of power, and the guardians of this requirement that there must be a constitutional basis for both legislative and executive acts are, of course, the federal courts. It is in the political genes of my country to insist that some objective reviewing body, independent of electoral fear or favor, should have the authority to hold both legislature and executive to account by constitutional standards. Some objective locus of power to determine whether the asserted lawmaking or administrative power exists at all and, even if it does, to ask whether it has been exercised according to the processes of law which the Constitution prescribes is central to the American tradition.

The distrust of power implicit in the federal system, explicit in the Bill of Rights, was designed to secure that freedom from coercion in which Friedrich Hayek puts such store in his *Constitution of Liberty*.[5] It is a keystone in the American foundation of a voluntary society.

But a nation's character and outlook on life is only in part a function of its governmental institutions. It is the individual experiences of a people that sometimes matter more. We Americans are a nation of people all of whom (with the exception of the American Indians) have immigrant ancestors. With the exception of the victims of the slave trade, our ancestors were voluntary refugees. The frontier, in turn, was pushed westward by "internal refugees." Escape from oppression, escape from boredom — whatever the negative cause — all were inspired by hope that the fields would be greener in some distant place.

As Oscar Handlin has pointed out in his classic book, *The Uprooted*, peasants from Europe were often miserable, alienated strangers in the ghettos into which they were dumped after a harsh passage.[6] Nevertheless they bore the burden, the moral burden of to some extent having chosen their lot.

There was no expectation that their children would die where they were born and grew up. They were kept alive in spirit by the hope, the plausible hope, that their sons and daughters would do better than they had done.

This hope was made plausible and was in many cases vindicated because of the country's geographical expansion. Even more important was its phenomenal economic growth. Ever-widening prosperity, although punctuated by occasional depressions and panics, meant that each generation outdid their parents. Yesterday's luxuries became today's necessities on the ever-rising tide of affluence.

---

[5] *The Constitution of Liberty* (Chicago: University of Chicago Press, 1960).
[6] *The Uprooted*, 2d ed. (Boston: Atlantic–Little Brown, 1973).

Some were left out because of race. Some regions, like the deep South at the turn of the century, did not share in the spread of industrialization. More recently, once-prosperous areas, like mine in New England, lost their historic economic base of industrial leadership. But migration of labor responded to the call of employment opportunity. "Depressed areas" were deserted as areas of growth beckoned. Mobility, mass mobility, probably had more to do with keeping life voluntary than any other aspect of the American experience. There was for many Americans, even if not for all, a sense of having a second chance, an opportunity for a fresh start, if not for yourself, at least for your children.

This fact, or at least the feeling, of being able to escape inherited, perpetual misery has, I believe, been the most central feature of American life.

Opportunity, of course, is not just a question of freedom of choice. Options depend upon capacities, too. But the higher and higher levels of economic prosperity, coupled with a tradition of compulsory public education in elementary and secondary schools and the spawning of state colleges and universities, did mean that the barriers to the acquisition of skill and talent were steadily lowered from generation to generation. Hayek and Friedman were right in that freedom from official coercion and freedom of market choice did provide a fruitful seedbed for the nurture and harvest of widely dispersed talent and skill, ingenuity and creativity. The resulting level of productivity and prosperity seemed well suited to provide not only a minimal but for many a prosperous life. Riches were thought to be fairly, albeit roughly, distributed in accordance with contribution. Margaret Mead was not excessively chauvinistic when she wrote in her wartime morale-boosting book *And Keep Your Powder Dry* that in America there was a widespread confidence that success was more related to skill and effort than it was to favor or status.[7]

[7] New York: William Morrow, 1942.

Possibly because of our reliance on escape, on mobility, on the fresh start and the second chance we had to invent synthetic "ligatures." Associations without roots abounded: Rotary Clubs, Y.M.C.A.'s, trade and professional associations, fraternal groups, all in the nature of "portable communities." The nation of joiners which de Tocqueville had earlier remarked became a nation of those who were fiercely loyal and sentimental — and happily generous — in the alumni associations tying them to schools and colleges which in later life they might see only through the spirited haze of alumni reunions.

In terms of keeping life voluntary, however, as long as the hope for improvement and the promise of choice were real for enough people, the gains of mobility were worth the loss of roots and ligatures.

Finally, although we cannot expect that personal purpose will be given to us in tablets from a latter-day Moses descending from the clouded mountain top; there is a sense in which life will be less than voluntary unless there is confidence in the ends and means of the society.

I would submit, Mr. President, that if the citizen does not feel that the society or nation of which he is a part has some worthy purpose, he may have all the personal capacity and opportunity he desires, his intimate bonds may be strong, but still life will not be truly voluntary, at least not as voluntary as it might be.

At times in our history Americans have exhibited a national self-confidence bordering on hubris. One need only recall Washington's farewell address, the era of Senator Benton's "Manifest Destiny," and Henry Luce's proclamation of the "American Century."

Almost everything I have said thus far might have been said by an optimistic American traditionalist of the late nineteenth century. At least it is in tune with the sentimental nostalgia which seems to be the current yearning of so many Americans.

What is it, then, that makes us feel instinctively that the validity of this traditional American dream is now challenged by reality? For the balance of this lecture I would like to try to touch on some of the factors which seem to challenge the historic American approaches to the task of keeping society as voluntary as possible.

Let me first state them cryptically and then return to their elaboration.

First there is the evolution of the welfare state into what I have referred to elsewhere as the "entitlement state." This poses seemingly intractable obstacles to keeping government accountable to the rule of law.

Second is the spreading fact and feeling of captivity in large, impersonal institutions, public and private, often directed from some remote headquarters.

Third is the barrier to a fresh start and the second chance erected by the degree of specialization increasingly required by all callings.

Fourth is the limits to growth, the disappearance of the physical frontier, the slow-down of economic growth; also what the late Professor Hirsch had in mind in his final work, *The Social Limits to Growth*.

Fifth is the difficulty of defining success in terms which make ambition worthy.

The responsibility of government, not only in the vast area of national security, but increasingly in the meeting of social needs and its responsibility for the level of economic activity generally, has made the citizen, both corporate and individual, more and more dependent upon public expenditures. I call this the entitlement state, not because it is literally confined to or even dominated by automatic entitlements such as social security, veterans' benefits, Medicare, and agricultural subsidies, but because increasingly there is a widespread sense of dependence upon discretionary federal outlay. Often the disbursement is in the name of national security. The defense budget is so enormous. The specifications for defense procurement are often so detailed and specialized as to defy effective competitive bidding. The political pressure for defense contracts is so important politically under the federal system. The "bail-out" is not limited to Lockheed, or Chrysler, the loan guarantee is not limited to merchant shipbuilding. The contractual allocation of discretionary federal support determines the fate of firms and of entire regions.

It is in the effort to assure minimal human capacity in health, education, and living conditions, however, that the scope of federal spending has burgeoned. Individuals as well as businesses are increasingly dependent upon federal largesse.

This role of government as dominant purchaser, significant lender and guarantor, and in the case of the arts and sciences as grantor, has radically changed the American vision of limited government, limited in its powers and accountable to the rule of law for the exercise of those powers.

Whole regions and states have become crucially dependent for their destiny on whether or not a large contract is lodged in the area. The economic sunburst in the sunbelt was not wholly disassociated from the location of the Space Agency in Texas. The vitality of the West Coast and the revival of New England has not been unrelated to defense contracts to firms appropriately named United Technologies, General Dynamics, and the industries applying the miracles of the microchip and the mini-computer, in areas bearing such names as "Silicon Valley."

The role of federal spending, of course, has changed the relationship between state and federal governments. The independence and self-determination of the states has been significantly eroded by the dependence of their economic prosperity on federal spending. Also the relationship between the executive and the Congress has been altered. In one sense the executive is more dependent than ever upon the Congress; for the power of the purse and the requirement of annual appropriations for an expanded scope and variety of substantive programs has enormously strengthened the hand of the legislature vis à vis the executive.

On the other hand, the power of the executive to decide on a case-by-case basis who will receive the federal bounty has created a degree of political dependence of Congressional delegations upon executive favor which was unknown in simpler times.

Perhaps the most significant aspect of the pervasive dependence of persons, companies, and communities on the allocation of federal funds is the fact that to a very large extent the exercise of this enormous power escapes the rule of law. Only in the case of alleged willful or grossly negligent abuse can the failure to award a contract be questioned. It is even more difficult to question the decision to extend or withhold a subsidized loan. Certainly the failure to award a grant is almost beyond legal scrutiny. This is because of the quaint fiction that receipt of the federal financial support is a privilege, not a right. Broad discretion is accorded to the administrator. The courts will not easily be persuaded to question its exercise. So, in large areas the citizen has become the dependent of the state, and to a very large extent he has no recourse to objective review if he feels poorly dealt with. A. V. Dicey may have been a premature calamity-howler when he viewed with alarm the consequences of the state's assumption of relatively primitive welfare responsibilities at the close of the nineteenth century.[8] If one takes seriously the citizen's non-dependence on his government as an important element in the voluntary society, perhaps Dicey's time has now come.

A second dimension of this relative immunity of the spending power from the rule of law is the ease with which the Congress can make the loans, the subsidies, or the grants contingent upon the recipient's compliance with a variety of conditions. These conditions may have nothing at all to do with the performance of the activity which the government is assisting. The conditional contract or grant, carrying with it the penalty of forfeiture for breach

---

[8] *Law and Public Opinion in England During the Nineteenth Century*, 2d ed. (London: Macmillan, 1962).

of condition, has been the principal instrument for securing federal compliance with various policies concerning the employment of women and minorities. Whatever the substantive merits of the policies involved, it is clear that the leverage afforded by attaching conditions to federal expenditures bypasses accountability to constitutional standards.[9] Covert regulation by way of the conditioned grant or subsidy or loan has subverted the ancient American effort to keep the government from intruding on the voluntary, self-determined life of the citizen, the institution, the locality.

The enormous expansion of government and the spreading sense of dependence upon political favor has been matched, maybe exceeded, by the growth of and the impersonalization of private organizations. As the number of firms producing a product or performing a service diminishes, and what they have to offer is differentiated from their few rivals only by the artistry of the electronic huckster, the fact and the feeling of consumer choice shrivels. Not only is choice narrowed and robbed of its meaning, but personal identification of customers with suppliers — commercial ligatures, if you will — may be lost. The papa–mama neighborhood store closes. The impersonal, computerized, saran-wrapped supermarket in some shopping center without any neighborhood at all takes its place.

By acquisition, merger, or raid or takeover, the bosses' bosses can change overnight. Effective control of policies governing the daily life of an enterprise can be removed to other states or to other countries which have no feeling for the local situation. The concentration of economic power can diminish the sense of identity and the reality of choice which were counted on to make life voluntary.

As centers of economic activity become more concentrated there are fewer doorbells to ring in order to find support for a new idea,

---

[9] See Kingman Brewster, Appendix to Annual Report of the President, Yale University (1975).

a new product, a new way of making an old product. If very large
outlays are needed to cultivate markets as well as to support the
research and engineering needed to turn invention into innovation,
the chance for the individual to "do his thing" will be confined to
the mazes and channels within existing, very large, hyper-organized
financial and corporate institutions. The sense of a fresh start, the
opportunity for a second chance may be less and less an individual
reality, and more and more dependent upon the ability to get on
the escalator of some organized institution whose management
is alert and perceptive enough to indulge the creative and risk
the new.

There are other new barriers to the fact and the feeling of
mobility which have nothing to do with "bigness," public or private. One is inherent in the degree of refined, specialized knowledge and skill which an increasing number of professions and
vocations now require. The fresh start, the second chance is less
realistic even for the most talented and accomplished. At least it
is not easy any longer to change ruts, once you have chosen one.
This is not new, of course. Transferability from medicine to engineering or vice versa was never a realistic prospect. However, I
suspect that the ruts have become narrower as all callings, including medicine and engineering, have become increasingly sub-
specialized.

In sum, the "point of no return" is reached sooner, as one
becomes committed by training to a highly specialized calling or
profession. And the point of "no transfer," even within a profession, is also likely to be reached early on, as you accumulate the
refined specialism of a particular career.

By all odds the most frightening challenge to the American
tradition of voluntary society is posed by the limits to growth. It
is not necessary to buy the model of our shrunken future produced
by the Club of Rome.[10] Nor is it even required that we adopt the

---

[10] Club of Rome, *Limits to Growth* (Washington, D.C.: Potomac Associates,
1972).

somewhat frightening projections of the United States government study entitled *The Year Two Thousand*[11] in order to conclude with some certainty that the phenomenal growth of the first thirty years after the Second War is not likely to be resumed. Or, if it is resumed, it is almost bound to be at the expense of our children's children. It is enough to say that the planet's resources of energy and materials are finite and that population will continue to expand, so that even if full employment without inflation is achieved, constant growth of consumption and production must be slower than it has been since the days of our grandfathers.

Obviously if the kitchen is not producing more and new guests are coming to the table, if they are to be fed the family must hold back. Or put from the outside looking in, those who ate crumbs had better not expect a place at the table if the larder is running low. Competition from immigrants, or in the case of the United States, from traditionally oppressed minorities, becomes a threat. More pervasively, the optimistic notion that riches may replace rags in a single generation carries with it for the first time the inference that rags must replace riches for someone else as a consequence. The pressure for "fair shares" replaces the reliance on infinite competitive opportunity. Conversely, "keeping the upstarts down" replaces the traditional energetic effort to see the American dream fulfilled, even for the most wretched among us. A generous openness becomes cast o'er by a selfish, tight-fisted meanness. Such a society can scarcely be called "voluntary," since eventually it becomes a continuous confrontation between the fearful "have's" and the envious "have-not's."

But even if the limits of material growth are overdrawn, or even if they can be pushed back in time by exploitation of the riches of the sea bed or the energy of the sun, there are, as Professor Hirsch has pointed out, severe social limitations on the "leveling up" promise of material growth.

[11] United States Government (Washington, D.C.: Government Printing Office, 1980).

The nub of Hirsch's message is best left to his own summary statement:

> The themes developed in this book qualify both the priority and the promise of economic growth in two major ways. First, the paradox of affluence — economic growth in advanced countries — carried some elements of built-in frustration: the growth process, when sustained and generalized, fails to deliver its full promise. The growth process runs into social scarcity. Second — the reluctant collectivism — continuation of the growth process itself rests on certain moral preconditions that its own success has jeopardized through its individualistic ethos. Economic growth undermines its social foundations. These then are the dual social limits to growth.[12]

The first point emphasizes the vast difference between material goods and what Hirsch calls "positional goods." Once the minimal material requirements are satisfied, the aspiration for the "positional goods" takes command. They are inherently scarce. Indeed, their value may be lost if they cease to be scarce, like a beach which hordes suddenly have access to, or tokens of community respect which, like prizes, cannot be awarded to all competitors without vitiating their value.

The second point — reluctant collectivism — is the inevitable consequence of the pressure to distribute as fairly as possible the "positional" goods which are inherently scarce. This becomes of vastly more consequence for society when the economic pie is large enough to allow all to live quite well materially. If infinite expansion will not make room for all, the rationing of positional goods must be guided by some process informed by a popularly accepted ethic other than a scramble of competitive self-interest.

This is obviously a dangerous oversimplification of a most comprehensive, perceptive, and analytically brilliant thesis. But I hope it is sufficient to indicate that the traditional American path to a

---

[12] *Social Limits to Growth* (London: Routledge & Kegan Paul, 1977), p. 175.

voluntary society by way of upward mobility may be obstructed by social limits to growth. Not only may the quest for higher and higher levels of satisfaction for all be frustrated, but the ethic of individual self-determination so central to the traditional American way of life may be inadequate.

Finally, it will be recalled that I mentioned in my preliminary summary of the challenges to the American way of achieving a voluntary society, the loss of enchantment with traditional American definitions of success. The quest for material gain and political power certainly have not lost their appeal. But to some extent their lustre has become tarnished. When a democratic polity accountable to a rule of law seemed to square with reality, political power was a worthy and respected goal. When financial success through an expanding free market seemed to reflect an ability to give people more of what they wanted at lower cost, affluence might be envied, but by and large it was more an object of respect than a target of resentment.

As the rule of law seems less able to constrain political favoritism, as the market seems less able to assure that reward correlates with contribution, the dream begins to fade. Most important, the fresh start, the sense of being able to make it on the merits becomes more dubious; at least the chances become more dependent upon someone else's decision and favor than on one's own skill and effort.

When I assumed responsibility for the direction of Yale University in 1963, I was acutely aware of what I then called the "crisis of purpose" of the student generation. That was well before the outbreak of what was later politely called "student unrest" in the late sixties. I suggest that this crisis of purpose has also outlasted that turbulent episode in American campus life. It persists today, despite the "eerie tranquility" which characterizes the surface stability of our campuses.

There is a new vocational seriousness extruded under economic pressure. There is a new patience, perhaps born more of cynicism than of satisfaction. I worry now about a patience without purpose. It promises boredom for the privileged. Among the less privileged purposeless patience can readily fester into resentment, particularly for the frustrated and the envious.

I am haunted by a warning suggested by Rebecca West's characterization of the state of Empire at the time of St. Augustine's birth, although it is so extreme that to apply it to the present American situation is perhaps a gross caricature. She wrote of the mood of the declining empire:

> Man could not use time in the only way it can serve him; he had no chance to devise a drama in which he could play his part and reveal the character of his self. Since he needed that revelation for his own enlightenment, since without it he goes out of the world knowing no more than the beasts of the field of anything beyond his sensations, it was as if life had been cancelled, as if he had unfairly been given over to death while his flesh still promised him preservation from it. The children of the time of his birth "sat in anguished lethargy." [13]

If our children's children are not to be robbed of their sense of purpose, are not to "sit in anguished lethargy," I submit that America must rediscover the path to a voluntary society; for without that promise there is little in the American prospect likely to give us heart.

II

In my first lecture I attempted to describe what I mean by a "voluntary society" and to discuss what I believe to be some of the distinctively American ways of achieving it. I indicated some of the tendencies in contemporary America which challenge these traditional ways of allowing life for most citizens of the United States to be as voluntary as possible.

---

[13] *St. Augustine* (London: T. Nelson, 1938), p. 16.

All of this could, perhaps, be stated in negative terms. How does a society minimize resentments? Most particularly, can America avoid becoming an increasingly resentful society as it faces the realities of pervasive government, ever-larger and increasingly impersonal private business and financial organizations, barriers to mobility imposed by specialization, and both physical and social limits to growth?

I suggest that a society which minimizes resentment, even though it may not be a "good" society in terms of perfect justice or optimum efficiency in the production and allocation of resources, is not an easy objective or an unworthy goal. The state's modest aim, then, should be to minimize justifiable resentments.

By justifiable resentments I would emphasize the distinction between those disappointments, frustrations, and envies which are simply the result of bad luck, attributable to fate and natural circumstance, and those which can be traced to conscious manipulation, or which systematically load the dice, as it were, or rig the outcome.

I do not mean to imply that resentment is justified only when the cause of disappointment or frustration or envy can be traced to some identified person, such as a malevolent public official or exploitative employer, buyer, or seller. The butt of resentment may be "the system." A political system, an economic system, a social system can breed justifiable resentment even though those who control it and benefit from it are not wicked.

Indeed, resentment against "the system" may be enduring, whereas the irritation at being done in by some malevolent wretch in a particular official incident or private transaction is transitory. If the whole system seems unfair, to the bitterness of the immediate hurt is added the feeling of being trapped for all time, even unto your children's children's generation.

Anyone can put up with the occasionally high-handed official. Resentment digs in its heels, however, if you become convinced that all officials can get away with being high-handed. In private transactions, too, hostility may be sparked by an individual outrage, but if crass exploitation is ubiquitous then resentment sours all of life.

I would venture the opinion that the two most fundamental causes of a resentful society are: first, the widespread feeling that the power to push other people around is able to perpetuate itself; and, second, the widespread feeling of being trapped in an inescapable, perpetual disadvantage which is not your own fault. (I would also, at the risk of chauvinistic smugness, suggest that the reason why our two societies are as voluntary as they are is precisely because we have been convincing in our determination to rid power, particularly political power, of its ability to perpetuate itself by abuse; and because of our credible determination to lift the curse of perpetual social and economic disadvantage.)

So, when I ask "can we keep society voluntary?" I could just as well ask can we prevent the attitude of most of its members from becoming resentful? In either case I am concerned primarily with these two provocations to resentment, the same two enemies of a voluntary life: self-perpetuating power and the trap of hopeless, perpetual disadvantage.

I suggested in my first lecture that the American approach to these objectives emphasized, first, the limitations on and accountability of power, and second, a sense of opportunity and mobility, the fresh start and the second chance. Can American society long remain voluntary, or avoid becoming resentful, if the prospects of limits on power and the vision of unlimited individual mobility have lost their promise? What can be done to revive their hope?

First, the reach of government cannot be rolled back if the nation is to avoid the wasteful neglect of its citizens' capacities, whether in terms of their health, their development, or their conditions of life.

It was one of your turn-of-the-century philosophers, Bernard Bosanquet, who made the point that freedom is, after all, a product of capacity times opportunity.[14] In modern society there is no way of assuring physical capacity in the face of the costs of sophisticated health care; nor can intellectual ability be fully developed given the costs of higher levels of education; nor can housing and minimal conditions of life be provided to the poor and the disabled without supplementing what would be provided simply by leaving the task to a wholly free market.

Indeed, if I were to single out one point of emphasis which marks contemporary conservatives from their progressive critics in both our countries, it would be the conservatives' preoccupation with choice and their relative neglect of the capacity side of the freedom equation. Conservatives in their turn were quite properly critical of the New Deal, Fair Deal, New Frontier, and Great Society succession because of the excessive preoccupation of these programs with governmental responsibility for underwriting capacity without sufficient regard for its vulnerability to political abuse on the one hand or its tendency to sap initiative and self-reliance on the other.

For a while it seemed as though right and left in these terms were to find common ground in the substitution of some form of automatic guaranteed income, whether by a "negative income tax" or otherwise, as an alternative to administered welfare. The scope of specific proposals varied widely between Nixon and McGovern. Daniel Patrick Moynihan, then a Nixon staff member, made a strenuous effort to do battle with that latter-day professionalized version of Tammany Hall, the welfare administrators' lobby.[15] The government lost, but they tried.

The American experience in the provision of low- and middle-income housing is instructive. Instead of relying primarily upon public housing, which requires the citizen to be a tenant of the

---

[14] "Life and Philosophy" in *Contemporary British Philosophy*, J. H. Muirhead, ed. (London and New York: Macmillan, 1924), p. 69.

[15] For a chronicle and analysis of this fight, see Moynihan, *The Politics of Guaranteed Income* (New York: Random House, 1973).

state, in the administration of Herbert Hoover the government
turned to the federal guaranty of mortgages. The federal guaranty
permitted lower interest rates. More important, by providing a
secondary market for such guaranteed mortgages, the government
made it possible for the house owner to obtain a term for his
mortgage loan far longer than a bank could otherwise afford to
offer. Of course the government as well as the bank had to be sure
that location, design, and construction made economic sense. These
requirements could be governed by standards of general applica-
bility which defined eligibility of both plans and borrowers. The
government, however, did not know who the individual beneficiaries would be, nor did the citizen have any detailed negotiation
with public officials. It was the bank, not the government guarantor who did the financing and monitored compliance with the
government guarantor's regulations. This device illustrates, if
you will, the possibilities of using the power of government to rig
markets rather than supplant them. Like free markets, govern-
mentally rigged markets can rely upon myriads of private transactions made by thousands of private centers of self-interested
decisions. This is vastly preferable to a monolithic centralized
allocation by officials who have a discretionary power to give or
withhold the federal bounty. The rigged market as the distributor
of public assistance is a healthy buffer between the citizen and his
government.

Given my own background in the university world, it is natural
that I should have been particularly sensitive to the growing need
in the sixties and seventies to tap the resources of the society as a
whole to help meet the mounting costs of higher education and
research. At the same time I was fearful of the burden of red tape
at best, political abuse at worst, if government were given the
power to make discrete decisions about which students or which
universities should receive support. Again, taking a cue from the
Federal Housing Administration, it seemed possible to devise a
scheme which would leave the decision about who goes where,

and which institution receives the subsidy, to private, market-type decisions by students and university admissions officers.

The society could invest in its successor generations without requiring the government to deal directly with either the student or the institution.

If lending institutions — savings banks, savings and loan institutions, insurance companies, for example — could be reimbursed by government, dollar for dollar, for any amount which they had advanced to students toward the cost of their education up to some stated ceiling, then the government would not have to deal directly with the students. The students would be entirely free to spend this advance at the institution of their choice, provided that institution would take them. The whole scheme could be made self-policing and self-liquidating over the life of a generation by requiring the student who received such an advance to accept a small income tax surcharge for his or her earning lifetime. Collection would therefore be done by the Internal Revenue Service, with all the penalties which attach for fraud, nonpayment, or underpayment of taxes generally. (I was pleased to read that Milton Friedman approved, indeed seems to have suggested, such a scheme back in the fifties.)[16]

By all odds the most difficult problem arises in those areas where individual need defies measurement, either because of its urgency, as in the case of those who become ill, or because of its intangibility, as in the case of the creative and performing artist. Without confidence, let alone pride, in my own solutions, I would suggest that ingenuity might produce ways in which health care could be less bureaucratically provided than its direct provision by the state involves, more equitably available than a free market in fee for services permits, and at less cost than third-party payments through insurance of private billings seems to entail.[17] Tax or

[16] *Freedom to Choose* (New York: Avon, 1979), p. 174.

[17] Brewster, "Health at Any Price?" Stevens Lecture, Royal Society of Medicine, London 1979.

other incentives for doctor-managed, pre-paid group practice seem to offer some range of intermediate solution, midway between the government and the free market, which would be vastly preferable to reliance upon either the state or the marketplace to do the job.

Although it represents a small part of the gross national product, the importance to the society of maintaining vitality in the work of succeeding generations in the fine arts, literature, and music seems to me crucial; not so much for the benefit of the artists as for the sake of their beneficiaries: the beholders, the readers, the listeners. Yet here the dead weight of bureaucracy on the one hand or the philistine standards of the marketplace on the other make political choice and consumer choice, to say the least, inadequate to the task of nurturing the creative talents of the oncoming generations. Again, I have no brief for any particular device or arrangement, but there is room for ingenuity along the same lines mentioned in the case of housing, education, and health care.[18] It should be possible to create and support intermediaries who would not be beholden to a bureaucracy whose views they had to consider in deciding whether to show a particular painter, publish a particular poem, or commission a particular piece of music.

The common denominator of all of these examples is the "rigged market" as a far preferable alternative to government abdication of concern for the development of the citizen's capacities on the one hand, or government assumption of direct administrative responsibility for distributing favors on the other.

However, no amount of ingenuity will enable the government to avoid the need to make some noncompetitive, selective awards, particularly in the research-intensive, high-technology fields, whether in biomedical research, nuclear energy development, communications systems, or monster weapons production. As men-

---

[18] Brewster, "Paternalism, Populism, and Patronage," unpublished lecture, Victoria and Albert Museum, 1978.

tioned in my first lecture, on these federal awards the fate of industries, sometimes whole regions, may depend. There will always be the temptation to be influenced by political or personal friendships or antipathies. Whether in the allocation of procurement, public investment, or guaranty of private financing, the government wields a power of economic life and death far more potent than any conceivable administrative regulatory sanction or criminal penalty. Yet unlike the exercise of the police and regulatory power, the exercise of the discretionary spending power is, generally speaking, not subject to judicial review. A society which does not even try to curtail this discretionary power, or at least to make it accountable to objective standards to the extent possible, can no longer pretend that the government's power to affect the citizen is insulated by a rule of law from the temptations to abuse. If I am right, that in large part the voluntary spirit in a society depends upon the citizens' confidence that what happens to them is their own fault, more the result of effort and skill than of status or favor, then it behooves those who support or at least accept the responsibilities of the "entitlement state" to be sure that its entitlements are handed out in such a way that they cannot be used to play favorites.

I am not pessimistic about this. The proliferation of the regulatory state, first under President Wilson, more broadly under the second Roosevelt, did give rise to doctrines and procedures of administrative law. There was a conscious effort to balance the need for administrative discretion to get the job done with the need for judicial review in the name of fairness to those regulated. A comparable effort of legal invention ought to be possible in the area of discretionary spending. The right of redress against abuse should not require the stultification of the contractual or the financing powers of government.

Big government is not the only threat to voluntary life. More and more of the economy is dominated by centers of private economic power which seem immune from accountability either to government or to the marketplace. The closed shop and the captive market both run against the grain of the American tradition of being able to take your custom elsewhere without having to give reasons. If there is no elsewhere, or if the elsewhere's are all identical, the right to choose loses much of its meaning.

In their efforts to assure a dispersion of and limitation upon economic power in the American tradition, the Sherman Act and its progeny are of almost constitutional significance. In many ways they seek to achieve economic pluralism and limits on "economic sovereignty" comparable to the dispersion of and limitation upon power which the Constitution sought to achieve in the political sphere.

The antitrust laws cannot fairly be used to strike down bigness which is merely the evolutionary result of competitive survival.[19] But they could be used to prevent expansion by merger or acquisition which holds no promise of increased efficiency. They could be used to strike down practices which are more restrictive than efficient conduct of business requires. In short, they could call all mergers and all restraints on dealers and suppliers into question, putting the burden of persuasion on the defendant to demonstrate the efficiencies which would be lost if the merger or the practice were banned.

The conglomerate merger, for example, could be made vulnerable unless it could show demonstrable operating joint costs and savings through the combination of seemingly unrelated products or services. It would not outrage my sense of fairness to have a double standard for the large firm with few competitors and the smaller firm with many rivals. The latter might be absolved by a failure to show a purpose to restrain or monopolize. The former, the large or dominant firm, might be held to a higher standard, be required to make a positive effort to exhaust all less restrictive

---

[19] Brewster, "Enforceable Competition; Unruly Reason or Reasonable Rules?" *American Economic Review* (May 1956).

options. It is the difference between "not meaning to" and "meaning not to."

This, it will be argued, is a change in presumption; from the presumption of innocence to the presumption of guilt. Not so. My suggestion simply would say that restraints and acquisitions are presumptively illegal. Public concern is not limited to their economic effect on the degree of competition in the market for the benefit of consumers generally. There is also a social presumption against higher degrees of monopoly power or higher levels of concentration than managerial, technological, and distributional efficiencies require. The dispersion of private power is no less worthy a goal for those who would keep society voluntary than is the dispersion of political power.

Even if such a rigorous deconcentration policy were to be pursued, however, it is still true that economies of scale in many industries would create what might be called politely "centers of economic dependence." Even in such cases it would be better to leave them in private hands in order to avoid the even heavier hand of centralized authority. Rivalry is a dynamic thing, even if the rivals are few. As long as there are plural centers of initiative, at least no one can afford to become set in his ways. Innovation in distribution and service as well as in products and ways of making them will still afford vastly more choice over time than would any centralized monolithic commissariat. If government permission had to be obtained before major capital decisions could be made, even if there were no official abuse, bureaucratic timidity would tend toward a "riskless capitalism," which is a contradiction in terms. However, if "private centers of economic dependence" are to be tolerated, they should have a legal obligation to treat their satellites in a nondiscriminatory way, whether such satellites are dependent distributors or dependent suppliers.[20]

[20] Brewster, "The Corporation and Economic Federalism," in Mason, *The Corporation in Modern Society* (Cambridge: Harvard University Press, 1959).

Furthermore, as in the case of decentralized political power, so the dispersed centers of economic power ought not to be able to erect barriers to the mobility of people. Retirement plans should be transferable; so should contingent or deferred compensation programs. Even if corporate "sovereigns" cannot be deprived of much of their power, the barriers to mobility among them should be kept as low as possible. It is not private profitability of each firm that is the goal. It is the voluntariness of the society as a whole which is the ultimate objective. The feeling of the possibility of escape, of mobility, of a fresh start has its claim which must be weighed against both the public and the private economies of continuity of association and employment.

Finally, without penalizing bigness, it is possible to encourage new entrants to a market. This may urge relief of new or smaller business from the burdens of regulation. It may even warrant special tax incentives for small or new businesses.

Even when the ways of limiting both public and private power are exhausted, however, it will not make life voluntary for those at the bottom of the social or economic heap if they feel that their chance to escape upward is forever frustrated by circumstances about which they can do nothing. It is the narrowing of horizons, the lowering of general expectations which pose the greatest threats to the mobility, the second chance, the fresh start, which have played such an important role in keeping American life voluntary. How do we prevent a society which is bound to be cabined by limits to growth from becoming riddled with resentment among those stuck on its bottom rungs?

If life in the constricted society is to be voluntary, much more emphasis than ever before must be placed on measures to assure that, insofar as possible, even if there is not room at the top for everyone, the paths to the top are open on the basis of merit. Perhaps the best we can hope for is to have those who end up at the bottom feel that "I had my chance, and I muffed it."

Recently, in the United States, equality of opportunity has been clumsily and not very effectively advanced by requiring "affirmative action" by employers to seek out qualified members of "under-represented" groups. Also, progressive taxation, especially progressive estate and inheritance taxation, has somewhat reduced the power of wealth to perpetuate itself from generation to generation. Mandatory regulation and taxation, however, can only deal with the extreme cases. If upward mobility in the constricted society is to be reinvigorated, it will depend far more upon the provision of the chance to develop talent and capacity than it will on "leveling down" by taxation or the prohibition of willful exclusionary practices.

A widespread chance for self-development has long been an important part of the American dream. Jefferson saw it as the only way to assure an "aristocracy of talent." Horace Mann and his followers persuaded the states to require education through the high school. The land grant legislation assumed a federal responsibility to assist the training of farmers in modern agriculture and workers in the mechanic arts. The provision of educational opportunity for all veterans of the Second World War through the so-called G.I. Bill probably did more than any previous measure to make higher education available to substantially all male members and a number of women of my generation. I have already suggested ways in which federal financing could assist all those with the motivation and the talent for it to go on to as high a level as their drive and ability warranted. This could be done without undue burden on them, and without requiring the government to deal directly with either the student or the institution.

If the sense of mobility, with its special emphasis on the fresh start and the second chance, is to be made real in a relatively static society, educational opportunity must not be limited to traditional degree-granting institutions or confined to the early years of life. Correspondence schools, community colleges with their part-time enrollments and after-hours classes have long been major resources for adult self-improvement. And, as in the case of the working-men's college movement in your country, improvement has not been limited to vocational or career-related study. Liberal learning, too, has its place in mid-career education. Already we have borrowed bits and pieces of your experience with the Open University which has been followed with admiring scrutiny by American educators.

Now, suddenly, the communications revolution is upon us. Its potential must be seized to bring within the reach of every family access to audio-visual educational materials at the convenience of the viewer.

The first trouble, of course, is the difficulty of knowing which technology to bet on. The art and the science are moving so fast that if you invest in the cassette, then the disc looks better. Both may be made obsolete by the video recorder. Channels will seem to proliferate as cable television fans out across the land. But no sooner will capital be sunk in the cable spiderweb than direct transmission via satellite will become economically accessible to the average set owner. And computer technology will make it possible to store and retrieve upon instant demand any number of sequences.

We are, at the moment, so bemused and distracted by all kinds of entertainment from video pornography to star wars in the parlor, that it is easy to overlook the immense self-education potential in this communication and computer revolution.

Education is, I fear, inherently paternalistic. It is somewhat officiously missionary. Learning may not have to be compelled, but it does have to be "sold," if all those who would benefit most from it are to be provoked to learn. This does not call for the salesmanship of the huckster. It demands rather the genius of the inspired teacher, the dedication of the devoted headmaster, the vision of the gifted educational administrator.

Government has its role, but it must not smother either invention or innovation, which are far more likely to be fostered by a broad variety of initiatives. Universities and other established institutions of learning have a role, if for no better reason than because their identification with the effort will give self-education the prestige and cachet to whet the status ambition of the potential students. However, universities, particularly their faculties and staffs, are notoriously resistant to academic change. They are quick to be snobbishly scornful of any but the tried and true way of performing the educational task. (Indeed, Lord Perry's technical and pedagogical achievements were nothing compared to his winning a place among the Committee of Vice Chancellors and gaining full accreditation for Open University degrees.)

It is hard to predict where the drive and the breakthrough will come from. The self-education revolution may have to rely more on the tradition of encyclopedia or insurance salesmen than it does on dons and professors. It may be spawned by some middle-level manager in a conglomerate giant who has a sharp eye for the main chance. It may be a byproduct of some new technology which has a higher potential for educational materials than has yet been revealed. Or it may spring first from the training demands of the military or of the giant public and private bureaucracies which cannot afford to see their thousands of employees be undertrained or become vocationally obsolete.

The fashioning of the new techniques for self-education will probably come from a mixture of several or all of these motivations and interests. But the new era of mid-life self-education will come — soon. And with it will come an opportunity for a fresh start, the second chance, the shift sideways to a new path as well as a chance to step up the ladder you are already on.

Organizing mid-life education in this new day may not be the job of a Department of Education. It may not be within the purview of a Public Broadcasting Corporation. But government can make a powerful difference in the acceleration of this new potential for vindicating the tradition of mobility as a primary way of keeping American society voluntary. The important thing is to recognize what the self-education potential of the communications revolution could mean to the voluntary spirit of American life. The significance, the success of such a program of turning the communications revolution to the service of public education without walls is not to be measured by the numbers who enroll or even by their potential achievements. Its availability alone has the supreme value of making it easier to convince people that if they do not pull themselves up by their own bootstraps they have only themselves to blame. It is a powerful antidote to the virus of resentment. Self-blame is not a bad alternative to blame of "the system."

If life is to be voluntary it must have not only freedom from coercion. It requires more than promise of choice. It must not be frustrated by lack of capacity. Even with capacity, a person must have purpose by which choice can be guided. And, at least for most Americans, that purpose cannot be dictated by some all-embracing ideology or theology.

Many of us have found our greatest purpose and satisfaction not in the pursuit of political power or private wealth, but in callings motivated neither by popularity in the marketplace nor by popularity in the polling place. In addition to whatever is meant by the private sector or the public sector, there is a third, not-for-profit, sector. Some would call it the independent sector, but it is really no more independent than many undertakings motivated by profit. Some would call it the voluntary sector, but it has no exclusive claim on the voluntary motivation. Politics and business can be highly voluntary for their participants, particularly their successful participants.

Perhaps self-determination connotes the special quality of those activities which do not aim to please either a political or a commercial constituency. Anyway, I shall call this area the "self-determined sector." Some activities, such as hospitals, may be found in all three sectors: public, proprietary, and charitable. In my country universities, for example, may be equally strong and significant whether they are publicly supported state universities or privately supported independent universities.

For their participants, voluntary organizations and activities may provide more binding ties and loyalties than any group outside the family. Their emotional spur can be fierce. (The tribal loyalties of the alumni of American schools and colleges illustrate the point.) The demands of time and energy and worry exacted by nonprofit institutions may be far greater than is asked by any nine-to-five government or business job. Their satisfactions, too, can be more rewarding than permits measurement in terms of income or political power. They may provide a path to community appreciation and status far more reliable than any public or industrial or commercial or financial, or even elected office. This may be true for the paid hands, the compensated executives and staffs, of not-for-profit institutions. It may be equally true for the volunteers, from the senior trustees of a foundation, school, or hospital to the helper at the county fair, the alumni fund raiser, or the amateur docent who guides visitors through the local art gallery.

Most voluntary organizations arise from a shared sense of community needs. They are, for the most part, intensely local. They provide the special satisfaction of being able to see and touch and feel the impact of what you do. Even if the organization is as complex as a hospital or a university, it still is likely to be a local establishment, small enough so that it does provide a community for its members in which relationships are personal. Not only are they local, but most nonprofit organizations are self-governing. Those who run them may have to be recruited by fraud, duress, or other forms of arm-twisting, whether they are asked to be commodores of yacht clubs or trustees of prestigious medical, artistic, or educational institutions. Nevertheless the trustees and executives are not imposed on the organization by some remote, absentee public or private authority. Most self-determined institutions do not have to submit to the sameness and the conformities which the size and the standards of microprocessed managerial efficiency impose upon the remote outposts of monster organizations. The self-determined sector will, by its inherently local nature, sustain the richness which only variety permits. Such variety will persist as long as the activity, the organization, the institution are reflections of the needs and idiosyncrasies and traditions of local communities, not the fine print of some federal regulation or corporate directive. The "self-determined" sector may, in an otherwise impersonal society, help the citizen to shed his anonymity. It may provide the "ligatures" to compensate for the shrinkage of mobility in modern America.

I suggest that precisely because of the inevitability of bigness and the spreading impersonality in both the governmental and the corporate worlds, the vitality of the self-determined sector is more important than ever, if life is to be voluntary for the citizen. It may be that in the next century it will be in the self-determined sector that freedom from coercion, freedom of choice, and ligatures will be most likely to provide the "life chances" for the majority of citizens, whatever their public or private work-day vocation. There are many reasons to prefer nonprofit institutions for particular functions. But their most important contributions to the society as a whole may be the promise they hold for keeping life in the society as voluntary as possible.

This seems to me an important enough element in any strategy to keep America voluntary to warrant positive public encouragement.

There are people, of course, who feel that all expenditures in the public interest should be channeled through the democratic processes of public revenue allocated by legislative appropriations. Such people are made very unhappy by the ability of the taxpayer, especially a wealthy taxpayer, to support the charitable or educational activity of his choice and thereby reduce his taxable income. Because the size and vitality of the self-determined sector seems to me crucial to the spirit and the morale of American society, for the average person — not just the elite of wealth — there should be an expansion, not a reduction, of opportunity and tax incentives for its private support.

But when all is said, even if it were all done, is not this just tinkering, dealing with a few eddies and currents, when it is a tide that threatens to drown the voluntary life? Do bring, if you can, a rule of law to the exercise of the growing public spending power. Do what you can to bolster the antitrust laws, at least so that the growth of corporate gargantuas is not made easy. Make whatever use you can of the promise of modern communications and computer technology for a new educational spur to upward mobility. Proliferate the opportunities for self-fulfillment in the self-determined, nonprofit sector. Still, where are the successor generations to find their reason for being, a rationale which makes sense of themselves? Where can they find a satisfying, purpose-giving vision of the society of which they are a part? If both social and physical limits to growth rudely belie the vision of ever-widening opportunity upward, driven by acquisitive self-interest, is there another dream to take its place which will keep the society from becoming resentful, which will keep it, in my sense of the word, voluntary?

Are there goals worthy of aspiration which might supplement, although not necessarily replace, the drives for wealth and power? In order to respond to Hirsch's warning about the social limits to growth, they must be goals which can be pursued without the traditional competitive ethic of grab, grab, grab. Or to use his phrase, they must not be dependent upon a competitive struggle for inherently scarce "positional goods."

There are some recent studies, more anecdotal than statistically persuasive, which would indicate that more and more Americans are finding their greatest satisfaction in nonmaterial accomplishments. Daniel Yankelovich's recent book *New Rules* brims over with warm optimism as he follows defectors from the rat-race of the metropolis to the creative or service life in communities small

enough to give life a personal meaning.[21] Another recent book by
Angus Campbell, *The Sense of Well-Being in America*, charts
with a rather broader empirical base a widespread search for satisfactions which cannot be measured in terms of either material
wealth, political power, or conventional status.[22]

I can only offer clues from purely personal experience and
observation. The experience is admittedly atypical, for I have
spent all my life in institutions and callings which were not driven
by either money or political power. That is not to say I was unin-
terested in the paycheck or in popular plaudits. But the principal
satisfactions as a student, as a naval aviator, as a law professor,
and as an academic administrator lay elsewhere. Even if my own
life has been thus sheltered, however, I have had a chance to
observe many friends in public life and many friends in trade.
Although I have known many in both business and government,
I have yet to meet the person who is really unconcerned with the
impact he has on others. Their concern for their impact as persons
on other human beings is something different from their ambition
for power, their acquisitive drive for wealth, or their consciousness
of status.

I have called it the drive for "selfish usefulness." [23] For those
in politics or those in business, a very large part of life's energies
and thought's attention is spent on how to make a constructive
difference in the lives of those they affect. There is, I think, in all
of us a desire to be valued by someone, whether that someone is
another individual, a family, an institution, or a community; the
desire to be someone known and needed, as Oscar Handlin
suggests in his epilogue chapter to the revised edition of *The
Uprooted*.[24]

21 Daniel Yankelovich, *New Rules* (New York: Random House, 1981).

22 Angus Campbell, *The Sense of Well Being in America: Recent Patterns and
Trends* (New York: McGraw-Hill, 1980).

23 Baccalaureate Address, Yale University, 1976.

24 *The Uprooted*, p. 296.

By what standard is this difference, this impact on the lives of others to be judged constructive? Whether your impact is in a small circle, your family, for instance, or whether it is in a larger circle of friends, colleagues, institutions, organizations, or constituencies, the feeling of usefulness depends upon the belief that because of something you did or promoted or prevented you enlarged either the capacity or the opportunity of others.

The scientist, the scholar, the artist are propelled by the hope that by what they discover, by what they reveal, they will add new dimensions to the lives of those who come to understand their thoughts, appreciate their insights, or behold their works.

Teachers, from the most elementary levels to the heights of universities such as this one, obviously build their life satisfaction on the hope that they will contribute to both the capacities and the opportunities of their students.

I could go on with those professions to which people turn for help or to vindicate their hopes. Architects, doctors, even lawyers share the full measure of this satisfaction of selfish usefulness.

Certainly the motivation of selfish usefulness is the engine which drives what I have called the self-determined sector of nonprofit institutions, organizations, and activities.

And despite their sheepish reluctance to admit it, the much-maligned bureaucrats in the public sector, and even the most philistine managers in the private sector, derive their greatest satisfactions from those occasions or events which entitle them to believe that they have so organized the activity of others who work with them or for them that capacities have been developed or opportunities have been seized which they might otherwise never have known.

In my wildest spasms of utopian optimism, I can glimpse a vision of a society which encourages each citizen to develop his own abilities in order to enlarge the capacities or opportunities of others. It would be a sort of chain reaction, where each developed his own potential in order to contribute to the potential of others, and so on until the ripples set moving reached the outer limits of the sea. It would be a kind of breeder reactor which liberated capacity and expanded opportunity all around — not born of righteousness, therefore free of moralizing; but spurred on by the delight of voluntary, selfish usefulness.

At least I would suspect that the goodness of a society has something to do with the extent to which it rewards the instinct for usefulness. If so, then, just as war is too important to leave to the generals, perhaps the economy is too important to leave to the economists. Accomplishment of material welfare may be the largest task of economic organization, but we should also have a concern about giving people the widest possible chance to prove that they have something to offer which other people want. The incentive and the variety of opportunity for material usefulness are at least as important as the promise of efficiency in the allocation of resources. Capitalism is not just an economic system, it is a system of rewards and incentives for usefulness, too, and should be judged as such.

The encouragement of usefulness puts some conventional responsibilities of government in perspective too. It suggests that government's first and foremost responsibility is to deter conduct or arrangements which are designed to limit or to shrink people's capacities and opportunities. Physical harm, neglect, abuse of person or property — the catalogue of criminal coercion or wrongful taking heads the list. Most heinous of all, perhaps, is the systematic exercise of public or private power to hold down or oppress people because of their race, their color, their national origin or their religion or any other class attribute. Even if no gain to the bigot or the oppressor is involved, the willful deprivation of either capacity or opportunity for whole classes or groups of people is the evil most deserving of opprobrium.

On the positive side, development of a capacity for usefulness is an urgent government concern. But care must be taken to go about it in ways which minimize the citizen's dependence upon official favor. All available technology should be mobilized to try to assure that it is never too late to start, that the citizen should feel that he has only himself to blame if he does not stretch to the limit of his potential.

Perhaps more basic than the negative and positive roles of government to the revival of faith in the voluntary life is the proliferation of the self-determined sector of organized nonprofit activity and the redefinition of success in terms of usefulness rather than in terms of material advantage or exclusiveness.

At least such a course for American society would take us out of the deadening calm of "anguished lethargy."

Ethics, Law, and the Exercise of Self-Command

THOMAS C. SCHELLING

THE TANNER LECTURES ON HUMAN VALUES

Delivered at
The University of Michigan

March 19 and 21, 1982

THOMAS C. SCHELLING did his graduate work at Harvard University immediately after World War II and joined the Marshall Plan, first in Europe and then in Washington, D.C. He taught at Yale University for five years, and became Professor of Economics at Harvard in 1958. Most of his work has been in the study of bargaining and conflict, much of it applied to diplomacy, strategy, and arms control. A special interest has been the unintended collective consequences of individually purposive behavior. *The Strategy of Conflict* and *Micromotives and Macrobehavior* reflect these interests. Recently he has turned his attention to the ways people try to control their own behavior, and some of the policy issues in self-management.

A few years ago I saw again, after nearly fifty years, the original *Moby Dick*, an early talkie in black and white. Ahab, in a bunk below deck after his leg is severed by the whale, watches the ship's blacksmith approach with a red-hot iron which, only slightly cooled by momentary immersion in a bucket of water, is to cauterize his stump. As three seamen hold him he pleads not to be burnt, begging in horror as the blacksmith throws back the blanket. And as the iron touches his body he spews out the apple that he has been chewing, in the most awful scream that at age twelve I had ever heard.

Nobody doubts that the sailors who held him did what they had to do, and the blacksmith too. When the story resumes there is no sign that he regrets having been cauterized or bears any grievance toward the men who, rather than defend him against the hot iron, held him at the blacksmith's mercy.

They were not protecting him from an involuntary reflex. And he was not unaware of the medical consequences of an uncauterized wound. Until the iron touched him he knew exactly what was afoot. It was a moment of truth. He was unmistakably all there. He made his petition in clear and understandable language. They had neither personal interest nor legal obligation to subject him to torture. And they disregarded his plea.

When the iron struck he went out of his mind, still able, though, to communicate with perfect fidelity that all he wanted was the pain to stop. While the iron was burning his body we might declare him to have been not fully present, but until that instant it is hard to claim that he didn't understand better than we do what the stakes were.

* * *

Ahab and his wound dramatize a phenomenon that, usually not so terrifying, all of us have observed in others and most have

observed in ourselves. It is behaving as if two selves were alternately in command. A familiar example is someone who cannot
get up when the alarm goes off. More poignant is someone who
cannot commit suicide.

I say only that people act *as if* there were two selves alternately
in command. I'd rather not commit myself on whether there really
are two different selves or cognitive faculties or value centers that
alternate and compete for control. But the ways that people cope,
or try to cope, with loss of command within or over themselves are
much like the ways in which one exercises command over a second
individual. Putting the alarm clock across the room is a familiar
example. The varied behaviors and decisions that can display this
quality range from merely troublesome to deadly serious:

— smoking, drinking, using drugs
— gambling
— scratching
— eating
— beating children while drunk
— procrastinating
— attempting suicide
— exercising
— diving off a high board
— staying awake
— panicking
— having stage fright
— spending on binges
— being sexually aroused

Let me try to be precise about what I have in mind. I shall
state what it is and contrast it with some things that it isn't.

What I have in mind is an act or decision that a person takes
decisively at some particular point in time, about which the person's preferences differ at the time of action from what they were
earlier, when the prospect was contemplated but the decision was

still in the future. If the person could make the final decision about that action at the earlier time, precluding a later change in mind, he would make a different choice from what he knows will be his choice on that later occasion.

Specifically, if I could decide now not to eat dessert at dinner, not to smoke a cigarette with my coffee, not to have a second glass of wine, and not to watch the late movie after I get home, I would make those decisions because *now* I want *not* to do those things *then*. And I know that when the time arrives I shall want to do those things and will do them. I now prefer to frustrate my later preferences.

Finding ways to anticipate those decisions, to make them irreversibly with the preferences of this moment and not leave them to be made differently when other preferences reign, can be difficult or impossible. *Decision theory* is the science of choosing in accordance with one's existing preferences, maximizing the satisfaction of one's values. When the values that govern one's preferences are liable to displacement by values that one deprecates, we need in addition something that we might call *command theory* — the theory of self-command, or self-management.[1]

Let me be clear about what I do not have in mind. People can undergo changes in mood. They like different foods at breakfast and at dinner. There are times when they want to hear music, other times when they want to talk, to be alone, to play with children, to play golf, or to go to bed. One can be a warrior during the day and a romantic at night, or absorbed in a laboratory for days on end and then spend a weekend above timberline. These are not unstable values. Even when someone is described as "a different person" in the evening from what he was during the day, or after a good night's sleep, the different persons are not in a quarrel with each other. If the warrior cannot savor, during the

---

[1] Some of the ways that people cope with themselves, or try to, are explored in Schelling, "The Intimate Contest for Self-Command," *The Public Interest* (Summer 1980), pp. 94–118.

heat of battle, the gentler nocturnal sport that requires a different mood, he can remember it when he needs to, can appreciate it, and can be sure that when the time comes his mood will respond.

The alternate moods do not discredit each other. They do not deny each other's legitimacy. A conscientious adult is able to allocate resources among these alternating activities and to be considerate of one mood while in another. The fact that my interest in dinner is at a nadir after breakfast does not mean that, asked what I want for dinner, I shall give a negligent answer. Just as a parent can allocate benefits among children, one can be one's own manager or referee and maintain a long-run perspective on his own biorhythms, changing moods, and seasonal interests, and not see the alternating moods and interests as contradictions. In economics this is the normal case. Decision theory treats people as able to mediate among points in time.

The contrast between this normal case and the case that I introduced with Ahab is that in deciding this morning what I would choose for this evening, or during summer whether to reserve a ski holiday eight months later, I normally want my preferences at that later time to be controlling. Those later preferences, as best I can anticipate them, are the ones that matter to me now. They may compete with the present, if my budget will cover only a seashore holiday this week or a ski holiday next winter, or if I cannot enjoy Sunday a movie that I already saw Wednesday. But however much those anticipated future preferences about a future action compete for resources with my current preferences about current action, my *current* preferences about that *future* occasion are those future preferences as I foresee them and appreciate them now. There can be competition but there is no conflict.

In this normal case I know that I shall want to watch the movie on television tonight and I make sure there is TV in my hotel room. In the other case I know that I shall want to watch the movie and for that reason I ask for a room without television. (I would even pay extra for a room with the TV disconnected.)

The phenomenon, then, that I want to deal with can be described as alternating preferences, or alternating values that are incompatible or uncompromisable. In the normal case there is a dynamic programming self that looks over wants and desires that continually change, anticipating preferences and attempting to satisfy them. It is as if there were a succession of momentary selves, each with its own wants and desires, all under the supervision of a timeless superself, an overall manager or referee who treats the transient selves evenhandedly.

In the case I want to discuss, that superself, that dynamically programming referee, does not exist. Instead, there is a succession or alternation of impermanent selves, each in command part of the time, each with its own needs and desires during the time it is in command, but having — at least some of them — strong preferences about what is done during the period that another one is in command. One of us, the nicotine addict, wants to smoke when he is in command; the other, concerned about health and longevity, wants not to smoke ever, no matter who is in command, and therefore wants *now* not to smoke *then* when he will want to. In the normal case a person's sexual interests wax and wane and, subject to the difficulty of imagining or remembering the alternate appetites, one tries to accommodate them; the case that concerns me is the person who some of the time wants sexual satisfaction and the rest of the time wants to be a virgin.[2]

* * *

[2] The richest, most varied, and most comprehensive approach to this subject that I have discovered is George Ainslie's "Specious Reward: A Behavioral Theory of Impulsiveness and Impulse Control," *Psychological Bulletin* 82 (July 1975), pp. 463–496, and some later unpublished work of Ainslie's. An intriguing philosophical approach to these issues is Jon Elster's "Ulysses and the Sirens: A Theory of Imperfect Rationality," *Social Science Information* 41 (1977), pp. 469–526, and his book *Ulysses and the Sirens*, mentioned in note 5. In economics there are attempts to accommodate self-management or self-control within traditional consumer theory and, more recently, some efforts to break out of the tradition. A pioneer work was Robert H. Strotz, "Myopia and Inconsistency in Dynamic Utility Maximization," *Review of Economic Studies* (1955–56), pp. 165–80. The best-known effort to fit this subject within the economics tradition is George J. Stigler

I have tried to describe a phenomenon that generates the problem of self-command, or self-management. Self-management is not unilateral. It occurs in a social environment. People are helped or hindered in their self-management by social arrangements. They have friends who offer cigarettes and friends who chide them when they smoke, hostesses who tempt them with chocolate and hostesses who cooperate with an earlier self by serving grapefruit, firms that advertise temptations and fraternities that support abstinence. There are prohibitions, taxes, regulations, and public education that impinge on self-management. Custom and etiquette are involved. Work environments make a difference. Even strangers can help.

The questions I want to call attention to are those of ethics and social policy. If somebody now wants our help later in constraining his later behavior against his own wishes at that later time, how do we decide which side we are on? If we promise now to frustrate him later, and he later releases us from the very promise that we were to honor despite his release, must we — may we — keep our promise against his express wishes? Should we rescue Ahab from his tormentors? Should people be able to surrender to a "fat farm" that legally may keep them, or legally must keep them, until their weight loss reaches the pounds they speci-

and Gary S. Becker, "De Gustibus Non Est Disputandum," *American Economic Review* 67 (March 1977), pp. 76–90; their formulation denies the phenomenon I discuss. On the edge of traditional economics are C. C. von Weizsacker, "Notes on Endogenous Change of Tastes," *Journal of Economic Theory* (December 1971), pp. 345–72, and Roger A. McCain, "Reflections on the Cultivations of Taste," *Journal of Cultural Economics* 3 (June 1979), pp. 30–52. Outside the tradition, and viewing the consumer as complex rather than singular, are Amartya K. Sen, "Rational Fools: A Critique of the Behavioral Foundations of Economic Theory," *Philosophy and Public Affairs* 6 (Summer 1977), pp. 317–45; Gordon C. Winston, "Addiction and Backsliding: A Theory of Compulsive Consumption," *Journal of Economic Behavior and Organization*; and Howard Margolis, *Selfishness, Altruism, and Rationality* (Cambridge University Press, 1982). Winston and Margolis recognize the referee, or superself, that I find lacking; whether the difference is one of perception or of methodology I am not sure. The only genuinely multidisciplinary work of any great scope by an economist that I know of is Tibor Scitovsky's brilliant small book *The Joyless Economy: An Inquiry into Human Satisfaction and Consumer Dissatisfaction* (New York: Oxford University Press, 1976).

fied when they entered captivity? May a majority of the voting population ban dessert in the dining room, or outlaw cigarettes throughout the nation, not to keep others from eating or smoking but to discipline themselves?

In the cases that come quickly to mind, a conscientious bystander has little difficulty deciding which side he is on, between the two rival selves that occur in a friend or stranger. We excuse or discount what is said or done in anger, under stress or the influence of alcohol. We are expected to protect a drunk person from excessively generous as well as destructive impulses, to impede any momentous and irreversible action like giving all his money away, joining the foreign legion, or quitting his job. When begged for a cigarette by someone who we know is trying to quit, or asked for his car keys by someone who is drunk when it's time to go home, we may comply, but not without guilt. And we don't hesitate to be forceful with someone who will be late for work if he doesn't get out of bed.

But not all cases offer an easy choice. People trying to lose weight do not receive universal sympathy. A mother is expected to consider it unhealthy for a daughter to starve herself to be skinny, and she and her daughter may have different definitions of skinny. When the fear of fat takes on the proportions of a phobia, as among anorexic girls who learned to control their food intake by vomiting and are unable now not to vomit, our usual sympathy for abstinence gets a challenge. The dilemma is most poignant in deciding one's obligation when an opportunity presents itself to frustrate an attempt at suicide.

Still, the frequent and familiar cases usually seem to be easy cases, not hard ones. It may be hard to decide how far our obligation extends to someone who asks in advance that we use all necessary force when he has drunk too much to see that he does not become too candid in public about his wife or his employer or his host, or to keep him from driving his own car, or to keep him from drinking any more; but whatever obligation we feel is usually to

that earlier self that asked our help and elicited a promise, the one
to whom we have to explain our own behavior tomorrow when
he's sober, and not the one who tells us to ignore the earlier inhibited sober self that never had the courage to speak out about
his wife or his employer.

What are the familiar cases, and how do we decide them?
How would we explain to ourselves why we just don't credit the
person who refuses to get up in the morning? Why did nobody
rescue Ahab, and why did I think that you would agree that anyone who loved Ahab, or even a conscientious stranger, should have
held him down?

*   *   *

In some cases the person just doesn't seem to be all there. He
is his usual self with something subtracted. The person who prefers not to get out of bed is thought to be not fully alert; his
engine hasn't warmed up; he cannot remember or visualize the
consequences of staying in bed or assess their importance. We
may even believe that there are chemical inhibitors of brain activity
that play a role in sleep, and until they have been washed or
metabolized away his brain is not working. It is not a different
he, just an incomplete one. The same may be thought of the person overtaken by fatigue or drowsiness, the person under sedation,
and some of the people — the quieter ones — whose brains are
awash with alcohol.

Then we have contrary cases, the people who are not only "all
there" but too much. They are overstimulated or exhilarated.
There are drugs that will do it, but so will success. So will relief —
from anxiety or fear or suspense. In contrast to the drowsy, these
people need restraint, not arousal. They can suffer a transient self-
lessness and generosity, not withdrawal but hyperactivity. If the
half-awake person can be described as somebody whose preference
map is not fully illuminated, the overstimulated person is like one
whose preference map, though illuminated everywhere, is too

brightly lit in some places. The contrast has the same effect as partial darkness.

A third case is passion, or infatuation. We have the expression "marry in haste and repent at leisure," and some that convey the same thing more bluntly. But I include anger, patriotism, religious fervor, revenge, disgust, and all of those transient overwhelming moods that elevate certain values to absolute domination. Proposing marriage, joining the foreign legion, placing large wagers in support of one's opinion, abandoning one's family, and tearing up one's will are among the things that may be done in haste and repented at leisure.

Next is capture, or captivation. It is being glued to TV, absorbed in a novel, caught in a mathematical puzzle, engrossed in a symphony, or absorbed in frustration trying to fix a recalcitrant piece of equipment. This may be where to include fantasy; some of us are as readily captivated by daydreams as by that late movie or unfinished novel. A simple interruption will sometimes rescue the captive; other times he can still hear the siren song and may be as sneaky as an addict in getting back to that puzzle, story, or daydream.

My next set consists of phobias, panic, and extreme terror. The person who cannot dive off the high board or make the parachute jump, who cannot face an audience without an urge to flee, who suffers vertigo or claustrophobia, cannot make himself pick up a spider or put a kitten to death. I saw a movie in which a Scottish fisherman had his thumb caught in a giant clamshell. The tide was rising. With his knife he severed his thumb. I've wondered whether I'd have drowned before I could remove mine. The friendlier illustration is a child's loose tooth; tying the tooth by a string to a doorknob and slamming the door was the solution when I was a boy, and it illustrates how short the interval may be between the preference that the tooth be yanked and the succeeding preference that it not be.

Some of these are easy cases. But I mean easy to decide, not easy to cope with. If we've come across someone sitting in the winter woods freezing to death, drowsy and feeling no cold, and he refuses to jump to get warm, getting him to do it may be impossible; but deciding whether to obey his command to leave him alone should not be hard.

Some of these cases I no longer find easy. But there are at least some easy cases in every category I mentioned, and I tried to describe them with sufficiently prejudiced language to make you think of some easy cases. I have two more categories. The first is appetite. By that I mean food, drink, tobacco, and any substance that a person can eat or sniff or inject or rub on his skin that generates an addiction or habituation. (I could include here addictive activities, like gambling or golf or the morning newspaper; but they may be more at home in my earlier category of capture than here with nicotine and chocolate.) What keeps these appetites from being easy cases is that not everybody is more likeable sober than drunk. Some of the addictive narcotics may be harmful only because they are disapproved of and prohibited. And some attempts to quit cigarettes may be so doomed to failure, or to periodic relapse, that surrender is preferable to a fruitless pursuit of victory.

One more category is perseverance. Its obverse is procrastination, quitting. People who set themselves regimes of daily exercise, piano practice, or periodontal care often fall by the wayside. Joggers do not enjoy universal sympathy. Some good intentions abort for plain lack of serious dedication; and people who could bind themselves to a program might in the end find it a bore and regret it. I see all around me, and inside me, the occupational disease of procrastination. Many of us have to burden ourselves with deadlines or short-term goals to get anything written. Social controls play a role; the *Times Literary Supplement* for January 22, 1982, contained a splendid example, a review article by George Steiner on the life and work of the Hungarian radical Georg Lukacs. "When I first called on him, in the winter of 1957–8, in a house still pockmarked with shellbursts and grenade splinters, I stood speechless before the armada of his printed works, as it crowded the bookshelves. Lukacs seized on my puerile wonder and blazed out of his chair in a motion at once vulnerable and amused: 'You want to know how one gets work done? It's easy. House arrest, Steiner, house arrest!' "

*   *   *

Let me reexamine a few of these characterizations. The person who won't get up in the morning I said was not quite all there. Why does that count against him? Apparently because he cannot fully appreciate what it will be like to be late to work. But does the self who sets the alarm fully appreciate the discomfort of getting out of bed? My answer is yes. But notice: I am not in bed. I don't expect that to change your mind, but in more difficult cases I find it important to remind myself that when I think about these issues I am not impartial. I write only when I am awake, and the self that might prefer bed goes unrepresented.

In another respect we are not impartial. We have our own stakes in the way people behave. For my comfort and convenience I prefer that people act civilized, drive carefully and not lose their tempers when I am around or beat their wives and children. I like them to get their work done. Now that I don't smoke, I prefer people near me not to. As long as we have laws against drug abuse it would be easier all around if people didn't get hooked on something that makes them break the law. In the language of economics, these behaviors generate externalities and make us interested parties. Even if I believe that some poor inhibited creature's true self emerges only when he is drunk enough to admit that he despises his wife and children and gets satisfaction out of scaring them to death, I have my own reasons for cooperating with that repressed and inhibited self that petitions me to keep him sober if I can, to restrain him if he's drunk, or to keep his wife and children safely away from him.

And what about Ahab? When I first thought of mentioning him I thought him a dramatic illustration of an easy case. If I were Ahab, I thought, I would thank you afterwards for holding me down. But now I wonder what that proves.

If you hurt somebody so that I may live, my thanking you doesn't prove that you did right. If I say that in Ahab's condition I would like to be cauterized, you will notice that I say it with a fearlessness that makes my decision suspect. It is hard to find a way to call my bluff. I'm not about to be burned. If I were, I'd behave like Ahab, and you would not credit me with now having a full appreciation of where my interest lay.

Suppose I were to be burned and Ahab in the next room were to be burned also. Would you, while disregarding my personal plea, ask my advice concerning what to do about Ahab?

After you burn me and I recover and thank you, you give me the bad news: the other leg is infected and must be burned the same way to save my life, perhaps after a delay. Do I withdraw my thanks, in fear you'll think I want it done again? Does the delay matter?

How do we know whether an hour of extreme pain is more than life is worth? The conclusion that I reach tentatively is that we do not. At least, I do not. The question entails the kind of undecidability that many economists attribute to the interpersonal comparison of utilities. Most economists believe we have no way of testing, or even defining, what we mean by whether one person gets greater joy or utility or satisfaction out of a meal or a holiday or a warm room than another person, or out of spending some amount of money, and whether my enjoying something at your expense, my pleasure and your pain, can be added algebraically. That means that if you must cauterize Ahab's leg to keep me from dying there is no way to determine whether the little two-person society consisting of Ahab and me enjoys a net gain in utility when you spare him the pain and let me die.

The conclusion I come to is that I can no more decide this for myself, if it is I being burned and I dying, than I can decide for two other people.

Does it make it easier or harder if I imagine Ahab to be old, with only a few years of life to save at the cost of an hour's torture? You may well ask how, if I have just alleged that a judgment is impossible, it can then be easier or harder. What I have done is slip into the position that many economists take after acknowledging the impossibility in principle of that interpersonal comparison. It is to acknowledge that as a practical matter we do make decisions. We do not hesitate interminably over whether to favor some extra income for a poor person at the expense of a wealthy person, or whether to give our concert ticket to an enthusiast or to someone who merely likes music. Because we have to, we make such decisions.

So I must conclude that these decisions are not based on utility comparisons. What are they based on? In Ahab's case I think mine is taking sides. Which side am I on? Facing no pain I seem to be on the side of the Ahab that wants to live. I do not think I know how to make the effort really to decide whether his life is worth the pain. When I try, I find myself succumbing to the pain, and to keep my resolve for Ahab's sake I abandon the effort at comparison.

*   *   *

This ambivalence makes a difference in welfare economics, social choice, and political philosophy. In economics there is a well-explored field of individual rational choice. There has also been an interesting field of social choice, in which the singular behavior of a rational individual is compared with a collective decision. We got used to the fact that in a collectivity there is no unanimous preference; we discovered that majority decision will not reliably point to a collective preference. And with continued work (of which Kenneth Arrow's is most widely cited) we have become convinced (some of us) that it is futile to model collective decision on the analogy of a single individual. I suggest that the ordinary human being is sometimes also not a *single* rational individual. Some of us, for some decisions, are more like a small collectivity than like the textbook consumer. Conflict occurs not only when two distinct human beings choose together but also within a single one; and individuals may not make decisions in accordance with the postulates of rationality, if by individuals we mean live people.

If we accept the idea of two selves of which usually only one is in charge at a time, or two value systems that are alternate rather than subject to simultaneous and integrated scrutiny, "rational decision" has to be replaced with something like collective choice. Two or more selves that alternately occupy the same individual, that have different goals and tastes, even if each self has some positive regard for the other (or one feels positively and the other does not reciprocate), have to be construed as engaged not in joint optimization but in a strategic game. There is no agreed weighting system for taking the alternate preferences simultaneously into account. And even the possibility of bargains and compromises is limited, if not precluded, by the absence of any internal mediator. It is hard for the different selves to negotiate if they cannot be simultaneously present. (Not impossible, perhaps, but hard.)[3]

So we should not expect a person's choices on those matters that give rise to alternating values to display the qualities typically imputed to rational decision, like transitivity, irrelevance of "ir-

---

[3] It is proposed by Jon Elster that typically one of the "selves" engages in forward planning and strategic behavior, making arrangements to constrain the other self's options, while the alternate self is preoccupied, when in command, only with the current episode. (He proposes that this asymmetry in strategic attitude is a basis for choosing the authentic self.) In the perhaps rarer cases of reciprocal strategic behavior, each party might engage an attorney to represent that self, empowering the attorneys to reach and enforce a mutually advantageous bargain. While this possibility has no legal standing, and, if it did, enforcement of the bargain might still not be manageable, it affords a conceptual possibility of negotiation between two selves that never simultaneously exist.

relevant" alternatives, and short-run stability over time. We should expect the kinds of parliamentary strategies that go with small-group voting behavior and the second-best choices that have to be made when rights and contracts are not enforceable. Depriving oneself of certain preferred opportunities — suppressing certain states that economists call "Pareto superior" — because the other self would abuse the opportunity becomes an expected tactic:

— not keeping liquor (food, cigarettes) in the house
— not keeping television in the house
— not keeping sleeping pills in the house
— not keeping a gun in the house
— not keeping the car keys in the house
— not keeping a telephone in the house
— not keeping the children in the house

Dramatic cases of a *latent* rather than a *regular* alternate self are the anticipation of a self that will emerge under torture, truth serum, or extreme privation. Less dramatic are anticipated somnambulism and talking in one's sleep, scratching or removing dressings while asleep, and social affairs at which one is likely to lose his temper. Other familiar instances are choosing a restaurant where desserts or liquor are not served or luncheon partners who do not drink, doing embarrassing business by telephone to avoid loss of poise, and leaving money at home to avoid a shopping binge.

There is even a possibility that within a single human body a nervous system and brain and body chemistry can alternately produce different "individuals," no one of which is uniquely *the* person or self. In science fiction a human body can be an arena in which several extraterrestrials play out their careers. When several aliens come to inhabit an Earthling's body, one of them may sleep during daytime and another nighttime, one may have access only to certain memories or sensory systems, and they may compete to extend their spans of control over the Earthling body.

Is there anything like this among human beings? Maybe. Surgically, an individual is changed into "another individual" through frontal lobotomy. Lobotomy is irreversible as it has been practiced; but in principle one can imagine an irreversible removal (lobectomy) and a reversible lobotomy. With the latter, a person alternates between the self whose lobe is deactivated and the one whose lobe is functioning. The changes are described as dramatic enough to constitute a new personality. (The judicial system has had to decide, for purposes such as marriage annulment, whether it is the same person afterward.) Castration was an equivalently potent way of changing hormonally the value system of male human beings. It, too, is irreversible; but if we imagine castration accomplished chemically rather than surgically, it might be reversible.

Possibly the human being is not best modelled as a unique individual but as several alternates according to the contemporary body chemistry. Tuning in and tuning out perceptual and cognitive and affective characteristics is like choosing which "individual" will occupy this body and nervous system. When pressed I insist only that people can usefully, for some purposes, be viewed *as if* they were two or more alternative rival selves, but the more I reflect on it the more I wonder whether there is any reason for excluding the literal possibility.

*   *   *

The law does not like to distinguish these different selves, or to differentiate an authentic self from impostors. In America I cannot go to a fat farm, a non-smoking resort, or an exercise camp and legally bind the management to hold me when I ask to get out. The management cannot claim that it has contracted with the authentic "me" to make me stay even if my impostor self, the one that I went to the farm or camp to guard against, claims that "I" now want to get out. I can contract that they get no fee unless they succeed in keeping me; but the authentic "I" cannot sue them afterwards for improper release if they let me go when the wrong "I" insists on leaving. And they cannot protect their investment by impeding my departure when that other self gets control and says he is leaving and to get out of his way.

The law does not permit me to write a will that I cannot change, nor promise a gift and be held to my promise. If I think I am potentially dangerous, to myself or to others, the law does not permit me to commit myself voluntarily to the custody or guardianship of an institution that may hold me captive. I have to demonstrate that I am so dangerous, to myself or to somebody else, that I qualify for involuntary commitment. Dr. Jekyll can ask to be locked up for his own good, but when Mr. Hyde says "let me out" they have to let him out.

There are ways of getting around the law, but they do not involve straightforward recognition of a person's right to bind himself against himself. If I think it would be good for me to change my habits and location, to be kept away from people and places I know, to learn discipline, I can enlist in the Army. My enlistment is a contract in which the other party has an interest that can be legally protected against my defection. Legally the Army is not conspiring with my authentic self to frustrate the other self when it wants to go AWOL.

But if I cannot prevent my impostor self from asserting his (my) rights when it is his turn to be in charge, cannot lock him up against his will or make it a legal offense to sell him liquor, can I nevertheless deny him legally certain faculties that he might exploit when he is in charge? Can I claim that he was impetuous when he made that gift, and I'd like it returned; that he enlisted in a fit of patriotism after seeing an inspiring movie, or as a heroic gesture after being turned down by the woman he loved? Can I claim that he married under the influence of passion or liquor or a biorhythmical euphoria, and the marriage vow should be void? Can I arrange with my bank not to honor his check if he fails to pass a diagnostic test that determines whether he is the authentic

I or that impostor? The answer seems to be, not easily. Indeed, only very exceptionally. And usually only by claiming and demonstrating some recognized mode of mental incompetence. If I can be proved mentally impaired as I made a bequest the bequest can be invalidated and you have to give it back; but if I was simply out of my mind with joy, and suffering one of my occasional fits of impulsive generosity, I cannot claim that it wasn't "I" and that the gift wasn't "his" to give.

There are statutory ways of guarding against certain actions that might be taken by one's wayward self. But the ways that I know of merely constitute denial of legal sanction for actions that might be taken impetuously or under duress. The political process itself guards against impetuous decisions by requiring two readings of a bill, time intervals between announcement of intent and consummation of some activity, public notice, and other dilatory procedures. The chief mechanism seems to be mandatory delay, or the requirement that certain things, like marriage licenses, be issued only during daytime hours. Mainly they can guard against decisions taken by an impetuous self that gains control long enough to do the business but not long enough to outlast the delay.

The law can try to help one self guard against the other by protecting private efforts of "third" parties to cooperate with one of them. Surgeons may be privileged to tranquilize the patient who, if his head were clear, would in mid-surgery overrule the surgeon's decision. That, of course, is taking sides. The law may protect me in restraining you from some impetuous or violent act against yourself, an act that your other self would ultimately deplore. The law may protect me if I restrain you from rushing into the burning building to recover your negotiable securities, the family dog, or one of your children, especially if I unquestionably did it believing it to be for your own good, and more especially if it is judged indeed to have been to your benefit. But I probably cannot get away with kidnapping you to keep you from smoking or from getting tattooed, or to keep you a virgin, although your later recovery will probably protect me from your taking civil action. Recapturing you from a religious cult and washing out your brain is still in undecided legal status. The most serious cases are those that involve, one way or another, actively or passively, taking your own life — one of your selves taking the one life that you share.

Helping you die is not allowed. Attempts at suicide surely must often involve divided selves. The lesser acts that people seem incapable of making themselves perform, including those that involve a palpable phobia, suggest that taking one's own life except in the most painful or utterly hopeless situations or where it constitutes a desperate act of heroism, is bound to be internally controversial. Two selves alternate in hoping for death or life. The law takes sides. In effect and in explicit intent, the law sides with the self that will not die. Someone who lives in perpetual terror of his own suicidal tendencies can welcome the law's sanctions against people who might be importuned to help with the suicide. People for whom life has become unbearable but who cannot summon the resolve to end it have the law against them in their efforts to recruit accomplices. The self that wants to live, if there is one, has the law on its side.

*   *   *

There is a paradox. Full freedom entails the freedom to bind oneself, to incur obligation, to reduce one's range of choice. Specifically, this is freedom of contract; and it works through expectations. The behavior of others depends on what they expect of me; by restricting my own freedom of choice I gain influence over the choices of others. The results can be called "cooperation," "immunity," "bargaining power," or even "coercion." A textbook on the legal attributes of corporations emphasizes not only the right to sue but the right to be sued. The *promise* is an instrument of great power, but only if it is believed that one has to keep the promise (or make restitution).[4] The law recognizes this principle as long as the promise — the commitment, the obligation, the impairment of one's own freedom of choice — has a reciprocal quality and is *to* somebody else. The promise requires an addressee. One may not contract with himself.

This is a stunning principle of social organization and legal philosophy. One cannot make a legally binding promise to oneself. Or perhaps we should say that the second party can always release the first from a promise; and if I can promise myself never to smoke a cigarette I can legally release myself from that promise whenever I choose to smoke. It comes to the same thing.

Charles Fried provided me with the name for what has no standing at law — the *vow*. The vow has standing if directed to a deity and is enforced by whatever authority the deity exercises. And the vow as an expression of intent can receive social and institutional support if it is recognized by an established church. Religious and fraternal orders differ from the common law in providing moral support, even coercive support, for vows like abstinence, celibacy, penury, and dedication to prayer, good works, and even heroism. But the vow has no standing at law.

People nevertheless seek to make binding decisions through physical constraints and informal social arrangements. People ingest chemical antagonists against alcohol to induce nausea upon drinking. If people cannot lock the refrigerator they can wire their jaws shut. Devices can be implanted in people that will emit a signal to tell on them if they drink, or immobilize them if they

---

4 "In order that I be as free as possible, that my will have the greatest possible range consistent with the similar will of others, it is necessary that there be a way in which I may commit myself. It is necessary that I be able to make non-optional a course of conduct that would otherwise be optional for me. By doing this I can facilitate the projects of others, because I can make it possible for those others to count on my future conduct, and thus those others can pursue more intricate, more far-reaching projects. If it is my purpose, my will that others be able to count on me in the pursuit of their endeavor, it is essential that I be able to deliver myself into their hands more firmly than where they simply predict my future course." Charles Fried, *Contract as Promise* (Cambridge: Harvard University Press, 1981), p. 13.

do. Castration and lobotomy have been mentioned as surgical techniques for permanently changing motives and incentives, and there are tranquilizers and negative aphrodisiacs to keep certain fears and passions in check. I have mentioned tying the tooth to the doorknob; one can ask a friend to pull the string instead. People avoid cues and precursors, the sights and smells that subvert their abstinent intentions; people dare not eat the first peanut, start an argument, begin the novel they can't afford to take the time to read, or turn on the TV because it is harder to turn off than merely not to turn on. The friend who will pull the string attached to the tooth, or extract a splinter, can also monitor calories and police cigarettes, or even push a person out of the airplane to help launch a skydiving hobby. But one can sometimes arrange a coercive environment, like offices in which smoking is not allowed or a job in an explosives factory, or make bets that are informally enforceable about weight control or cigarettes; and there are buddy systems, like Alcoholics Anonymous, whose moral support can be enlisted. We could invent some unconcealable testimony to one's dedication — dyed hair, or a tattooed forehead, imploring bartenders not to serve drinks and waiters not to serve desserts.

But nothing like contract law is available. I am not endorsing the idea that the law should be available to enforce unilateral vows. But there is little speculation about how the law might help and what the dangers and abuses might be.[5]

Actually, there is no a priori basis for confidence that enforceable contract is a generally good thing. People might just get themselves tied up with all kinds of regrettable contracts, and the custodians of legal wisdom might have decided that enforceable contract is a mischief. Suppose promises to second parties tended usually to get people into trouble, so that a wise legal tradition

---

[5] There is stimulating discussion throughout Jon Elster, *Ulysses and the Sirens* (New York: Cambridge University Press, 1979). I am indebted to his work and to his comments on this lecture. Most of the legal discussion I have found deals with mental illness and informed consent. See the reference to Rebecca Dresser's work in note 6.

would readily excuse people from promises incurred in haste, or in passion, or in disgust. Duress is recognized; if impetuosity were a problem, legally binding contracts might require something like a second or third reading before acquiring status. It is an empirical question whether the freedom to enter contract, the freedom to make enforceable promises, or the freedom to emancipate oneself from a nicotine habit would prove generally to be a good thing. But the social utility of recognizing the vow, the unilateral promise, through social or legal innovation is not much discussed. It may therefore be worthwhile to imagine what form such legal innovation might take.

A possibility is that the state become an enforcer of commitments that people would voluntarily incur and submit to authority. How would the state enforce my commitment to give up smoking, reading the comics at breakfast, or terrorizing my children? A possibility is that I grant the state a perpetual search warrant: the authorities may enter my home or search my person at any time without warning or court order, confiscating anything they find that is authorized in my original disposition to be confiscated. Another would be to allow denunciation: any observer, or anybody on a list that I authorize, could have me locked up or examined or searched, even punished — I having relinquished rights of cross-examination or immunity. House arrest might be voluntarily incurred; I can be locked up, kept in my home that has been purified of television, alcohol, tobacco, or inventories of food. I can be incarcerated and denied things I want or required to perform what I want to be required to perform — physical exercise, rapid reading, or writing this lecture. There could be a parole system: I oblige myself to report daily and be examined for weight, nicotine, heroin, or bloody cuticles. Curfews, and placing gambling casinos or bars off-limits to me, might be enforced by circulating my picture. I could be obliged to pay forfeit when caught in violation of my vow, giving up money or privileges or freedom; this would be like designing criminal law specifically for those who sign up to be subject to it. I could have license plates that do not permit me to drive at night, or that authorize any policeman to stop me and check for alcohol without regard to the First or Fifth Amendments. Or I might legally submit to a guardian; this would be like power of attorney, but would give somebody authority to have me subdued, to command that I not be served, to sequester me without my consent, or to control my bank account and my car keys.

The state might enforce contracts that I entered into for purposes of self-restraint. I make a bet that I will not smoke. A bet is equivalent to a penalty on my smoking. I can already make a somewhat enforceable bet if I bring a friend into it, but if he or she is a real friend, what I commit is respect rather than money, and if he or she is not a real friend and the amount of money is large, I probably do not have to pay because the bet is not enforceable. (Surrendering the money to a third party could help.) Still, the social coercion of bets among friends, especially small groups of more than two, in losing weight or giving up cigarettes is impressive. Insurance contracts might help: that medical insurance should be cheaper for people who do not smoke, because they make fewer claims on their medical insurance, is an idea that has some appeal even though it may not have much logic. (Smoking may kill people less expensively than most ways of dying.) But as an incentive people might be allowed to enter insurance contracts that imposed heavy penalties on proven relapses from declarations of abstinence, if there were unambiguous tests like body weight or cigarette stains that would permit a person to incur a high price for delinquency.

There has recently been some attention to the liability of bartenders for serving drinks to people who were already drunk and subsequently suffered accidents or violence. (There have been societies in which recognizable ethnic or racial types were ineligible for service of some kind.) We can imagine a category of voluntary outlaws, people who have irreversibly chosen never again to

be served liquor, the law cooperating by making it a misdemeanor
to serve such a person in a public place or even in private, there
being some form of identification to establish liability. There
might even be "citizen's arrest" of anyone caught smoking or
drinking in public who had voluntarily enrolled among those for
whom it is forbidden to smoke or drink.

An innovation might permit people to make contracts from
the terms of which they could not release the second party. We
contract that you may and must expel me from the airplane if I
am unable to make myself jump, when I have signed up for parachute instruction. Or you may keep me in a cell until I sober up,
lose weight, or go thirty days without smoking. When I scream
to be released there must be some provision for inspection to see
what it is that I am screaming about; but when it becomes clear
that I am screaming only for cigarettes or heroin, or complaining
that they don't feed me enough, the authorities will certify that the
contract is merely being enforced and that my screams needn't be
attended to any further.[6]

A difficulty with enforcing my vows is that there needs to
be somebody with an interest in enforcing the rule on me. If you
finance my business and I promise to return your investment, there
is no need for the state to take any initiative; you take the initiative if I don't come through. But when I vow to do twenty push-
ups before breakfast, even if there are techniques by which to

---

[6] There is one proposal for a legally binding act of "self-paternalism" that has
received attention, most recently in an exhaustive analysis by Rebecca S. Dresser,
"Ulysses and the Psychiatrists: A Legal and Policy Analysis of the Voluntary Commitment Contract," *Harvard Civil Rights–Civil Liberties Law Review* 16 (1982),
pp. 777–854. This is letting a patient give a psychiatrist authority to have the
patient committed for treatment to an institution during an episode in which the
psychiatrist prescribes such treatment and the patient refuses. In some ways this
proposal is the epitome of our subject. It does, however, represent an extreme
method, incarceration. All kinds of constitutional rights are impinged on, from the
right to travel to the proscription of involuntary servitude. And it abuts the issue of
involuntary commitment, which has a long civil-rights history. The careful analysis
cited above demonstrates that concern for the merits of the case is only part of the
matter; what might appear best for the rights and welfare of such patients could
conflict with constitutional principles of much wider scope.

establish whether or not I comply, there is no one to bother unless we make it in somebody's interest to spy on me and denounce me to the authorities. We might offer rewards to people who catch me overweight and bring me in for weighing; that means assimilating the self-directed promise to criminal rather than civil law, which I think is a strike against it.

*   *   *

When I contemplate the aloofness of the law and the needs that so many of us have for help, including legal help, in binding ourselves for our own good (as we can bind ourselves in contractual exchange), I see a gap in our legal institutions. The law has grasped the paradox that freedom should include the freedom to enter into enforceable contracts; it seems to overlook the need that people often have, and perhaps the right that they should have, to constrain their own behavior for their own good. And this could mean, as I have mentioned, either submitting oneself to a personal "criminal law" with rewards for private enforcement, or entering into contracts entailing reciprocal obligations from which one could not release the second party. But having identified an important legal right that seems to be missing, I have to ask myself whether I really think it would be a wise society that permitted me to make irrevocable decisions, or decisions that I could revoke only at a high and deterrent cost. Do I really wish that there were some magical way that I could put certain acts forever beyond reach? Do I really wish that I could swear out a warrant for my own arrest in the event I violate some pledge, offering a large reward and complete immunity for anyone who apprehends me?

It is ultimately an empirical question whether even the right to enter a contract is a good one. If people were continually entering contracts shortsightedly we might want to protect them by requiring every contract to be ratified three times with prescribed time intervals between, to avoid contracts entered in haste. We have laws that deny minors the right to borrow money. We forbid indentured labor. People may not assign their earnings. Involuntary servitude may not constitutionally be voluntarily incurred. One cannot offer a pound of flesh as collateral, even if there is no other security to offer and one is desperate for a loan. But except for some constitutional and paternalistic safeguards, enforceable contract is popular because it has proved itself. Would the legal power of unilateral determinism, of eliminating options, of entering an enforceable vow, prove to be a blessing or a curse?

I do not know, but we can identify some dangers. One is that the wrong self gets the jump and legally protects its power to beat up the kids, keep liquor in the office, get fat or get skinny — I forget which is the "wrong one" here — or never to go jogging again. It is one thing to ask the law to recognize an individual's right to become legally forbidden or legally obligated to engage in certain acts or to live a certain way; it is something quite different for the law to select the authentic or legitimate or socially approved self and deny Mr. Hyde the right to oblige Dr. Jekyll to keep some of that stuff around that he drinks to become Mr. Hyde, or deny him the right to move away to where Mr. Hyde will have no place to play or people to play with when it is his turn to emerge.

Then there is changing your mind. I have arranged to pay a forfeit if I am observed smoking, and my informer draws a reward from that forfeit. I later discover that I am terminally ill and may as well smoke; or harmless tobacco is developed; or new research discovers that not everybody is susceptible to the hazards of tobacco, and specifically that I am not, and I'd like to enjoy smoking again. Can we design procedures for backing out of a commitment that was skillfully designed to make it impossible to back out?

Then there will be unforeseen emergencies in which people who were never to lay eyes on their children again need to see them, people who wanted their licenses revoked need to drive, or people who wanted to be confined need to be released. Procedures that cannot be abused to undo the virtues of the original commitment would have to be devised.

I have heard expressions of concern that struggle builds character and the merchandising of "instant self-control" will weaken the human spirit. I acknowledge the possibility but cannot help comparing the argument to a similar argument we used to hear against taking the pain out of childbirth.

We would want to avoid frivolous commitments — showing off, momentary demonstrations, excursions into martyrdom while under some kind of infatuation. (I conjecture that the tattoo has been popular among youngsters precisely because it is indelible; it is a permanent mutilation; it is an act of daring, precisely because it admits no change of mind and shares if ever so slightly the finality of suicide, loss of virginity, or enlistment in the foreign legion.)

As both law and medicine deprecate suicide, they both deprecate castration of children. Sterilization is allowed for adults, but I understand that psychiatrists are not at ease about sterilization that may be undertaken for convenience by people who haven't the maturity to appreciate how they may react at a later age. Children under the age of contract can probably be dismissed from these problems; but there is a slightly desperate quality to this whole subject which suggests that this legal opportunity would be of least interest to the people who could best claim sanity, adulthood, maturity, responsibility, and emotional stability.

The objection that appeals to me most strongly is that people may be coerced into "voluntary" self-denial, self-restriction, even self-removal. A Los Angeles judge offered probation to a welfare mother convicted of fraud on condition she let herself be sterilized, thereby saving herself six months' incarceration; he was giving her a free option only if — which was doubtful — six months was the sentence he would have given her had her childbearing not been at issue. Employers, parole boards, judges and probation officers, even school admissions officers and spouses, not to mention various

moral minorities in the electorate, may demand assurances of both
good behavior and good intentions as conditions for what they
can offer, once those assurances are publicly available. Certain
rights, like early retirement (even early death), can come to carry
some implied obligation. (Imagine an option, perhaps upon
application for marriage license, legally to forswear forever one's
right to a divorce. Who could believe it was voluntary?) The
"vow" itself, in its more traditional meaning as a profession of
faith, was sometimes coerced by the vilest means. (Religious
minorities have at least one advantage when the majority religion is
one that a person must be born into — no coercive proselytising.)[7]

Coercion shows up in two ways, the one I just mentioned and
the direct act of enforcement. If the government itself is responsible for enforcing the sanctions one has voluntarily incurred, in
the manner of criminal law, there is both unpleasantness and an
enlargement of that domain of government, the manipulation or
harassment of individuals, that many of us like least. Enforcement
by a private party, in the manner of civil law, would probably be
felt to involve a noticeably lesser governmental role in the coercive
enforcement. If damages only, not actual performance, could be
claimed, the arrangements might be less effective but less threatening to society. Finally, there is the question whether the government should void or deny or prohibit privately available means of
binding ourselves. Thomas Nagel has remarked that few governments any longer make it easy to enter into a permanently indis-
soluble marriage. Governments might regulate measures that

---

[7] Voluntary submission to polygraph testing is a perfect example. "In addition
to its uses in prisons, the military, police work, FBI and CIA investigations, and
pretrial examinations both for the prosecution and for the defense, the polygraph
has also found its way into corporate America, where it is widely used for detecting
white collar crime and for screening potential employees. This year, it is estimated,
half a million to a million Americans, for one reason or another, will take a lie
detector test." Alfred Meyer, "Do Lie Detectors Lie?" *Science 82* (June 1982),
p. 24. Refusal to submit "voluntarily," like pleading the Fifth Amendment or declining to make financial disclosure, is construed as an admission of having something to hide.

operate directly on the brain. The implantation, requiring the services of a surgeon, of devices that monitor behavior could be discouraged by several means. I tend to feel that the dangers in allowing long-term renunciations of freedom are least when they do not depend on the government for enforcement; that leaves open whether government should deny the freedom to impair freedom where enforcement of contract by the government is not involved.

I do not conclude that the dangers are so overwhelming that we should continue to deny any legitimacy to the demand for legal status for these unilateral self-commitments. But I also do not conclude that we should discover a new disadvantaged minority, those that need help in self-defense against themselves, and acknowledge their right to enlist the law in their behalf. I conclude instead that there are probably innovations along the lines I have suggested, and that with care there might be some tentative exploration, with adequate safeguards and the expectation that it may be years or generations before we converge on a reasonable legal philosophy. The law is still groping for how to cope with rights to life and rights to death, rights of children and rights of the unborn, rights of separated parents, rights of the emotionally unstable or the mentally retarded, and the proper legal sanctions on drugs, adultery, contraceptive advice to minors, and the entrapment of drunken drivers. There should be no easy solution to this one.

I have spoken of the *legal* status of vows, but the issue could be more broadly formulated as one of social *policy*. The method could be legislative as well as judicial. Bartenders have been found liable for serving drinks to people who had already drunk too much and went on to get themselves destroyed by automobile. The liability could be established by legislation as well as by judicial interpretation. There have been and are societies in which particular kinds of individuals may not be served alcohol; what would be new is the provision for voluntarily putting oneself, perhaps with some indelible mark like a tattoo on one's forehead, in the statutorily recognized category of persons who may not be served.

*　　*　　*

The law aside, there are difficult discriminations in determining the authenticity of a request for help in somebody's dying.

If your moral convictions never permit you to help someone die, or even to let someone die in the belief that that is what he wants, no authentication is necessary, no request being admissible no matter how authentic. But if you wish to credit a request to be allowed to die, or a request to be helped to die, authenticating the source of the request — which self it is that is in command and controls the decision to make the request — is certainly important and probably difficult.

It is hard to imagine there being no question of authenticity. Death is so complete, so final, so irreversible, that a self that controls the decision may be unable to command the action. Inability to produce one's own death does not seem to be reliable evidence that one "really" prefers to live, any more than inability to cut one's own thumb out of its socket testifies to one's preferring to drown. Even asking for help may be subject to inhibition, and only a transient surge of determination could galvanize it. And while the self that is created by that transient surge may be the one that deserves recognition, it is not the only self involved.

We are dealing with an even more unambiguously "divided self" when the requests vacillate. To plead in the night for the termination of an unbearable existence and to express relief at midday that one's gloomy night broodings were not taken seriously, to explain away the nighttime self in hopes of discrediting it, and then to plead again for termination the next night creates an awesome dilemma.

How do we tell the authentic self? Maybe the nighttime self is in physical or mental agony and the daytime self has a short memory. Maybe the daytime self lives in terror of death and is condemned to perpetuate its terror by frantically staying alive, suppressing both memory and anticipation of the more tangible horrors of the night. Or perhaps the nighttime self is overreacting to nocturnal gloom and depressed metabolism, trapped in a nightmare that it does not realize ends at dawn.

The search for a test of the authentic self may define the problem wrong. Both selves can be authentic. Like Siamese twins that live or die together but do not share pain, one pleads for life and the other for death — contradictory but inseparable pleas. If one of the twins sleeps when the other is awake, they are like the two selves that alternate between night and day.

That both selves are authentic does not eliminate the issue. We must still decide which request to grant. But if both selves deserve recognition, the issue is *distributive*, not one of *identification*. We can do cost-benefit analysis and try to maximize their joint utility. But it is *we* and not *they* who are concerned with joint utility. The need for commensurable utility, for adding the desires of the one and the desires of the other, is like the need, under the authenticity formulation, for assessing the probabilities and the severities of the two errors: wrongly crediting the plea to die and wrongly crediting the plea to live. If the nighttime self is authentic we commit error in heeding the daytime self; but also vice versa. In the absence of certainty about which self is authentic, we have something like the distributive issue of dealing fairly with two selves that have opposite needs.[8]

---

[8] In discussion I find that responses to a hypothetical ambivalence about wanting to live and wanting to die are sensitive to the way the alternative preferences are described. If the choices are presented as symmetrical — a strong desire for life expressed at one time and a strong desire for death at another — people, while recognizing a grave conflict, elect to credit or defer to the voice in favor of life. But descriptions of actual patients who display the ambivalence often lend themselves to an alternative, nonsymmetrical formulation: there is a preference for *death*, and there is a horror of *dying*. Death is the permanent state; dying is the act, the transition — the awesome, terrifying, gruesome, and possibly painful event. Presented this way, the choice can be compared to Ahab's. Ahab can enjoy permanent relief — minus a leg, to be sure — only by undergoing a brief and horrifying event, as the

What about a promise made with certainty about the currently authentic self — authentic at the time the promise is made — to disregard the alternate self that may make an appearance? I ask you to promise to let me die, if necessary to help me, even to make me die, in certain gruesome and degrading circumstances that I specify in detail. Your promise is to disregard any countermand. No matter how much I plead to be left living you are to honor your obligation. And I urge you to contemplate, if tempted to heed the countermand, that it may be the voice of a terrified self that is incapable even of letting its terror be terminated.

The worst happens, and I plead persuasively. I claim that the self that demanded my execution couldn't know what I know now.

The same dilemmas can arise for pain rather than death. But the miraculous progress of anesthesia in our society makes Ahab's predicament uncommon, while the miraculous progress in medical life support is increasing the concern with dying.

If I can get relief from chronic pain only through an interval of acute pain and I cannot be sufficiently anesthetized to keep me from screaming for relief and pleading that the surgery be discontinued, there arises the ethical question. Do you let me change my mind when I discover how painful the ordeal really is that I committed myself to before I could ever know what it felt like to be in such pain? Or do you take note on my behalf that pain is short and life is long — or that pain will be past and life will be ahead — and not bother even to measure my pain's intensity?

Dying, killing, and suicide are unlike pain, confinement, disablement, and even torture, which, however horrendous, have a finiteness that death lacks in our culture. Imagine a patient allergic

---

permanent relief of death can be obtained only by undergoing a brief and horrifying event. Of course, the person whose momentary preferences are dominated by the terror of dying may not be able to cooperate in making this discrimination for us. Indeed he or she may misrepresent (even to himself or herself) the terms of the choice, just as people who face a frightening trip to doctor or dentist may misrepresent their symptoms. In somewhat the same way, the novice parachutist might be described as badly wanting *to have jumped* while frightened of *jumping*.

to anesthesia solemnly signing a request before witnesses that the operation about to be embarked on proceed irrespective of the patient's vehemently expressed later wishes that the pain and the operation stop. I expect the surgical team to abide by the request, secure in the belief that no punitive action could be taken against them until the operation had been completed and the pain had subsided, by which time the patient's original self, the one that signed the request, would again be gratefully in charge. I can even more easily imagine the surgeon's assuring the patient that the operation requires confining his head so that no request could be voiced, and confining his head, whether it were necessary for the surgery or not. (The rule might be: anesthetize the tongue if you cannot anesthetize where it hurts.)

Our thinking on this may be affected by the observation that, at our ages, examples of unbearable pain are usually episodes, like surgery or cauterization. When instead protracted intervals of pain are the lifetime price one pays for mobility or even for just living, doctors have to cope with patients who occasionally can't take it any more and who ask in desperation that the source of the pain, life itself, be removed.

We probably wouldn't hesitate to deny the request if it were a child. (It may be easier to cope with adults, especially elderly adults, the more childlike they become when at the mercy of a physician.) I don't know whether that is because we assume that the child's current self has a poor appreciation of the future, and other successive selves may be grateful that the younger self was not allowed to make that decision before they came on the scene. How many later selves have to endorse that early decision before we count a quorum and let those who have now spoken have their way at last?

Pain is often the obverse of dying. Dying is just the back side of the coin, when removing the source of the pain means removing life from the body. There is no later grateful self to express satisfaction if the doctor withholds relief, and no self able to thank him if he complies.

*   *   *

For centuries people were terrified by Hell, a condition worse than life itself, one that awaited after death, an inescapable sequel to which self-destruction made one especially susceptible. Death was no escape. But the audience for these remarks probably believes that death is the end of pain, an exit, not the entrance to an eternity of horror. And whatever the morality of suicide, it is probably not thought by many in my audience to be punishable by eternal damnation.

But the medical ability to keep people alive, to keep them alive irrespective of their wishes or despite them, and the legal obligation or ethical compulsion to do so — the obstinate unwillingness to recognize a right to death as well as a right to life — may have recreated Hell. While science and enlightenment were emancipating us from Hell after death, medical technology has recreated Hell as an end-stage disease. And our social institutions have made it a fate not easy to escape.

But expressing a wish to die or to live, when circumstances are tragic enough to make the choice genuine, is subject to multifarious dimensions of authenticity. The preferences themselves may not be voiced. Just as a person may be incapable of the initiative to commit so awesome an act, a person may be incapable of speaking about it. If the decision requires moral support or intellectual guidance, if one needs advice or at least an opportunity to discuss it, there is no way to discuss it without engaging another person; and the other person will be an interested party, perhaps himself unable to identify or to authenticate an expressed preference. Anyone intimate enough to be asked for help, even in arriving at a decision, is likely to have a selfish interest in the outcome, one that may conflict with his interest in identifying the authentic wish of the person whose death is at issue.

If I am the unhappy patient I may prefer to live but wish to die to stop being a burden to you. I may not want to burden you with guilt if I choose death, or to suggest that I think you resent my living. I may not be able to ask you to help me die to relieve you of the burden of me. And if I wrongly think you will benefit from my death, how can you persuade me my belief is wrong.

If you genuinely believe I prefer death, how can you be sure your own preferences are not mingled in your judgment of what is best for me, or of what I think is best for me? How can you avoid being suspected, even by legal authorities, of excessive zeal in helping me to relieve you of me? May the legal availability of a right to invite death acquire the character of an obligation? How can you keep your willingness to help me reach a decision to die from being, or appearing to be, an effort to persuade me? And how do several interested parties — kin and medical attendants — participate in the decision when they are themselves in dispute about the death and about responsibility for it?[9]

There is no graver issue for the coming century than how to recognize and authenticate the preferences of people for whom dying has become the issue that dominates their lives. This is the ultimate dilemma of authenticating the self, of discovering the legitimate sovereignty of the individual.

---

[9] I have written more on this in "Strategic Relationships in Dying," in Ernan McMullin, ed., *Death and Decision* (Boulder, Colo.: Westview Press, 1978).

Bombs and Poetry

FREEMAN DYSON

The Tanner Lectures on Human Values

Delivered at
Brasenose College, Oxford University

May 5, 12, and 19, 1982

FREEMAN DYSON was born in England and educated at the universities of Cambridge and Birmingham. During World War II he worked as a civilian scientist at the headquarters of the Royal Air Force Bomber Command. After the war he went to Cornell University and became Professor of Physics there. Since 1953 he has been Professor at the Institute for Advanced Study in Princeton. His professional work has been mostly on technical problems of mathematical physics, but he has written a number of articles on broader issues for a wider public. His autobiography, *Disturbing the Universe*, was published in 1979. He is now writing a book on war and weapons which will be an expanded version of these Tanner Lectures.

INTRODUCTION

I chose the title "Bombs and Poetry" for this series of lectures, because I want to discuss the gravest problem now facing mankind, the problem of nuclear weapons, from a literary rather than a technical point of view. Poetry means more than versification. It means the whole range of human reactions to war and weapons as expressed in literature. The main theme of the lectures will be the interconnectedness of the bombs and the poetry. I will be exploring the historical and cultural context out of which nuclear weapons arose, and at the same time looking for practical ways of dealing with the problem of nuclear weapons in the future. My hope is that an understanding of the cultural context may actually help us to find practical solutions. Basic to my approach is a belief that human cultural patterns are more durable than either the technology of weapons or the political arrangements in which weapons have become embedded.

The three lectures are independent of each other. You may come to any one or two of them without feeling obliged to come to the others. The first lecture, "Fighting for Freedom with the Technologies of Death," is a historical account of our involvement with weapons since 1914, giving special attention to the tactical nuclear weapons which now constitute the most immediate threat to our survival. The second lecture, "The Quest for Concept," examines various alternative doctrines or policies which have grown up around nuclear weapons, and tries to define a doctrine which may offer us some long-range hope of escape from the trap into which reliance on nuclear weapons has brought us. The third lecture, "Tragedy and Comedy in Modern Dress," places the problem of nuclear weapons into a wider context, as the contemporary manifestation of a human predicament which is as old as the Iliad

[83]

and the Odyssey, *the doom of Achilles and the survival of Odysseus. Each of the three lectures is arranged like an old-fashioned sermon, with historical examples at the beginning and a moral at the end.*

*   *   *

I. FIGHTING FOR FREEDOM WITH THE TECHNOLOGIES OF DEATH

The title of today's talk is borrowed from a recent book written by Steve Heims and published by the M.I.T. Press, *John Von Neumann and Norbert Wiener: From Mathematics to the Technologies of Life and Death.* I will be talking about warfare and technology from a historical point of view. I shall be trying to answer two questions. Why has war always been so damnably attractive? And what can be done about it?

In the impressions of World War I which I absorbed as a child, technology was a malevolent monster broken loose from human control. This view of technology was then widespread, not only among poets and literary intellectuals but also among scientists. The most memorable description of the war which I read as a scientifically-inclined teenager came from the biologist J. B. S. Haldane:

> A glimpse of a forgotten battle of 1915. It has a curious suggestion of a rather bad cinema film. Through a blur of dust and fumes there appear, quite suddenly, great black and yellow masses of smoke which seem to be tearing up the surface of the earth and disintegrating the works of man with an almost visible hatred. These form the chief parts of the picture, but somewhere in the middle distance one can see a few irrelevant-looking human figures, and soon there are fewer. It is hard to believe that these are the protagonists in the battle. One would rather choose those huge substantive oily black masses which are so much more conspicuous, and suppose that the men are in reality their servants, and playing an inglorious, subordinate and fatal part in the combat. It is possible, after all, that this view is correct.

Haldane published this vignette in 1924 in a little book with the title *Daedalus, or Science and the Future*, which I found in the school science library at Winchester. It sold well and was widely read in scientific circles. Haldane had been an outstandingly brave and conscientious soldier. His friends in the trenches had given him the nickname Bombo because of his attachment to a noisy experimental trench-mortar which he liked to carry around in the front lines and blast off unexpectedly from time to time. His cold and clinical view of the battles of 1915 extended also to the future: "The prospect of the next world-war has at least this satisfactory element. In the late war the most rabid nationalists were to be found well behind the front line. In the next war no-one will be behind the front line. It will be brought home to all concerned that war is a very dirty business."

The soldiers of all nationalities carried home from World War I memories of pain, death, and physical squalor. The lasting image of war was men sharing a mud-filled ditch with corpse-fed rats. The degradation of the living left in men's minds a deeper revulsion than the sacrifice of the dead. During the years leading up to the outbreak of World War II, when my school-friends and I looked ahead to the future, we were not sure whether being killed would be worse than surviving. Wilfred Owen's poem "Mental Cases," in which Owen is describing survivors of the battles of 1917, gave us a picture of what might await us if we were unlucky enough to survive:

> Who are these? Why sit they here in twilight?
> — These are men whose minds the Dead have ravished.
> Memory fingers in their hair of murders,
> Multitudinous murders they once witnessed.
> Wading sloughs of flesh these helpless wander,
> Treading blood from lungs that had loved laughter.
> Always they must see these things and hear them,
> Batter of guns and shatter of flying muscles,
> Carnage incomparable, and human squander,
> Rucked too thick for these men's extrication.

Most of us did, unexpectedly, survive. And then, only a few years later, the invention and use of nuclear weapons carried the technology of death a giant step further. The nuclear bombs with their mushroom clouds make Haldane's vision of war, the black explosions attended by doomed and puny human servants, look even more plausible. How could this have happened? How could supposedly sane people, with the stink of the trenches still fresh in their memory, bring themselves to create a new technology of death a thousand times more powerful than the guns of World War I? To answer these questions, I look again at the career of Robert Oppenheimer. Oppenheimer is a good example to illustrate how it happens that people get hooked on weaponry. A rich new source of historical facts has recently become available, throwing a fresh light on Oppenheimer and on the mental climate out of which nuclear weapons grew.

The new source is the volume of *Letters and Recollections* of Robert Oppenheimer edited by Alice Smith and Charles Weiner.* It gives us a far more authentic and many-sided picture of Oppenheimer's personality than we had before. In January 1981 I met Robert's brother Frank at a meeting in Toronto and thanked him for allowing Smith and Weiner to publish Robert's letters to him, which are in many ways the best and the most revealing in the whole collection. "Yes," said Frank. "At one time I had thought of publishing his letters to me in a separate book. But it is much better to have the five or six characters Robert showed to his various friends all together in one place."

In 1932, when Robert was twenty-seven and Frank was nineteen, Robert wrote a letter to Frank on the subject of discipline. "But because I believe that the reward of discipline is greater than its immediate objective, I would not have you think that discipline without objective is possible: in its nature discipline involves the subjection of the soul to some perhaps minor end; and that end

* Cambridge: Harvard University Press, 1980.

must be real, if the discipline is not to be factitious. Therefore,"
he concluded, "I think that all things which evoke discipline:
study, and our duties to men and to the commonwealth, war, and
personal hardship, and even the need for subsistence, ought to be
greeted by us with profound gratitude; for only through them can
we attain to the least detachment; and only so can we know
peace." I have pulled these sentences out of their context. It is
true, as Frank said, that Robert's letters to him show only one face
of a six-faced mountain. But still I believe that these two sentences
contain a key to the central core of Robert's nature, to the sudden
transformation which changed him eleven years later from bohe-
mian professor to driving force of the bomb project at Los Alamos.
Perhaps they also contain a key to the dilemmas we face today in
trying to deal wisely with the problems of nuclear weapons and
nuclear war.

How could it have happened that a sensitive and intelligent
young man in the year 1932 put war on his short list of things
for which we should be profoundly grateful? This little word
"war" appears in his letter untouched by any trace of irony.
Oppenheimer's gratitude for it is as sincere as the gratitude of
the poet Rupert Brooke, who greeted the international catastrophe
of 1914 with the famous words: "Now God be thanked who has
matched us with His Hour." But Brooke died in 1915, and his
reputation as a poet was irretrievably smashed in the years of
muddy slaughter which followed. The poets whose works survived
the war and were read by the literary intellectuals of Oppenheimer's generation were the poets of plain-speaking disillusion-
ment such as Wilfred Owen. It comes as a shock to find Oppenheimer in 1932 writing about war in the manner of Rupert Brooke.

There were of course other voices in the 1920's than Haldane
and Owen. I do not know whether Oppenheimer read *The Seven
Pillars of Wisdom* by T. E. Lawrence, a man whose many-sided
strengths and weaknesses curiously paralleled his own. Lawrence
was, like Oppenheimer, a scholar who came to greatness through

war, a charismatic leader, and a gifted writer who was accused
with some justice of occasional untruthfulness. *The Seven Pillars*
is a marvelously vivid and subtly romanticized history of the Arab
revolt against Turkish rule, a revolt which Lawrence orchestrated
with an extraordinary mixture of diplomacy, showmanship, and
military skill. It begins with a dedicatory poem, with words which
perhaps tell us something about the force that drove Robert
Oppenheimer to be the man he became in Los Alamos:

> I loved you, so I drew these tides of men into my hands,
>   And wrote my will across the sky in stars
> To earn you Freedom, the seven pillared worthy house,
>   That your eyes might be shining for me
>   When we came.

And with words which tell of the bitterness which came to him
afterwards:

> Men prayed that I set our work, the inviolate house,
>   As a memory of you.
> But for fit monument I shattered it, unfinished: and now
> The little things creep out to patch themselves hovels
>   In the marred shadow
>   Of your gift.

And there was Joe Dallet. Dallet was the first husband of
Robert Oppenheimer's wife Kitty. Born into a wealthy family, he
rebelled against his background, became a Communist, and organized a steelworkers' union in Pennsylvania. In 1937 he went to
Spain to fight on the losing side in the Spanish civil war. Kitty
tried to follow him to Spain, but only got as far as Paris when she
heard that he had been killed in action. Three years later she married Robert. Robert and Kitty were well suited to each other; they
settled down and raised a family and supported each other in sickness and in health, through all Robert's triumphs and tribulations,
until his death. But I often felt that it must have been hard for

Robert, at least in the early years, to be living in a silent ménage à trois with the ghost of a dead hero.

The Spanish war certainly captured Robert's imagination and caused him to become politically engaged. It was easy for Robert and his left-wing friends, viewing the war from a distance of six thousand miles through a screen of righteous indignation, to romanticize and oversimplify. They looked on the war as a simple fight for freedom, a heroic struggle of right against wrong. They did not read George Orwell's *Homage to Catalonia*, the best eye-witness record of the war, written by a man who fought in it as a private soldier and faithfully set down on paper the heroism and the sordidness, the tragedy and the folly. Orwell's book sold poorly in England and was not published in the United States. The right wing disliked Orwell because he was a Socialist, and the left wing disliked him because he told the truth. The truth was too complicated to fit into the ideological categories of left and right. To a man who kept his eyes open and was not afraid to say what he saw, the disasters of the war could not be blamed on one side alone. One of the minor side effects of the war in Spain was that it erased from the minds of left-wing intellectuals the hard-earned lessons of World War I. They saw the Loyalist cause in the Spanish war as clean, heroic, and virtuous. They forgot what Haldane and Wilfred Owen could have told them, that the conditions of twentieth-century warfare tend to make heroism irrelevant. In the romanticized view of the Spanish war which Robert Oppenheimer absorbed from his friends in Berkeley in the late 1930's, the legend of Joe Dallet, the rich man's son who fought on the side of the workers and laid down his life for their cause, fitted naturally into place.

Recently I learned from the historian Richard Polenberg at Cornell some facts about Joe Dallet's life and death. Dallet was unlike the majority of the left-wing intellectuals who flocked to Spain to fight for the Republic. Dallet took soldiering seriously. He believed, like Robert, in discipline. He quickly became an expert on the repair, maintenance, and use of machine guns. He drilled his troops with old-fashioned thoroughness, making sure that they knew how to take care of their weapons and how to use them effectively. In an anarchic situation, his unit was conspicuously well organized. His men caught from him the habit of competence, the pride of a steelworker who knows how to handle machinery. At moments of relaxation, when he sat down with his friends over a bottle of wine, he talked mostly about his beloved machine guns. This was the image of Joe which his friends brought to Kitty in Paris when they came to see her after his death. This was the image which Kitty brought to Robert when she married him.

From Joe's guns it was a short step to Robert's bombs. When Robert accepted in 1942 the job of organizing the bomb laboratory at Los Alamos, it seemed to him natural and appropriate that he should work under the direct command of General Groves of the United States Army. Other leading scientists wanted to keep the laboratory under civilian control. Isadore Rabi was one of those most strongly opposed to working for the Army. Robert wrote to Rabi in February 1943, explaining why he was willing to go with General Groves: "I think if I believed with you that this project was 'the culmination of three centuries of physics,' I should take a different stand. To me it is primarily the development in time of war of a military weapon of some consequence." Rabi did not join the laboratory.

Late in 1944, as the Los Alamos project moved toward success, tensions developed between civilian and military participants. Captain Parsons of the U.S. Navy, serving as associate director under Oppenheimer, complained to him in a written memorandum that some of the civilian scientists were more interested in scientific experiments than in weaponry. Oppenheimer forwarded the memorandum to General Groves, with a covering letter to show which side he himself was on: "I agree completely with all the comments of Captain Parsons' memorandum on the fallacy of regarding a controlled test as the culmination of the work of this laboratory. The laboratory is operating under a directive to produce weapons; this directive has been and will be rigorously adhered to." So vanished the possibility that there might have been a pause for reflection between the Trinity Test and Hiroshima. Captain Parsons, acting in the best tradition of old-fashioned military leadership, flew with the *Enola Gay* to Japan and armed the Hiroshima bomb himself.

Some of the people who worked under Oppenheimer at Los Alamos asked themselves afterwards, "Why did we not stop when the Germans surrendered?" For many of them, the principal motivation for joining the project at the beginning had been the fear that Hitler might get the bomb first. But that danger had disappeared by May 1945 at the latest. So the primary argument which persuaded British and American scientists to go to Los Alamos had ceased to be valid before the Trinity Test. It would have been possible for them to stop. They might at least have paused to ask the question, whether in the new circumstances it was wise to go ahead to the actual production of weapons. Only one man paused. The one who paused was Joseph Rotblat from Liverpool, who, to his everlasting credit, resigned his position at Los Alamos and left the laboratory on May 9, 1945, the day the war in Europe ended. Twelve years later Rotblat helped Bertrand Russell launch the international Pugwash movement; he has remained one of the leaders of Pugwash ever since. The reason why the others did not pause is to be seen clearly in Oppenheimer's assurance to General Groves, written on October 4, 1944: "The Laboratory is operating under a directive to produce weapons; this directive has been and will be rigorously adhered to." Oppenheimer had accepted on behalf of himself and his colleagues the subordination of personal judgment to military authority.

Fighting for freedom. That was the ideal which pulled young men to die in Spain, to take up armed resistance against Hitler in the mountains of Yugoslavia, and to go to work with Oppenheimer in Los Alamos. Fighting for freedom, the traditional and almost instinctive human response to oppression and injustice. Fighting for freedom, the theme song of the Spanish war and of World War II from beginning to end. In 1937 Cecil Day Lewis wrote a war poem called "The Nabara," a long poem, perhaps the only poem which adequately describes the spirit of those who went to fight against hopeless odds in the early battles of World War II, even though it was written before that war started. "The Nabara" is a dirge for fifty-two Spanish fishermen, the crew of an armed trawler which lost a battle against one of Franco's warships. It is also perhaps a dirge for all of us who have chosen to fight for freedom with the technologies of death. I quote here a few of the concluding stanzas:

> Of her officers all but one were dead. Of her engineers
> All but one were dead. Of the fifty-two that had sailed
> In her, all were dead but fourteen, and each of these half
>   killed
> With wounds. And the night-dew fell in a hush of ashen tears,
>   And Nabara's tongue was stilled.

> Canarias lowered a launch that swept in a greyhound's curve
> Pitiless to pursue
> And cut them off. But that bloodless and all-but-phantom
>   crew
> Still gave no soft concessions to fate: they strung their
>   nerve
> For one last fling of defiance, they shipped their oars
>   and threw
> Hand-grenades at the launch as it circled about to board
>   them.
> But the strength of the hands that had carved them a hold
>   on history
> Failed them at last: the grenades fell short of the enemy,
> Who grappled and overpowered them,
> While Nabara sank by the stern in the hushed Cantabrian sea.

They bore not a charmed life. They went into battle
                                    foreseeing
Probable loss, and they lost. The tides of Biscay flow
Over the obstinate bones of many, the winds are sighing
Round prison walls where the rest are doomed like their
                                    ship to rust,
Men of the Basque country, the Mar Cantábrico.

For these I have told of, freedom was flesh and blood,
                                    a mortal
Body, the gun-breech hot to its touch: yet the battle's
                                    height
Raised it to love's meridian and held it awhile immortal;
And its light through time still flashes like a star's
                                    that has turned to ashes,
Long after Nabara's passion was quenched in the sea's
                                    heart.

Day Lewis published this poem in a little volume with the title
Overtures to Death in 1938. It resonated strongly with the tragic
mood of those days, when the Spanish war was slowly drawing to
its bitter end and the Second World War was inexorably approach-
ing. I remember, when I was at Winchester in 1938, our chemistry teacher Eric James, who was the best teacher in the school,
put aside chemistry for an hour and read "The Nabara" aloud.
He is now, by the way, sitting in the House of Lords. I can still
hear his passionate voice reading "The Nabara," with the boys
listening spellbound. That was perhaps the last occasion on which
it was possible to read an epic poem aloud in all sincerity to honor
the heroes of a military action. At Hiroshima, the new technology
of death made military heroism suddenly old-fashioned and im-
potent. After Hiroshima, Day Lewis's lofty sentiments no longer
resonated. The generation which grew up after Hiroshima found
its voice in 1956 in the character of Jimmy Porter, the young man
at center stage in John Osborne's play *Look Back in Anger*. Here
is Jimmy Porter, griping as usual, and incidentally telling us im-

portant truths about the effect of nuclear weapons on public morality: "I suppose people of our generation aren't able to die for good causes any longer. We had all that done for us, in the thirties and forties, when we were still kids. There aren't any good, brave causes left. If the big bang does come, and we all get killed off, it won't be in aid of the old-fashioned, grand design. It'll just be for the Brave New nothing-very-much-I-thank you. About as pointless and inglorious as stepping in front of a bus."

Jimmy Porter brings us back to where Haldane left us in 1924. The two world wars seemed totally different to the people who fought in them and lived through them from day to day, but they begin to look more and more alike as they recede into history. The first war began with the trumpet-blowing of Rupert Brooke and ended with the nightmares of Wilfred Owen. The second war began with the mourning of Day Lewis and ended with the anger of Jimmy Porter. In both wars, the beginning was young men going out to fight for freedom in a mood of noble self-sacrifice, and the end was a technological bloodbath which seemed in retrospect meaningless. In the first war, the idealism of Rupert Brooke perished and the trench-mortars of Haldane survived; in the second war, the idealism of Joe Dallet perished and the nuclear weapons of Robert Oppenheimer survived. In both wars, history proved that those who fight for freedom with the technologies of death end by living in fear of their own technology.

Oppenheimer's activities as a scholar–soldier did not cease with the end of World War II. After the first Soviet nuclear test in 1949, he took the lead in pushing for a vigorous development of tactical nuclear weapons to be used by the United States Army for the defense of Western Europe. Here is the testimony of his friend Walt Whitman (the chemist, not the poet of that name) as a character witness on Oppenheimer's behalf during the security hearings of 1954:

> I should say that always Dr. Oppenheimer was trying to point out the wide variety of military uses for the bomb, the

small bomb as well as the large bomb. He was doing it in a climate where many folks felt that only strategic bombing was a field for the atomic weapon. I should say that he more than any other man served to educate the military to the potentialities of the atomic weapon for other than strategic bombing purposes; its use possibly in tactical situations or in bombing 500 miles back. He was constantly emphasizing that the bomb would be more available and that one of the greatest problems was going to be its deliverability, meaning that the smaller you could make your bomb in size perhaps you would not have to have a great big strategic bomber to carry it, you could carry it in a medium bomber or you could carry it even in a fighter plane. In my judgment his advice and his arguments for a gamut of atomic weapons, extending even over to the use of the atomic weapon in air defense of the United States, has been more productive than any other one individual.

As a consequence of his interest in tactical nuclear weapons, Oppenheimer traveled to Paris in November 1951 with three other people to talk with General Eisenhower, who was then in command of American forces in Europe. General Eisenhower was quickly persuaded that tactical nuclear weapons would help his armies to carry out their mission of defense. The six thousand NATO tactical warheads now in Europe are an enduring monument to Oppenheimer's powers of persuasion. I once asked him, long after he had lost his security clearance, whether he regretted having fought so hard for tactical nuclear weapons. He said, "No. But to understand what I did then, you would have to see the Air Force war plan as it existed in 1951. That was the Goddamnedest thing I ever saw. Anything, even the war plans we have now, is better than that." The 1951 war plan was, in short, a mindless obliteration of Soviet cities. I could sympathize with Oppenheimer's hatred of the Strategic Air Command mentality, having myself spent two years at the headquarters of the British Bomber Command. I recalled an evening which I spent at the bar of the Bomber Command Officers' Mess, at a time in 1944 when our bombers were still suffering heavy losses in their nightly attacks on German cities. I listened then to a group of drunken headquarters staff-officers discussing the routes they would order their planes to take to Leningrad and Moscow in the war with Russia which they were looking forward to after this little business in Germany was over. Oppenheimer had heard similar talk in his encounters with the American Air Force. Compared with that, even a nucle-arized army seemed to him to be a lesser evil.

Under the circumstances existing in 1951, the idea of tactical nuclear weapons made sense both militarily and politically. The circumstances included a substantial margin of superiority of American over Soviet nuclear forces, both in quantity of weapons and in means of delivery. The circumstances also included a war in Korea, with United States troops fighting hard to defend South Korea against a North Korean invasion supported by the Soviet Union. At that moment of history, Oppenheimer was facing a triple nightmare. He was afraid, first, that the Korean war would spread to Europe; second, that a local invasion of West Berlin or West Germany would be answered by the United States Air Force's 1951 war plan, which meant the nuclear annihilation of Moscow and Leningrad; third, that the surviving Soviet nuclear forces, unable to touch the United States, would take their revenge on Paris and London. It was reasonable to think that the worst part of this nightmare could be avoided if the United States could respond to local invasions with local use of nuclear weapons on the battlefield. Oppenheimer argued in 1951 that the possibility of a restrained and local use of nuclear weapons would strengthen the resolve of Western European governments and enable them to stand firm against Soviet demands. The same arguments for tacti-cal nuclear weapons are still heard today, long after the disap-pearance of the American superiority which made them realistic.

The military doctrine of the NATO alliance is still based upon the possibility of first use of nuclear weapons by the allied armies to counter a Soviet non-nuclear invasion. How far this doctrine departs from sanity can be vividly seen in the official U.S. Army field manual FM-101-31-1 on nuclear weapons employment. This field manual is an unclassified document, used for the training of United States officers and readily available to foreign intelligence services. It describes how the well-educated staff-officer should make his plans during tactical nuclear operations. Various examples are presented of fictitious nuclear engagements, each of them conducted in a style appropriate to an ROTC Field Day. Here is "an example of a corps commander's initial guidance to his staff":

> Aggressor has organized the area between our current positions and the BLUE River for a determined defense. The decisive battle during the coming operation will be fought west of the BLUE River. Although we have a limited number of nuclear weapons for this operation, I am willing to expend 30 to 40 percent of our allocation in penetrating the Aggressor main and second defense belts, and advancing to the BLUE River. Corps fires will be used to engage Aggressor nuclear delivery means and those reserve maneuver forces which have the capability of adversely affecting the outcome of the battle. These fires will be delivered as soon as the targets are located.
>
> Once we are across the BLUE River, we must be ready to exploit our crossings and move rapidly through the passes of the SILVER Mountains and seize the communications center of FOXVILLE. Be extremely cautious in planning the employment of nuclear weapons in the SILVER Mountains, as I want no obstacles to our advance created in these critical areas.
>
> Weapons over 50 KT yield will not be allocated to divisions.

The problems of securing adequate intelligence concerning prospective nuclear targets are also discussed: "Delay of nuclear attacks until detailed intelligence is developed may impede the effectiveness of the attack. On the other hand, engagement of a target without some indication of its characteristics may cause an unwarranted waste of combat power."

So the staff-officer receiving ambiguous reports of major enemy units moving through populated friendly territory must take upon himself the responsibility of deciding whether to risk "an unwarranted waste of combat power." Fortunately, his task will be made easier by a well-designed system of nuclear bookkeeping. "Suggested forms or methods by which needed information can be kept at various staff agencies are discussed below." Samples are provided of forms to be filled out from time to time, summarizing the numbers of nuclear weapons of various kinds expended and unexpended. Very little is said about the possible disruption of these arrangements by enemy nuclear bombardment. But at least the well-prepared staff-officer knows what to do in one possible contingency. Section 4.17.c on Nuclear Safety reads in its entirety: "Enemy duds are reported to the next higher headquarters."

I ought to apologize to the authors of FM-101-31-1 for holding up their work to ridicule. They lack practical experience of nuclear warfare. When experience is lacking, the handbook-writer does the best he can, using a mixture of commonsense and imagination to fill the gaps in his knowledge. The handbook represents a sincere attempt to put Oppenheimer's philosophy of local nuclear defense into practice. I have taken my quotations from the 1963 edition of FM-101-31-1, the latest edition that I have seen. But when all due allowances are made for the historical context out of which FM-101-31-1 arose, it is still a profoundly disquieting document.

No matter how FM-101-31-1 may have been revised since 1963, it remains true that the doctrines governing the use and deployment of tactical nuclear weapons are basically out of touch with reality. The doctrines are based on the idea that a tactical nuclear operation can be commanded and controlled like an ordinary non-nuclear campaign. This idea may have made sense in the 1950's, but it certainly makes no sense in the 1980's. I have seen the results of computer simulations of tactical nuclear wars under modern conditions, with thousands of warheads deployed on both sides. The computer wars uniformly end in chaos. High-yield weapons are used on a massive scale because nobody knows accurately where the moving targets are. Civilian casualties, if the war is fought in a populated area, are unimaginable. If even the computers are not able to fight a tactical nuclear war without destroying Europe, what hope is there that real soldiers in the fog and flames of a real battlefield could do better?

The doctrines displayed in FM-101-31-1 are doubly dangerous. First, these doctrines deceive our own political leaders, giving them the false impression that tactical nuclear war is a feasible way to defend a country. Second, these doctrines spread around the world and give the military staffs of countries large and small the impression that every army wanting to stay ahead in the modern world should have its own tactical nuclear weapons too. If FM-101-31-1 had been stamped Top Secret it would not have been so harmful. In that case I would not have been talking about it here. But since our military authorities published it unclassified in order to give it a wide distribution, there is no point in trying to keep its existence a secret. The best thing to do in these circumstances is to call attention to its errors and inadequacies, so that people in military intelligence services around the world may not take it too seriously.

Fortunately, leaders of government in the United States and in Europe have come to understand that the purpose of the deployment of tactical nuclear weapons is primarily political rather than military. That is to say, the weapons are deployed as a demonstration of the American political commitment to the NATO alliance, not as a system of military hardware which could actually provide a meaningful defense of Europe. But this separation between political and military purposes of weapons is necessarily hedged about with ambiguities. On the one hand, the political sensitivities of NATO have imposed on the administration of tactical nuclear forces a command structure of unique complexity to ensure that the weapons will not be used irresponsibly. On the other hand, the troops in the field have to be trained and indoctrinated using manuals like FM-101-31-1 which make the firing of nuclear weapons into a standard operating procedure. The whole apparatus for handling tactical nuclear weapons is schizophrenic, trying in vain to accommodate the incompatible requirements of multinational political control and military credibility.

In my opinion, tactical nuclear weapons deployed in forward positions overseas are fundamentally more dangerous to world peace than strategic weapons deployed in silos and in submarines. Tactical weapons are more dangerous for two major reasons. First, tactical weapons are in places where local wars and revolutions may occur, with unpredictable consequences. Second, tactical weapons are deployed, as strategic weapons are not, with a doctrine which allows United States forces to use them first in case of emergency. Many of the tactical weapons are in fact so vulnerable and so exposed that it would make no sense to deploy them in their present positions if the option of first use were renounced. The combination of local political instability with vulnerable weapons and the option of first use is a recipe for disaster. In many ways, it is a situation reminiscent of the Europe of 1914, when the instability of the Hapsburg Empire was combined with vulnerable frontiers and rigid mobilization schedules. Compared with the immediate danger that a local conflict in an area of tactical weapons deployment might escalate into nuclear chaos, the instabilities of the strategic arms race are remote and theoretical.

The United States has already made one important and unilateral move to mitigate the danger of the tactical weapons. The most absurdly dangerous of them all was the Davy Crockett, a nuclear trench-mortar with a low-yield warhead which was supposed to be carried by small mobile units. FM-101-31-1 says (p. 38), "Allocate some Davy Crockett weapons to the cavalry squadron." A nuclear-armed cavalry squadron is a fine example of military euphemism. In reality it meant that Davy Crocketts were deployed in jeeps which were theoretically free to roam around the countryside. The Army decided that this was carrying nuclear dispersal too far. It was impossible to guarantee the physical security of the Davy Crocketts if they were allocated to small units as originally intended. Dispersal in small units also increased substantially the risk of unauthorized firing in case of local hostilities or breakdown of communications. So the Army wisely withdrew the Davy Crocketts from service and shipped them home, achieving thereby a real diminution in the risk of war at no political cost.

The same logic which got rid of the Davy Crocketts would dictate a continued withdrawal, unilateral or bilateral, of other tactical weapons, starting with those which because of their short range have to be deployed closest to the front line. Nuclear artillery shells would be a good candidate for the next round of withdrawals. The chief virtue of nuclear artillery was its high accuracy compared with the rockets of twenty years ago. Now the accuracy of rocket guidance is comparable with the accuracy of artillery. Guns are considerably more cumbersome and more vulnerable than rockets. Nuclear guns have to be placed in forward positions to be effective, they are hard to move quickly, and they are in danger of being overrun whenever there is a local breakthrough of enemy forces. If nuclear shells were not already deployed in our armies overseas, nobody would now dream of introducing them. Their military value is marginal, and they increase the risk that small-scale battles may involve us in unintended nuclear hostilities. They could be withdrawn, like the Davy Crocketts, with a substantial net gain to our security.

It is a strange paradox of history that the greatest present danger of nuclear war arises from these tactical weapons which Oppenheimer promoted with such good intentions during his period of political ascendancy. Oppenheimer pushed tactical nuclear weapons because they offered a counterweight to the Strategic Air Command in the interservice rivalries of the Truman administration, and because they offered a counterweight to Soviet tank armies in case of a war in Western Europe. It is clear that his actions were dominated by short-term considerations. There is no evidence that he ever considered the long-range consequences tactical nuclear weapons would inevitably entail, the massive Soviet response and the permanently increased risk of nuclear war arising by accident or miscalculation.

What are we to learn from this melancholy story? The main lesson, it seems to me, is that if we want to save the world from the horrors of nuclear war we must begin by winning over the soldiers to our side. It is not enough to organize scientists against nuclear war, or physicians against nuclear war, or clergymen against nuclear war, or even musicians against nuclear war. We need captains and generals against nuclear war. We need to persuade the soldiers in all countries, and especially the young men who will be the next generation of military leaders, that they cannot decently fight with nuclear weapons. The elimination of nuclear weapons must be presented to the public as a response to the demands of military honor and self-respect, not as a response to fear.

It is good to make people afraid of nuclear war. But fear is not enough. The generation which grew up after World War I was well indoctrinated in the horrors of trench warfare. Whether or not they read Haldane and Wilfred Owen, they met every day the widows and orphans and crippled survivors of the war. They looked back to the slaughters of Verdun and Passchendaele as we look back to the slaughter of Hiroshima, and they were properly afraid. Pacifist movements flourished in the 1920's and 1930's, and disarmament programs enjoyed wide public support. The fear of a repetition of World War I was real and almost universal. But human beings, for better or for worse, are so constituted that they are not willing to let their lives be ruled for very long by fear. Pride, anger, impatience, and even curiosity are stronger passions than fear. Thousands of men, including one of my uncles, lost their lives in World War I because their curiosity got the better of their fear. They could not resist the urge to stick their heads up out of the trench to see what was happening. Thousands more, including Joe Dallet, lost their lives in a hopeless cause in Spain because their fear was weaker than their anger. There is a deep force in the human spirit which drives us to fight for our freedoms and hang the consequences. Even the fear of nuclear holocaust is not strong enough to prevail against this force. When the trumpets sound and the cause is perceived to be just, young men of spirit, whether they are revolutionaries like Dallet or scholars like Oppenheimer, will lay aside their fears and their misgivings to join the parade, joyfully submitting themselves to the necessities of military discipline; for as Oppenheimer wrote to his brother, "only through them can we attain to the least detachment; and only so can we know peace."

We cannot defeat with fear alone the forces of misguided patriotism and self-sacrifice. We need above all to have sound and realistic military doctrines, doctrines which make clear that the actual use of nuclear weapons cannot either defend our country or defend our allies, that the actual use of nuclear weapons in a world of great powers armed with thousands of warheads cannot serve any sane military purpose whatever. If our military doctrines and plans once recognize these facts, then our military leaders may be able to agree with those of our allies and our adversaries upon practical measures to make the world safer for all of us. If our soldiers once understand that they cannot defend us with nuclear weapons, they may contribute their great moral and political influence to help us create a world in which non-nuclear defense is possible. In England, Lord Mountbatten and Field Marshal Lord Carver have made a good beginning.

The human situation, sitting naked under the threat of nuclear war, is desperate but not hopeless. One hopeful feature of our situation is the demonstrable idiocy of the military plans and deployments typified by Army Field Manual FM-101-31-1. There is a real hope that the soldiers in various countries may rebel against such idiocies and demand a world in which they can fulfill their honorable mission of national defense. The scholar–soldier Robert Oppenheimer persuaded General Eisenhower in 1951 that the American army needed tactical nuclear weapons. The world is now waiting for another scholar–soldier, or for a soldier who is not a scholar, to help us move back along the long road from the illusory world of FM-101-31-1 to a world of sanity.

II. THE QUEST FOR CONCEPT

I borrowed my title "The Quest for Concept" from my Princeton colleague George Kennan. He wrote an essay with this title fifteen years ago. I decided that Kennan's way of looking at things is the best way to come to grips with the problems of nuclear weapons, and so I have adopted Kennan's title as my own. This does not mean that Kennan is responsible for what I shall say. It means that I have accepted Kennan's fundamental standpoint, that we shall not succeed in dealing with the political and technical problems of controlling our weapons until we have agreed upon a coherent concept of what the weapons are for.

Kennan wrote his "Quest for Concept" in 1967, when the Vietnam tragedy was still unfolding and no end was in sight. His final sentences express the hope that sustained him through those dark days, a hope that should also sustain us today as we struggle to deal with the enduring problems of nuclear armaments:

> It remains my hope that if the Vietnam situation takes a turn that permits us once again to conduct our affairs on the basis of deliberate intention rather than just yielding ourselves to be whip-sawed by the dynamics of a situation beyond our control, we will take up once more the quest for concept as a basis for national policy. And I hope that when we do, what we will try to evolve is concept based on a modest unsparing view of ourselves; on a careful examination of our national interest, devoid of all utopian and universalistic pretensions; and upon a sober, discriminating view of the world beyond our

borders — a view that takes account of the element of rela-
tivity in all antagonisms and friendships, that sees in others
neither angels nor devils, neither heroes nor blackguards; a
concept, finally, which accepts it as our purpose not to abolish
all violence and injustice from the workings of international
society but to confine those inevitable concomitants of the
human predicament to levels of intensity that do not threaten
the very existence of civilization.

If concept could be based on these principles, if we could
apply to its creation the enormous resources of intelligence and
ingenuity and sincerity that do exist in this country, and if we
could refine it and popularize it through those traditional processes of rational discussion and debate on the efficacy of
which, in reality, our whole political tradition is predicated,
then I could see this country some day making, as it has never
made to date, a contribution to world stability and to human
progress commensurate with its commanding physical power.*

Today I shall try to carry forward into the areas of weapons
and strategy the process of rational discussion and debate upon
which Kennan rested his hope for the future. We now possess
weapons of mass destruction whose capacity for killing and tortur-
ing people surpasses all our imaginings. The Soviet government
has weapons that are as bad or worse. We have been almost totally
unsuccessful in halting the multiplication and proliferation of
these weapons. Following Kennan's lead, I want to ask some
simple questions. What are these weapons for? What are the
concepts which drive the arms race, on our side and on the Soviet
side? Since the existing concepts have led us into a situation of
mortal danger with no escape in sight, can we find any new concepts which might serve our interests better? Can we find a concept of weaponry which would allow us to protect our national
interests without committing us to threaten the wholesale massacre
of innocent people? Above all, a concept should be robust; robust

---

* Published as "In American Foreign Policy: The Quest for Concept," in *Harvard
To-day* (Autumn 1967), pp. 11–17.

enough to survive mistranslation into various languages, to survive distortion by political pressures and interservice rivalries, to survive drowning in floods of emotion engendered by international crises and catastrophes.

General Sir Archibald Wavell, who commanded British forces in the Middle East in World War II, published an anthology of poetry and also a book on generalship. I quote now from his book on generalship. "Whenever in the old days a new design of mountain gun was submitted to the Artillery Committee, that august body had it taken to the top of a tower, some hundred feet high, and thence dropped onto the ground below. If it was still capable of functioning it was given further trial; if not, it was rejected as flimsy." Wavell remarked that he would like to be allowed to use the same method when choosing a general. His suggestion applies equally well to the choice of strategic concepts. Any concept which is to succeed in regulating the use of weapons must be at least as robust as the weapons themselves or the generals who command them. A test of robustness for a concept, roughly equivalent to Wavell's hundred-foot drop for a mountain gun, is the process of verbal mauling which occurs in the public budgetary hearings of the committees of the United States Senate and House of Representatives.

The present nuclear strategy of the United States is based upon a concept which was definitively stated by Secretary of Defense McNamara in 1967. "The cornerstone of our strategic policy continues to be to deter deliberate nuclear attack upon the United States or its allies by maintaining a highly reliable ability to inflict an unacceptable degree of damage upon any single aggressor or combination of aggressors at any time during the course of a strategic nuclear exchange, even after our absorbing a surprise first strike."

A year earlier, McNamara had given a less formal definition of the concept. "Offensive capability or what I will call the capability for assuring the destruction of the Soviet Union is far and away the most important requirement we have to meet."

The concept is called Assured Destruction because of Mc-Namara's choice of words. It is also sometimes called Mutual Assured Destruction, with the implication that the Russians possess the same capability for destroying us as we possess for destroying them and that Soviet strategy should be based on the same concept as our strategy. I will discuss Soviet strategy a little later. One thing that emerges clearly from Soviet doctrines is that the Soviet Union does not accept Mutual Assured Destruction as a strategic goal. The word mutual is therefore misleading. It is better to call our concept Assured Destruction and to let the Russians speak for themselves.

Assured Destruction has at least the virtue of robustness. McNamara never had any difficulty in explaining it to congressional committees. It survived untouched the Vietnam War and the attendant political upheavals which changed so many other aspects of American life and incidentally put an end to Mc-Namara's tenure as Secretary of Defense. It still survives today as the ruling principle of American weapons deployment and of American conduct of arms-control negotiations. The words "assured destruction" are clear and unambiguous, and their meaning survives translation into Russian. The ability to survive translation is an important virtue. Endless trouble and misunderstanding was caused by the word "deterrence," which is a slippery concept in English and is usually translated into Russian as *ustrashenie*. It turns out that the word *ustrashenie* really means "intimidation," and so it was not surprising that discussions with Russians about deterrence proved frustrating to all concerned. There is no such difficulty with Assured Destruction. Assured Destruction means exactly what it says. It means, no matter what you do and no matter what happens to us, we retain the capability to bomb you back into the Stone Age.

I make a sharp distinction between Assured Destruction as a fact and Assured Destruction as a concept. It is a fact that we can assuredly destroy any country in the world, including our own, any time we feel like it. It is a fact that the Soviet Union can do the same. These are facts with which I have no quarrel. But the concept of Assured Destruction means something else. The concept means that we adopt as the ruling principle of foreign policy the perpetuation of this state of affairs. The concept means that we actively desire and pursue the capability for Assured Destruction, with a priority overriding all other objectives. That is what McNamara said: "Assured Destruction is far and away the most important requirement we have to meet." That is still the concept underlying United States policy today. Assured Destruction must come first; everything else, including our own survival, second. It is this concept of Assured Destruction, making it into the primary objective of our policy, which I wish to challenge. The fact of Assured Destruction is at the moment inescapable. The concept of Assured Destruction as a permanently desirable goal is, to my mind, simply insane.

The new strategic doctrine enunciated by President Carter in Presidential Directive 59 in 1980 does not change this concept. I cannot discuss PD 59 in detail, because I do not know what it says, and I do not even know anybody who has seen the document itself. From Secretary of Defense Brown's description of PD 59 it is clear that it leaves intact the concept of Assured Destruction as the primary purpose of strategic forces. What PD 59 apparently does is to add to assured destruction a number of preliminary stages, so that we can theoretically carry out various "lower-level" nuclear attacks on military and political targets in the Soviet Union while keeping the weapons needed for assured destruction in reserve. It is irrelevant to my argument whether the idea of lower-level nuclear attacks is realistic or illusory. In either case, as Secretary Brown said, the new doctrine describes only an embellishment and not an abandonment of previous concepts.

There are three compelling reasons why we should oppose the concept of Assured Destruction. First, it is immoral. Second, it is in the long run suicidal. Third, it is not shared by the Soviet Union, and therefore it stands in the way of any satisfactory and permanent arms-control agreement. I think I do not need to spell out why it is immoral to base our policy upon the threat to carry out a massacre of innocent people greater than all the massacres in mankind's bloody history. But it may be worthwhile to remind ourselves that a deep awareness of the immorality of our policy is a major contributory cause of the feelings of malaise and alienation which are widespread among intelligent Americans and of the feelings of distrust with which the United States is regarded by people overseas who might have been our friends. An immoral concept is not only bad in itself but also has a corrosive effect upon our spirits. It deprives us of our self-respect and of the good opinion of mankind, two things more important to our survival than invulnerable missiles.

I also do not need to spell out why the concept of Assured Destruction is ultimately suicidal. The concept rests on the belief that, if we maintain under all circumstances the ability to do unacceptable damage to our enemies, our weapons will never be used. We all know that this idea makes sense so long as quarrels between nations are kept under control by statesmen weighing carefully the consequences of their actions. But who, looking at the historical record of human folly and accident which led us into the international catastrophes of the past, can believe that careful calculation and rational decision will prevail in all the crises of the future? Inevitably, if we maintain Assured Destruction as a permanent policy, there will come a time when folly and accident will surprise us again as they surprised us in 1914. And this time the guns of August will be shooting with thermonuclear warheads.

The third defect of Assured Destruction as a concept is that it is not shared by the Soviet Union. Soviet leaders have told us repeatedly in no uncertain terms that they reject it. They have told us that they consider the deliberate destruction of civilian populations to be a barbarous concept and that their strategic forces will never be used for that purpose. I am not an expert on Soviet strategic doctrine, but I think there is good reason to believe that they mean what they say. The counterpart to McNamara's statement of our concept of Assured Destruction is the statement made in 1971 by the Soviet Minister of Defense, the late Marshal Grechko. Here is Marshal Grechko speaking: "The Strategic Rocket Forces, which constitute the basis of the military might of our armed forces, are designed to annihilate the means of the enemy's nuclear attack, large groupings of his armies, and his military bases; to destroy his military industries; and to disorganize the political and military administration of the aggressor as well as his rear and transport."

I am not claiming that Marshal Grechko's concept is gentler or more humane than McNamara's, but it is certainly different. Grechko did not design his forces with the primary mission of doing unacceptable damage to our society. Their primary mission is to put our military forces out of action as rapidly and as thoroughly as possible. Unacceptable damage to our population will be a probable consequence of their use, but it is not their main purpose. The technical name for Marshal Grechko's concept is Counterforce. Counterforce means that your ultimate purpose is to ensure the survival of your own society by destroying the enemy's weapons. Your immediate objective is to disarm him, not to destroy him.

There are many cultural and historical reasons why the counterforce concept fits better into the Russian than into the American way of thinking about war. The first and most important fact to remember about Russian generals is that they start out by reading Tolstoy's *War and Peace*. Their whole experience of war and peace in the years since 1914 has confirmed the truth of Tolstoy's vision. War according to Tolstoy is a desperate chaos, largely beyond human understanding and human control. In spite of terrible blunders and terrible losses, the Russian people in the end win by virtue of their superior discipline and powers of endurance.

All this is entirely alien to the American view of thermonuclear war as a brief affair, lasting a few hours or days, with the results predictable in advance by a computer calculation like a baseball score, so many megadeaths on one side and so many megadeaths on the other. Assured destruction makes sense if war is short, calculable, and predictable. Counterforce makes sense if war is long-drawn-out and unpredictable, and the best you can do is to save as many lives as you can and go on fighting with whatever you have left. I happen to believe that the Russian view of war, being based on a longer historical experience, is closer to the truth than ours. That is not to say that their concept of counterforce is free of illusions. Neither assured destruction nor counterforce is to me an acceptable concept. If I had to make a choice between them, I would choose counterforce as less objectionable on moral grounds. But neither assured destruction nor counterforce answers our most urgent need, which is to find a concept which both sides can understand and accept as a basis for arms-control negotiations.

The tragedy of the SALT negotiations, in my opinion, arose out of the basic incompatibility of the American and Soviet strategic concepts. The Soviet concept of counterforce says, "whatever else happens, if you drive us to war, we shall survive." The American concept of assured destruction says, "whatever else happens, if you drive us to war, you shall not survive." It is impossible to find, even theoretically, any arrangement of strategic forces on the two sides which satisfies both these demands simultaneously. That is why no satisfactory treaty can emerge from arms control negotiations so long as the concepts on the two sides remain as they are. The SALT II treaty was better than no treaty at all, but it was a miserable thing, unloved even by its friends, demonstrating the bankruptcy of the strategic concepts that gave it birth. If that is the best that our present concepts can do for us, then let us in God's name look for some better concepts.

When one contemplates the barbarity and insanity of our existing weapons and the plans for their further multiplication, one is tempted to say that there is no hope of salvation in any concept that does not reject them unconditionally. Perhaps it is true that we would be better off rejecting nuclear weapons unilaterally and unconditionally, irrespective of what other countries may decide to do. But unilateral disarmament is not by itself a sufficient basis for a foreign policy. Unilateral disarmament needs to be supplemented by a concept stating clearly what we are to do after we have disarmed, if we are confronted by hostile powers making unacceptable demands. There is a concept which deals with this question in a morally and intellectually consistent way, namely the concept of nonviolent resistance. Nonviolent resistance is not the same thing as surrender. Morally, nonviolent resistance and surrender are at opposite poles. The concept of nonviolent resistance says simply: "You shall not obey unjust laws, you shall not collaborate with unjust authorities, and you shall not shed any man's blood except your own."

Everybody who thinks seriously about nuclear weapons must sooner or later face in his own conscience the question whether nonviolence is or is not a practical alternative to the path we are now following. Is nonviolence a possible basis for the foreign policy of a great country like the United States? Or is it only a private escape-route available to religious minorities who are protected by a majority willing to fight for their lives? I do not know the answers to these questions. I do not believe that anybody knows the answers.

Gandhi in the 1930's made nonviolent resistance the basis of an effective political campaign against British rule in India. All of us young Englishmen who were against the Establishment and against the Empire acclaimed Gandhi as a hero, and many of us became believers in his concept of nonviolence. Then came Hitler. Hitler presented us with a dilemma. On the one hand, we still believed theoretically in the ethic of nonviolence. On the other hand, we looked at what was happening in Europe and said, "But unfortunately nonviolent resistance will not be effective against

Hitler." So in the end, almost all of us abandoned our allegiance
to nonviolence and went to war against Hitler. It seemed to us
at the time that there was no effective alternative to guns and
bombs if we wanted to preserve our lives and liberty. Most people
today would say that we were right.

Now, forty years later, a book called *Lest Innocent Blood Be
Shed* has been written by Philip Hallie, telling the story of a
French village which chose the path of nonviolent resistance to
Hitler.* It is a remarkable story. It shows that nonviolence could
be effective, even against Hitler. The village of Le-Chambon-
sur-Lignon collectively sheltered and saved the lives of many hun-
dreds of Jews through the years when the penalty for this crime
was deportation or death. The villagers were led by their Prot-
estant pastor André Trocmé, who had been for many years a be-
liever in nonviolence and had prepared them mentally and spiri-
tually for this trial of strength. When the Gestapo raided the
village from time to time, Trocmé's spies usually gave him enough
warning so that the refugees could be hidden in the woods. German
authorities arrested and executed various people who were known
to be leaders in the village, but the resistance continued unbroken.
The only way the Germans could have crushed the resistance was
by deporting or killing the entire population. Nearby, in the same
part of France, there was a famous regiment of SS troops, the
Tartar Legion, trained and experienced in operations of extermina-
tion and mass brutality. The Tartar Legion could easily have ex-
terminated Le Chambon. But the village survived. Even Trocmé
himself, by a series of lucky accidents, survived.

Many years later Trocmé discovered how it happened that the
village had survived. The fate of the village was decided in a
dialogue between two German soldiers, representing precisely the
bright and the dark sides of the German soul. On the one side,
Colonel Metzger — an appropriate name meaning in German

* *Lest Innocent Blood Be Shed: The Story of the Village of Le Chambon and How
Goodness Happened There* (New York: Harper and Row, 1979).

"Butcher" — commander of the Tartar Legion, killer of civilians, executed after the liberation of France as a war criminal. On the other side, Major Schmehling, Bavarian Catholic and decent German officer of the old school. Both Metzger and Schmehling were present at the trial of Le Forestier, a medical doctor in Le Chambon who was arrested and executed as an example to the villagers. "At his trial," said Schmehling, when he met Trocmé many years later, "I heard the words of Dr. Le Forestier, who was a Christian and explained to me very clearly why you were all disobeying our orders in Le Chambon. I believed that your doctor was sincere. I am a good Catholic, you understand, and I can grasp these things . . . . Well, Colonel Metzger was a hard one, and he kept on insisting that we move in on Le Chambon. But I kept telling him to wait. I told Metzger that this kind of resistance had nothing to do with violence, nothing to do with anything we could destroy with violence. With all my personal and military power I opposed sending his legion into Le Chambon."

That was how it worked. It was a wonderful illustration of the classic concept of nonviolent resistance. You, the doctor Le Forestier, die for your beliefs, apparently uselessly. But your death reaches out and touches your enemies, so that they begin to behave like human beings. Some of your enemies, like Major Schmehling, are converted into friends. And finally even the most hardened and implacable of your enemies, like the SS colonel, are persuaded to stop their killing. It happened like that, once upon a time, in Le Chambon.

What did it take to make the concept of nonviolent resistance effective? It took a whole village of people, standing together with extraordinary courage and extraordinary discipline. Not all of them shared the religious faith of their leader, but all of them shared his moral convictions and risked their lives every day to make their village a place of refuge for the persecuted. They were united in friendship, loyalty, and respect for one another.

So I come back to the question: what would it take to make the concept of nonviolent resistance into an effective basis for the policy of a country? It would take a whole country of people standing together with extraordinary courage and extraordinary discipline. Can we find such a country in the world as it is today? Perhaps we can, among countries which are small and homogeneous and possess a long tradition of quiet resistance to oppression. But how about the United States? Can we conceive of nonviolent resistance as an effective concept for the foreign policy of the United States? Reluctantly I have to answer this question in the negative. Nonviolence is a noble concept, and in many domestic situations within the United States, a practical concept, as Martin Luther King and others have demonstrated. But for the guiding concept of American foreign policy, nonviolent resistance lacks the essential quality of robustness. It could never survive the shock of a major international crisis, nor even the sniping of congressional committees going about their political business as usual.

I led you into this digression and spoke about André Trocmé and Le Chambon because I consider that our existing weapons and concepts are morally unacceptable and that every possible alternative road, no matter how radical or impractical, ought to be examined carefully. The digression is now at an end. Reluctantly I have to end the discussion of nonviolence, so far as United States foreign policy is concerned, with the question which Bernard Shaw puts at the end of his play *Saint Joan*:

> O God that madest this beautiful earth,
> when will it be ready to receive Thy
> Saints? How long, O Lord, how long?

I come back to the main road, the Street without Joy of national nuclear policies. I am trying to find a middle way between the concepts of Assured Destruction and nonviolent resistance, between Robert McNamara and André Trocmé. I believe there is such a middle way, and I believe my friend Donald Brennan knew roughly where it lies. Donald Brennan, alas, died two years ago at the age of fifty-four. I quote now from his testimony to the House

Foreign Affairs Committee of the U.S. Congress on July 17, 1969: "Let us consider two principles. The first principle is that, following any Soviet attack, we should be able to do at least as badly to the Soviets as they had done to us." Donald Brennan liked to call this principle the "Brass Rule," meaning that it is a debased form of the Golden Rule which says you should do unto others what you wish they would do unto you. Note that this principle does not require us to do very badly unto the Soviets if they cannot do very badly unto us.

"The second principle is that we should prefer live Americans to dead Russians, whenever a choice between the two presents itself. The Soviets may be expected to prefer live Russians to dead Americans, and therein resides the basis for an important common interest; we may both prefer live Americans and live Russians." Brennan ends by explaining why his second principle, the preference for live Americans over dead Russians, is controversial. It is controversial because it says that Assured Destruction is not desirable as a way of life. Assured Destruction may be necessary when no alternative is available, but we should not prefer it.

The concept which Donald Brennan advocated is called by the experts in arms control "Parity plus Damage-Limiting." I prefer to call it "Live-and-Let-Live." Perhaps it may be important to use a name for it which the public can understand. Donald Brennan was unfortunately an experts' expert, expressing his strategic concept in technical language which had little public impact. I believe the name "Live-and-Let-Live" accurately describes his concept and does not conceal its profound moral implications. To summarize Brennan's statement once again, his concept says: "We maintain the ability to damage you as badly as you can damage us, but we prefer our own protection to your destruction." I believe that this concept fits, as Assured Destruction does not, George Kennan's requirement that a concept should be modest, unpretentious, and free from apocalyptic overtones.

Live-and-Let-Live is a concept which should rule over all areas
of our foreign policy, not only over the technical issues of the
strategic arms race. Live-and-Let-Live should have a major impact
on the weapons which we and our allies deploy in Western Europe
and on the political problems which surround the control and use
of these weapons. The tactical nuclear weapons in Western Europe
make sense only as a component of an Assured Destruction strategy. If they are ever used, they will bring Assured Destruction
immediately to Western Europe and with high probability to the
Soviet Union and the United States too. The Live-and-Let-Live
concept implies that we no longer regard tactical nuclear weapons
as a satisfactory solution to the problem of European security. The
ultimate objective of our policy must be to get rid of tactical
nuclear weapons altogether. I have no illusion that we can get
rid of tactical nuclear weapons quickly or easily. I am saying only
that it is an even greater illusion to imagine that we can go on living with them forever.

Two technical factors ought to help us to move toward a Live-
and-Let-Live strategy in Europe. First, our professional soldiers
recognize the cumbersomeness of the nuclear weapon command
structure and the extreme vulnerability of the whole tactical nuclear weapon apparatus to a Soviet preemptive strike. Second, the
development of precision-guided munitions — which is the technical name for small, cheap, accurate, non-nuclear missiles capable
of destroying tanks and airplanes — offers a realistic substitute for
tactical nuclear weapons in the defense of Europe against a Soviet
invasion. It is quite wrong to claim, as some enthusiasts for
precision-guided munitions have claimed, that these are magic
weapons which will solve our military problems in Europe overnight. There are no magic weapons. But there are good as well
as bad military technologies. A good military technology is one
which leads away from weapons of mass destruction toward weapons which allow people to defend their homeland against invasion
without destroying it. The technology of precision-guided muni-

tions is good in this sense. It is reasonable to imagine a hopeful evolution of affairs in Europe, with the technology evolving away from nuclear weapons toward precision-guided non-nuclear weapons, and with the political authorities evolving away from Assured Destruction toward Live-and-Let-Live. Technical and political development must go hand in hand, each helping the other along.

The defense of Western Europe lies at the heart of our fatal involvement with nuclear weapons. Both tactical and strategic nuclear forces grew up in the context of the military confrontation between East and West in Europe. It is important to understand the difference between the Eastern and the Western concepts of nuclear weapons as they relate to the European situation. And it is important to understand the difference between the concepts of first use and first strike. The American doctrine says that we are prepared to use tactical nuclear weapons first if this is necessary to stop a non-nuclear invasion of Western Europe, but we do not contemplate using strategic weapons first in a direct attack on the Soviet Union. That is to say, American doctrine allows first use but forbids first strike. Soviet doctrine says that the Soviet Union will never be the first to introduce nuclear weapons into a non-nuclear war, but that the Soviet Union is prepared to respond to any Western use of tactical nuclear weapons on the battlefield with a strategic attack on the United States and its allies. That is to say, Soviet doctrine forbids first use but allows first strike. There are good and valid geographical reasons why first use seems good to us and bad to them while first strike seems good to them and bad to us. Unfortunately, the general public and the politicians on both sides do not understand the difference. Our people feel threatened when they hear that Russian doctrine allows first strike, and the Russians feel threatened when they hear that our doctrine allows first use.

What hope is there of escape from this web of threats and misunderstandings? A useful first step would be to educate the public so that the public knows the difference between first use and first strike. After that, it might be possible to discuss strategic doctrines publicly with some degree of rationality. Ultimately, we might be able to negotiate some kind of bargain with the Soviet Union in which we agree to give up the capability for first use while they give up the capability for first strike. A trade-off of first use against first strike capabilities would not only improve the security of both sides but would also, more importantly, diminish the psychological anxieties which drive the arms race. Such a trade-off should certainly be one of the immediate objectives of a Live-and-Let-Live strategy.

George Kennan has been the most thoughtful and consistent opponent of our first use doctrine, and I am delighted to see in a recent issue of *Foreign Affairs* that McNamara has publicly joined him in opposition to First Use. "I would submit," Kennan wrote in 1959, "that the first thing we have to do in order to put ourselves in a position to negotiate hopefully for an abolition of nuclear weapons, or indeed to have any coherent strategy of national defense, is to wean ourselves from this fateful and pernicious principle of first use." Kennan's words are as true now as they were twenty-three years ago. A simple No-First-Use declaration by the United States would be of enormous importance in lessening the risk of the outbreak of nuclear war. Recently a distinguished panel of military experts contemptuously dismissed the idea of a No-First-Use declaration on the ground that "declarations like that get put aside in the first moments of conflict." This shows that the panel did not understand what a No-First-Use declaration is designed to do. The purpose of a No-First-Use declaration is not to constrain the use of weapons in wartime but to constrain the deployment of weapons in peacetime. When Country A signs a No-First-Use declaration, the effect is to force the military authorities in Country A to take into account the possibility that the political authorities in Country A may actually mean what they say. This means that Country A is forced to go to the trouble of hardening and concealing its weapons or withdrawing them from exposed positions where they would be vulnerable to preemptive attack. The effect is to make Country A's deployments more survivable and at the same time less threatening to neighboring countries. The risk of war is reduced by these changes in peacetime deployments, not by any possible direct effect of a No-First-Use declaration in wartime.

Now suppose that two hostile countries A and B both sign a No-First-Use declaration. The effectiveness of the declaration in constraining Country A's deployments does not depend at all upon Country A believing that Country B is sincere. On the contrary, the more Country A mistrusts Country B's intentions, the stronger the effect of the declaration in discouraging Country A from unstable deployments. For the declaration to be effective, it is necessary only that Country A considers Country B not entirely trustworthy and Country A not entirely untrustworthy and vice versa. These conditions are rather well satisfied in the real world in which we are living.

The practical relevance of these considerations is most clearly seen in the contrast between U.S. deployment policies for strategic and tactical weapons. The U.S. strategic forces are deployed under our No-First-Strike policy, with the result that there is strong emphasis on hardening and concealment. Our tactical nuclear weapons in Europe and elsewhere are not subject to No-First-Use constraints, with the result that they are far more exposed and vulnerable. I believe that the tactical weapons are more likely than the strategic weapons to get us into bad trouble, and I believe that a No-First-Use declaration covering the tactical nuclear weapons of the NATO alliance would substantially reduce the danger of nuclear war. Of course, a NATO No-First-Use declaration would imply a drastic change in NATO force-structure and strategy, which just goes to show that the declaration would not be as empty of meaning as the panel of military experts supposed.

But I will not digress further into the complexities of First Use and First Strike. Let me come back to the strategic weapons.

I must try to tell you briefly what Live-and-Let-Live means for our strategic policy. First of all, it means no MX. And it means not just saying no to the Racetrack deployment of MX, but saying no to the MX missile in any shape or form. MX is a big step in the wrong direction from almost every point of view. But the question whether or not we deploy a particular weapon such as the MX is not the crucial issue. The far more important consequence of the Live-and-Let-Live concept is that it allows us, or rather compels us, to reorient our deployment strategies and our negotiating policies so that we are prepared in principle to go all the way to a world from which nuclear weapons have been eliminated entirely. So long as we stay with the concept of Assured Destruction, we cannot even contemplate negotiating the numbers of nuclear weapons all the way down to zero; we cannot even offer to our grandchildren any realistic hope of living in a non-nuclear world. The essence of the Live-and-Let-Live concept is that it releases us from inevitable and permanent dependence upon nuclear weapons. It allows us to work toward a future in which strategic offensive deployments are drastically reduced or altogether prohibited. It allows us to prepare in a realistic way to deal with the problems of international security in a non-nuclear world.

To achieve agreements drastically reducing numbers of offensive weapons, and to provide some assurance against clandestine violations, a deployment of non-nuclear missile defenses is likely to be helpful. In the long run, the transition from a world of Assured Destruction to a world of Live-and-Let-Live must be accompanied by a transfer of emphasis from offensive to defensive weapons. When we are talking about defensive weapons in general and about ballistic missile defense in particular, it is essential to make a sharp distinction between ends and means. Our experts in the arms control community have never maintained this distinction. They are so convinced of the technical superiority of offensive over defensive weapons that they let the means determine the ends. I say that we have no hope of escape from the trap we are in unless we follow ends which are ethically acceptable. The end must determine the means, and not vice versa. The only acceptable end that I can see, short of a disarmed world, is a non-nuclear and defensively-oriented world. Perhaps we may be lucky enough to jump to the disarmed world without going through the intermediate step of a defensive world. But at least we ought to consider seriously the question whether the defensive world is an end worth striving for. This question must come first. Only afterwards comes the question of means.

Defense is not technically sweet. The primal sin of scientists and politicians alike has been to run after weapons which are technically sweet. Why must arms-controllers fall into the same trap? There is a terrible arrogance in the statement that defense is hopeless and should therefore be forbidden. Nobody can possibly foresee the state of the world ten years ahead, let alone fifty. If a defensively-oriented world is an end worth striving for, and if we pursue it diligently with all the available means, especially with moral and political as well as technical means, we have a good chance of success. The burden is on the opponents of defense to prove that a defensive world is politically impossible. It is not enough for them to say, we didn't solve the decoy discrimination problem.

Opponents of defense often claim that a defensive strategy is unfeasible because defensive weapons don't work. Whether this claim is valid depends on what we mean by the word "work." If we mean by "work" that a weapon should save our lives in the event of a nuclear war, then defensive weapons do not work and offensive weapons do not work either. If we mean by "work" that a weapon should save those targets which are not attacked, then defensive weapons work very well and offensive weapons do too. In the real world the question whether weapons "work" is equally ambiguous and uncertain, whether the weapons are offensive or defensive. We cannot be sure that weapons of any kind will save our skins if worst comes to worst. We cannot be sure that either defensive or offensive weapons will be useless in discouraging

madmen from murdering their neighbors. So there are no compelling technical grounds for choosing an offensive rather than a
defensive strategy as a basis for our long-term security. The choice
ought to be made on political and moral grounds. Technology is a
good servant but a bad master. If we decide on moral grounds
that we choose a non-nuclear defense-dominated world as our
long-range objective, the political and technological means for
reaching the objective will sooner or later be found, whether the
means are treaties and doctrines or radars and lasers.

I have described in very brief and inadequate fashion some
possible steps by which we might move from a nuclear offensive-
dominated world to a non-nuclear defensive-dominated world,
from a world of Assured Destruction to a world of Live-and-Let-
Live. This great and difficult transition could only be consum-
mated if both the United States and the Soviet Union were to
adopt the Live-and-Let-Live concept as the basis of their policies.
As we know from Marshal Grechko and others, the Soviet Union
at present believes in Counterforce and not in Live-and-Let-Live.
That is to say, the Soviet Union in general prefers to be able to
destroy our weapons rather than to defend itself against them. It
is likely that the Soviet preference for counterforce will last for
some time. So long as the Soviet Union stays with the counterforce concept, we shall not achieve a defense-dominated world.
But even now, we shall be in a safer and more stable situation if
we unilaterally move to a Live-and-Let-Live policy than if we stay
with Assured Destruction. For us to adopt unilaterally a Live-and-
Let-Live concept does not mean that we let down our strategic
guard or that we put our trust in Soviet good will or that we
change our opinions of the nature of Soviet society. It merely
means that we change the primary objective of our strategic deployment from the Assured Destruction of Soviet society to the
Assured Survival of our own.

I would like to end as I began with some words of hope. I
shall quote again from the essay of George Kennan which gave

me the theme for this lecture. Kennan is describing the concept which he advocated as a basis for a rational American foreign policy in the years immediately following the Second World War.

> We in the Planning Staff were concerned to restore an adequate balance of power in Europe and eventually in Asia. We thought that once such a balance had been restored, we would negotiate a military and political Soviet retirement from Central Europe in return for a similar retirement on our part. We saw no virtue in keeping our military forces nose to nose with those of Russia. We welcomed the prospect of the emergence, between Russia and ourselves, of a Europe that would be neither an extension of Soviet military power nor of our own. We thought all this could be achieved by indirect, political means. It was our hope that if we could make progress along the lines I have described, there would be a good chance that the world would be carried successfully through the crisis of instability flowing from the defeat of Germany and Japan. New vistas might later open up — vistas not visible at that time — for the employment of our great national strength to constructive and hopeful ends.

This concept is still as valid today as it was in 1947. And today it carries with it an even greater promise, the promise of a first decisive step back from our fatal addiction to the technology of death.

III. TRAGEDY AND COMEDY IN MODERN DRESS

I begin with a quick summary of the first two lectures. In the first lecture I described the central tragedy of our century, the history of the two World Wars. I told how in both wars the just cause with which the war began, the fight for freedom, was corrupted and almost obliterated by the growth of the modern technology of killing. The culmination of this history was the development of nuclear weapons in quantities so large as to obliterate any conceivable just cause in which they might be used. Nevertheless, the cultural patterns of the past persist, and the safeguards regulating the use of these weapons are not proof against technical accidents and human folly. In the second lecture I discussed the concepts underlying our strategic doctrines and reached the conclusion that a concept which I call Live-and-Let-Live offers the best chance of escape from the predicament in which we are now caught. The essence of the Live-and-Let-Live concept is a determination to move as rapidly as possible away from offensive and nuclear weaponry towards defensive and non-nuclear weaponry. The means for bringing about this movement are moral, political, and technical, in that order. Morally, we must arouse the conscience of mankind against weapons of mass murder as we roused mankind against the institution of slavery a hundred and fifty years ago. Politically, we must negotiate international agreements to reduce offensive deployments and strengthen defensive capabilities. Technically, we must push further the development of non-nuclear defensive systems which may enhance the stability of a non-nuclear world.

This third lecture is concerned not with details of weapons but with human psychology and human values. I must apologize for disappointing those of you who may have been expecting me to provide a political program for the cure of the world's ills. I am not a politician and I have no program. I believe there is a chance that we may now be at a historical turning-point, with mankind as a whole beginning to turn decisively against nuclear weapons. If this turning is real, it will find appropriate political forms in which to express itself. If the turning is not real, no political program can succeed in bringing us to nuclear disarmament. So I decided in my last lecture to follow the wishes of Mr. Tanner and talk about humanity and morality rather than about weapons and politics. This has the consequence that I shall be talking today on a more personal level than before. I cannot discuss human values in the abstract but only in terms of particular people and particular events. I shall talk mostly about American people and American events, because America has been my home for thirty years and I prefer to speak of things which I know from first-hand experience.

Napoleon said that in war the moral factors are to the material factors as ten to one. The same ratio between moral and material factors should hold good in our struggle to abolish nuclear weapons. That is why I said that the moral conviction must come first, the political negotiations second, and the technical means third in moving mankind toward a hopeful future. The first and most difficult step is to convince people that movement is possible, that we are not irremediably doomed, that our lives have a meaning and a purpose, that we can still choose to be masters of our fate.

Polls taken among young people in American schools and colleges in recent years have shown that a consistently large majority believe, on the one hand, that their lives are likely to end in a nuclear war, and on the other hand, that there is no point in worrying about it since it is bound to happen anyway. We are all to some extent affected by this paralysis of the will, this atrophy of the moral sense. We shrug off with silly excuses our burden of responsibility for the impending tragedy. We behave like the characters in a Samuel Beckett play, sitting helplessly in our dustbins while the endgame of history is played out. Or we fritter away our days like John Osborne's Jimmy Porter, waiting for the big bang to come and convinced that nothing can be done about it, accepting the inevitability of a holocaust which is, as Jimmy says, "about as pointless and inglorious as stepping in front of a bus." Why have we become so apathetic and fatalistic? What is wrong with us? The subject of my third lecture will be the restoration of a sense of meaning to the modern world. If we can recover a sense of meaning, then we may also find the moral strength to tackle the institution of nuclear weaponry as resolutely as our ancestors tackled the institution of slavery.

The first step toward dealing effectively with the problem of meaninglessness in modern life is to recognize that it is nothing new. When the difficulties of modern living are discussed in magazines and on television, we often hear statements implying that our generation is unique, that never before in history did people have to cope with such rapid changes in social and moral standards, and so on. If people believe that their difficulties are new and never happened before, then they are deprived of the enormous help which the experience of past generations can provide. They do not take the trouble to learn how their parents and grandparents struggled with similar difficulties. They never acquire the long perspective of history which would let them see the littleness of their own problems in comparison with the problems of the past. If people lack a sense of proportion and a sense of kinship with past generations, then it is not surprising that they become anxious and confused and fall into the mood of self-pity which is one of the most unattractive aspects of the contemporary scene.

The beginning of a cure for this disease is to convince the patient that, as a matter of historical fact, past generations were as troubled as we are by the psychological disorientation associated with rapid change. I could give many examples to prove it, but since time is limited I will give only one. I ask you to consider the Pilgrim Fathers at Plymouth in Massachusetts, three hundred and fifty years ago. We all have a mental image of the society in which the Pilgrims lived after they settled in New England. The village clustered around the church, the hard work in the fields, the shared privations and dangers, the daily prayers, the old-fashioned puritan virtues, the simple faith in divine providence, the ceremony of thanksgiving after harvest. Surely here was a society that was at peace with itself, a community close-knit through personal friendships and religious loyalties. This traditional image of the Pilgrim society is not entirely false. But the reality is stranger and more complicated.

Here is the reality. William Bradford, passenger in the *May-flower* and historian of the Plymouth colony, is writing in the year 1632, twelve years after the first landing.

> Also the people of the Plantation began to grow in their outward estates, by reason of the flowing of many people into the country, especially into the Bay of the Massachusetts. By which means corn and cattle rose to a great price, by which many were much enriched and commodities grew plentiful. And yet in other regards this benefit turned to their hurt, and this accession of strength to their weakness. For now as their stocks increased and the increase vendible, there was no longer any holding them together, but now they must of necessity go to their great lots . . . . By which means they were scattered all over the Bay quickly, and the town in which they lived compactly till now was left very thin and in a short time almost desolate.

So you see, suburban sprawl and urban decay were already rampant within twelve years of the beginning. But let me go on with Bradford's account.

> To prevent any further scattering from this place and weakening of the same, it was thought best to give out some good farms to special persons that would promise to live at Plymouth, and likely to be helpful to the church or commonwealth, and so tie the lands to Plymouth as farms for the same; and there they might keep their cattle and tillage by some servants and retain their dwellings here. . . . But alas, this remedy proved worse than the disease; for within a few years those that had thus got footing there rent themselves away, partly by force and partly wearing the rest with importunity and pleas of necessity, so as they must either suffer them to go or live in continual opposition and contention. And others still, as they conceived themselves straitened or to want accommodation, broke away under one pretence or other, thinking their own conceived necessity and the example of others a warrant sufficient for them. And this I fear will be the ruin of New England, at least of the churches of God there, and will provoke the Lord's displeasure against them.

So I leave William Bradford, already in 1632 lamenting the breakdown of the old moral standards and the disintegrating effects of rapid economic growth. The remarkable thing is that these people who broke away from the Plymouth community were not yet the rebellious sons and daughters of the Pilgrims. The sons and daughters had not even had time to grow up. These people who broke away were the Pilgrims themselves, corrupted within twelve years of their landing by the temptations of easy money.

I conclude from this example and from many others that the psychological confusion and shifting values of the modern world are not new. Even the speed with which values shift is not new. Except in a few particularly stable and sheltered societies, moral standards have usually been in turmoil, and our psychological reference-points have rarely endured for longer than a single generation.

The next question is now: granted that past generations shared our problems, what can past generations do to help us? The most helpful thing they did was to leave us their literature. Through the writings of the war poets we can share and understand the meaning of the agonies of the two World Wars. Literature ties us together. Through literature we can know our roots. Through literature we become friends and colleagues of our predecessors. Through literature they talk to us of their troubles and confusions and give us courage to deal with our own. William Bradford understood this very well. His purpose in writing his history of the Plymouth colony was, as he says, "that their children may see with what difficulties their fathers wrestled in going through these things in their first beginnings; and how God brought them along, notwithstanding all their weaknesses and infirmities. As also that some use may be made hereof in after times by others in such like weighty employments." Bradford also understood that if his account was to be useful to future generations it must be totally honest. That is the greatness of Bradford. He shows us the Pilgrims as they really were, not a group of pious saints but a bunch of people like ourselves, mixed-up in their motives and purposes, feuding and quarreling with one another, keeping one eye on heaven and the other eye on the cash-box, and finally, in spite of all their muddles and mistakes, building a new civilization in the wilderness. Proudly Bradford tells how in the eighteenth year of the settlement, standing firm against the murmuring of the rude and ignorant, they hanged three Englishmen for the murder of an Indian.

If we are searching for meaning in a world of shifting standards, literature is one place where we can find it. Meaning is a subtle and elusive quality. It cannot be dished out to patients like a medicine. It is a matter of feeling, not of fact. All of us have periods in our lives when meaning is lost, and other periods when it is found again. It is an inescapable part of the human condition to be constantly borrowing meaning from one another. No man is an island. Or as William Blake said it:

> The bird a nest,
> The spider a web,
> Man friendship.

If we are lucky, we have friends or children or wives or husbands to lend us meaning when we cannot find it for ourselves. But often there come bad times when there are more borrowers than lenders, when a whole society becomes demoralized and finds meaning to be in short supply. Perhaps the present is such a time. In such times, those of us who have a taste for reading can turn to literature and borrow meaning from the past. Literature is the great storehouse where the meanings distilled by all kinds of people out of all kinds of human experience are preserved. From this storehouse we are all free to borrow. Not everybody, of course, reads books. Some cannot read and others prefer television. But there are still enough of us who love literature and know how to find meaning in it, so that we can take care of the needs of the rest by lending out what we have found.

Let me turn now to another writer, closer to us than William Bradford. Some of you in the audience may have had occasion to read a book called *The Siege* by Clara Park of Williamstown, Massachusetts.* Some of you may also have been lucky enough, as I have been, to know Clara Park personally. If I have any wisdom to share with you today, if I have anything to say worth saying on the subject of human values, I owe most of it to her. *The Siege* is the story of the first eight years of the life of Clara Park's autistic daughter. In the book the daughter is called Elly. It is a book about a particular autistic child and her family. And it is also, indirectly, a book about people in general and their search for meaning. We are still quite ignorant of the nature and causes of autism, but we know at least this much. The autistic child is deficient in those mental faculties which enable us to attach meaning to our experiences. We all from time to time have difficulty in grasping the meanings of things which happen to us. The autistic child has the same difficulty in an extreme degree. So the siege by which Clara and her husband and her three older children battered their way into Elly's mind was only an extreme case of the struggle which every teacher must wage to reach the minds of his pupils. The task is the same, to bring a sense of the meaning of life to minds which have lost an awareness of meaning or never possessed it. The story of Clara's siege has many connections with the theme of human response to nuclear weapons. The metaphor of a siege is a good one to describe the struggle we are engaged in. We are trying to surround the sterile official discussions of nuclear strategy with an aroused public concern, to break down the walls of hopelessness and indifference which keep us from feeling the urgency of our danger. Clara is telling us that the search for human values is a two-sided thing. We must be borrowers as well as lenders. The measure of Clara's achievement is that she not

---

* *The Siege: The First Eight Years of an Autistic Child; With an Epilogue, Fifteen Years Later* (Boston: Little, Brown and Co., 1982). Earlier editions were published in 1967 and 1972.

only planted in Elly's meaningless solitude an understanding of
the meaning of human contact and conversation, but also distilled
out of Elly's illness insights which gave added meaning to her own
life, to the life of her family, and to her work as a teacher.

But I did not come here to praise Clara. It is better to let her
speak for herself. She is a scholar and a teacher as well as a wife
and a mother. Here is her own summing-up, describing how a
teacher is ready to receive as well as to give meaning.

> I learn from Elly and I learn from my students; they also
> teach me about Elly. In the early years, I knew a student who
> was himself emerging from a dark citadel; he had been to the
> Menninger Clinic and to other places too, and he knew from
> inside the ways of thought I had to learn. "Things get too
> much for her and she just turns down the volume," he told me.
> I remembered that, because I have seen it so often since, in Elly
> and in so many others. Human beings fortify themselves in
> many ways. Numbness, weakness, irony, inattention, silence,
> suspicion are only a few of the materials out of which the per-
> sonality constructs its walls. With experience gained in my
> siege of Elly I mount smaller sieges. Each one is undertaken
> with hesitation; to try to help anyone is an arrogance. But Elly
> is there to remind me that to fail to try is a dereliction. Not all
> my sieges are successful. But where I fail, I have learned that
> I fail because of my own clumsiness and inadequacy, not be-
> cause the enterprise is impossible. However formidable the
> fortifications, they can be breached. I have not found one per-
> son, however remote, however hostile, who did not wish for
> what he seemed to fight. Of all the things that Elly has given,
> the most precious is this faith, a faith experience has almost
> transformed into certain knowledge: that inside the strongest
> citadel he can construct, the human being awaits his besieger.

Clara does not need to tell us, because anybody reading her
book knows it already, that outside the first circle of her family
and the second circle of her students there is a third circle, the
circle of her readers, a great multitude of people, teachers, doctors,
parents, friends, and strangers, who all in their different ways can

gather the gift of meaning from her story. And once again the gift works both ways. The book itself gave perspective and illumination and meaning to Clara's private struggle, a struggle which continued for many long years after the book was finished. Clara had always been a natural writer and a lover of literature. She had always believed in the power of written words to redeem the dullness of day-to-day existence. But it was Elly's illness and slow awakening which gave Clara a theme to match her capabilities as a writer. Elly gave Clara the strength of will and the understanding of human suffering which shine through the pages of her book. Through this book Clara reached out and touched the multitude in the third circle. She found herself embarked on a mission like the prophet in Pushkin's poem, who meets an angel at the crossroads and is sent out:

> Over land and sea,
> To burn the hearts of people with a word.

When Elly was twelve years old, I had the impression that she came close to being a totally alien intelligence, such as we might expect to encounter if we were successful in finding an intelligent life-form in some remote part of the galaxy. Astronomers have often asked themselves how we could hope to communicate with an alien intelligence if we were lucky enough to discover one. Perhaps Elly throws a little light on this question. At twelve years old she still had no sense of her own identity. Like many autistic children in the early stages of learning to speak, she used the pronouns "I" and "you" interchangeably. Her mental world must have been radically different from yours and mine. And yet she could communicate quite well with us through the medium of mathematics. While I was staying at her house, a letter arrived for Elly from one of her friends, another autistic child. Elly opened the letter. It contained nothing but a long list of prime numbers. I could see that the numbers were all the primes between one and a thousand. Elly glanced through the list rapidly, then took a pencil and gleefully crossed out the number 703. She was laughing and singing with joy. I asked her why she didn't like the number 703, since it looked to me like a perfectly good prime. She wrote down in large figures so that everyone could see, "703 $= 19 \times 37$." With that there could be no argument. So I knew that even the most alien intelligence has something in common with us. Her prime numbers are the same as ours.

One more public glimpse of Elly was provided by her father, showing her a little later at a crucial stage in her search for meaning. David Park and Philip Youderian published in the *Journal of Autism and Childhood Schizophrenia* an article with the title "Light and Number: Ordering Principles in the World of an Autistic Child." They described a marvelously elaborate and abstract scheme by which Elly at that time attached numbers to her emotions and to the comings and goings of the sun and moon.

> The numbers 73 and 137 are there, carrying their burden of magic, and the concept of the days in general belongs to their product $73 \times 137 = 10001$. What does it all mean? It is not hard to share Elly's meanings to some extent. One may react much as she does to sun and cloud, and see the humor of imagining horrible disasters as long as they cannot possibly happen. Some people respond to the individual qualities of numbers and think it splendid that 70003 is a prime. But these are only fragments of adult thought. For Elly they unite into a harmonious whole, capable of profoundly influencing her mood and her reaction to events. In essence, someone from whom the gift of words has been largely withheld has built a world of light and number . . . . It is clear if one talks with Elly that many of the actions of the people around her, and most of their interests and concerns, have no meaning at all for her. It is our conjecture that Elly's system of ideas represents her effort to fill the deficiency by establishing her own kind of meaning . . . . Elly now talks more than she did when her system was new, though still with great effort and concentration, and she has begun to share with others what she has seen during the day and what has happened at school. Re-

cently, when asked a question about her system, she smiled and said, "I used to care about that last year." Not that it is gone now, but only that there are more and more things to think about now that do not fit into the system.

With these words I will say goodbye to Elly. She has come a long way in the nine years since they were written. It took Elly's parents twenty years to nurture in her a sense of meaning and of human values so that she can now communicate with us as one human being to another. Perhaps in twenty years we can likewise break through our barriers of apathy and denial and face honestly the human implications of our nuclear policies. Elly is now no longer a case-history but a real person, a grown-up person whose privacy needs to be respected. If you want to see for yourselves what she has been doing recently, you can buy one of her paintings, signed with her real name, Jessica Park.

But I have not finished with Clara. Three years ago she published in the *Hudson Review* an article with the title "No Time for Comedy," which speaks more directly than *The Siege* to the concerns of these lectures. I took from her *Hudson Review* article the title and the main message of my talk today. The *Hudson Review* is a writers' magazine, read mostly by people with a professional interest in literature. Clara is saying to her literary colleagues that modern literature in its obsession with gloom and doom has lost touch with reality. She quotes from the Nobel Prize speech of Saul Bellow, my illustrious predecessor as Tanner Lecturer, who stands on her side in this matter: "Essay after essay, book after book . . . maintain . . . the usual things about mass society, dehumanization, and the rest. How weary we are of them. How poorly they represent us. The pictures they offer no more resemble us than we resemble the reconstructed reptiles and other monsters in a museum of paleontology. We are much more limber, versatile, better articulated; there is much more to us; we all feel it."

My message to you is the same. Literature has been, and will be again, the great storehouse of human values. Only at the moment it seems that a large fraction of our writing is dominated by a fashionable cult of meaninglessness. When literature deliberately cultivates meaninglessness, we can hardly look to it as a source of meaning. Literature then becomes, as psychoanalysis was once said to be, the disease of which it is supposed to be the cure. It is no wonder that ordinary people find it irrelevant to the real problems with which they are confronted.

Perhaps a restoration of our spirit may go hand in hand with a restoration of our literature. When we can write truly about ourselves, we shall also be better able to feel truly and act truly. And this brings me back to Clara Park. In *The Siege* she showed what it means to write truly. In the *Hudson Review* article she is saying that the fundamental malaise of our time is a loss of understanding of the ancient art of comedy. Comedy, not in the modern sense of a comedian who tries to be funny on television, but in the ancient sense of comedy as a serious drama ending in a mood of joy rather than sorrow. *The Siege* itself is, in this ancient sense of the word, a comedy. It is a classic drama of courage and love triumphing over obstacles, written in a style and language appropriate to our times.

Let us hear a little of what Clara has to say about tragedy and comedy:

> The Iliad and the Odyssey are the fundamental narratives of Western consciousness, even for those who have not read them: two masks, two modes, two stances; minor chord and major; two primary ways of meeting experience. The Iliad sets the type of tragedy, as Aristotle tells us, where greatness shines amid violence, error, defeat and mortality. The Odyssey celebrates survival among the world's dangers and surprises, and then homecoming, and order restored. It is the very archetype of a prosperous outcome, of Comedy . . . .
>
> Tragedy and Comedy: though the words are paired, their order is not reversible . . . . We can imagine Iliad and Odyssey in only one sequence. To turn back from the long voyage home to the fall of the city, from Odysseus in Penelope's arms to

Hector dead and Achilles' death to come, would be to turn experience upside down . . . . Historically indeed, but above all emotionally, the Odyssey comes last.

Last, as Sophocles at ninety, his proud city collapsing around him, in defeat returned to the bitter legend and brought old Oedipus to the healing grove of Colonus, insisting that though suffering is disproportionate, it is not meaningless but mysteriously confers blessing: last, as Matisse with crippled fingers cut singing color into immense shapes of praise . . . . Shakespeare's sequence makes the same statement; what comes last is not the sovereign Nothing of King Lear but the benign vision of Winter's Tale and The Tempest . . . .

Here on stage stand Ferdinand and Miranda, undertaking once more to live happily ever after, — the young, our own, that simple investment in the future we're all capable of, our built-in second chance. For them the tragic past is only a story that grownups remember. Untendentiously, insouciantly, they will go about their business, the business of comedy, making new beginnings of our bad endings, showing us that they were not endings at all, that there are no endings . . . .

What is at issue today is whether we have grown too conscious and too clever for comedy's burst of good will. In every age but this the creators of our great fictions have regularly accorded us happy endings to stand beside those others that evoke our terror and our pity. Happy endings still exist, of course. But they have lost their ancient legitimacy . . . . They awaken an automatic distrust . . . . And so for the first time since the beginning of our literature there is no major artistic mode to affirm the experience of comedy: healing, restoration, winning through . . . . It is a grand claim we make when we reject happy endings: that we are very special, that whatever songs previous ages could sing, in our terrible century all success is shallow or illusory, all prosperity a fairy-tale; that the only responses to our world which command adult assent are compulsive ironies and cries of pain; that the world which seems to lie before us like a world of dreams, so various, so beautiful, so new, hath, in short, really neither joy nor love nor light, nor certitude, nor peace, nor help for pain, and we are here as on a darkling plain waiting for Godot.

Clara goes on to say that the essential feature of comedy is not the happy ending but the quality of the characters which enables them to earn a happy ending. Odysseus, the prototype of the comic hero, earned his happy ending by being clever, adaptable, devious, opportunistic, and not too much concerned with his own dignity. When it was necessary to escape from a bad situation in the Cyclops' cave, he was willing to take a ride hanging onto the under-belly of a sheep. Here is Homer's image of the human condition, an image which has helped to keep us sane for three thousand years and can still keep us sane if we do not close our eyes to it: the Cyclops stroking the back of his favorite ram, telling it how grievously Odysseus has injured him and asking it where Odysseus has gone, while Odysseus precariously hangs onto the wool underneath, silently hoping for the best. The art of comedy is to make happy endings credible by showing us how they are earned.

"Was Homer's vision," Clara asks, "so much less searching than our own? There is an ugly arrogance in the insistence that our age, alone among all, is too terrible for comedy. In the city of York, in the years when Shakespeare was writing, only ten percent of the population lived to the age of forty. Aristocrats indeed did better; they had nearly an even chance. We cannot imagine what the words 'the shadow of death' meant to our forefathers. The Thirty Years' War left two of every three in Germany dead. Chaucer's pilgrims rode to Canterbury through a countryside which a generation before had been devastated by the Black Death . . . . Any realistic consideration of the life of the past, both in its day-to-day precariousness and its vulnerability to repeated holocaust, will show up our claims to unique misery as uniquely self-centered."

The heroes of comedy are people who do not pity themselves. They take the rough with the smooth. When they are lucky they are not ashamed of it. When they are unlucky they do not despair. Above all, they never give up hope.

There is in the literature of our own century another fine example of tragedy and comedy in action. In December of the

year 1911 the Norwegian explorer Amundsen reached the South
Pole. A month later the British explorer Scott arrived at the Pole.
After heroic exertions, Scott and his companions died in a blizzard
on the way home, only eleven miles from the depot where they
would have found supplies and safety. The story of Scott's expedi-
tion was written ten years later by Apsley Cherry-Garrard in a book
which he called *The Worst Journey in the World*. Cherry-Garrard
was one of the survivors who went out in search of Scott and
found him dead in his tent. Here is his description of the scene.

> Bowers and Wilson were sleeping in their bags. Scott had
> thrown back the flaps of his bag at the end. His left hand was
> stretched out over Wilson, his lifelong friend. Beneath the
> head of his bag, between the bag and the floor-cloth, was the
> green wallet in which he carried his diary . . . .
> We never moved them. We took the bamboos of the tent
> away, and the tent itself covered them. And over them we
> built the cairn.
> I do not know how long we were there, but when all was
> finished and the chapter of Corinthians had been read, it was
> midnight of some day. The sun was dipping low above the
> Pole, the Barrier was almost in shadow. And the sky was blaz-
> ing — sheets and sheets of iridescent clouds. The cairn and
> Cross stood dark against a glory of burnished gold.

Cherry-Garrard ends his last-but-one chapter with the text of
Scott's message to the public, found among the papers in the
tent. After summarizing the causes of the disaster, Scott finishes
on a more personal note: "For four days we have been unable to
leave the tent — the gale howling about us. We are weak, writing is difficult, but for my own sake I do not regret this journey,
which has shown that Englishmen can endure hardships, help one
another, and meet death with as great a fortitude as ever in the
past. We took risks, we knew we took them; things have come out
against us, and therefore we have no cause for complaint, but bow
to the will of Providence, determined still to do our best to the

last . . . . Had we lived, I should have had a tale to tell of the
hardihood, endurance and courage of my companions which would
have stirred the heart of every Englishman. These rough notes and
our dead bodies must tell the tale."

Those are the immortal words of the tragic hero Robert Scott.
But Cherry-Garrard does not stop there. Immediately after those
words he begins a new chapter, his last chapter, with the title
"Never Again." It starts with a quotation from the poet George
Herbert:

> And now in age I bud again,
> After so many deaths I live and write;
>   I once more smell the dew and rain,
> And relish versing. O my onely light,
>   It cannot be
>   That I am he
> On whom thy tempests fell all night.

Then Cherry-Garrard goes on:

> I shall inevitably be asked for a word of mature judgment
> of the expedition of a kind that was impossible when we were
> all close up to it, and when I was a subaltern of twenty-four,
> not incapable of judging my elders, but too young to have
> found out whether my judgment was worth anything. I now
> see very plainly that though we achieved a first-rate tragedy,
> which will never be forgotten just because it was a tragedy,
> tragedy was not our business. In the broad perspective opened
> up by ten years' distance, I see not one journey to the pole, but
> two, in startling contrast one to another. On the one hand,
> Amundsen going straight there, getting there first, and return-
> ing without the loss of a single man, and without having put
> any greater strain on himself and his men than was all in the
> day's work of polar exploration. Nothing more businesslike
> could be imagined. On the other hand, our expedition, running
> appalling risks, performing prodigies of superhuman endur-
> ance, achieving immortal renown, commemorated in august
> cathedral sermons and by public statues, yet reaching the Pole
> only to find our terrible journey superfluous, and leaving our

best men dead on the ice. To ignore such a contrast would be ridiculous; to write a book without accounting for it a waste of time . . . .

The future explorer . . . will ask, what was the secret of Amundsen's slick success? What is the moral of our troubles and losses? I will take Amundsen's success first. Undoubtedly the very remarkable qualities of the man himself had a good deal to do with it. There is a sort of sagacity that constitutes the specific genius of the explorer: and Amundsen proved his possession of this by his guess that there was terra firma in the Bay of Whales as solid as on Ross Island. Then there is the quality of big leadership which is shown by daring to take a big chance. Amundsen took a very big one indeed when he turned from the route to the Pole explored and ascertained by Scott and Shackleton and determined to find a second pass over the mountains from the Barrier to the plateau. As it happened, he succeeded, and established his route as the best way to the Pole until a better is discovered. But he might easily have failed and perished in the attempt; and the combination of reasoning and daring that nerved him to make it can hardly be overrated. All these things helped him. Yet any rather conservative whaling captain might have refused to make Scott's experiment with motor transport, ponies and man-hauling, and stuck to the dogs; and it was this quite commonplace choice that sent Amundsen so gaily to the Pole and back, with no abnormal strain on men or dogs, and no great hardship either. He never pulled a mile from start to finish.

This is as much as I have time for of Cherry-Garrard's post-mortem examination. You can find another glimpse of Amundsen in John McPhee's recent book *Coming into the Country*.* McPhee's book is about Alaska. He describes how on a wintry day in 1905, with the temperature at sixty below, Amundsen quietly and unobtrusively walked into the post office at Eagle, Alaska, to send a telegram home to Norway announcing that he had completed the first crossing of the Northwest Passage. The last four hundred

---

* New York: Farrar, Straus and Giroux, 1977.

miles he had traveled alone with his sled and dog-team. No fuss, no cathedral sermons. That was six years before he arrived at the South Pole.

Cherry-Garrard's final verdict on the two South Pole expeditions was simple. "There is a sort of sagacity that constitutes the specific genius of the explorer." Amundsen had it. Scott didn't. The word "sagacity" is carefully chosen. Sagacity is not the same thing as wisdom. Wisdom is the greater virtue, but it is too rare and too solemn for everyday use. Sagacity is by comparison rather cheap, rather slick, rather undignified, but nine times out of ten it is sagacity that will get you out quicker when you are stuck in a bad hole. The shipwrecked mariner in Kipling's Just-So story "How the Whale Got His Throat" was "a man of infinite resource and sagacity," and so he naturally knew how to trick the whale into giving him a free ride back to England. Three thousand years earlier, Odysseus showed the same sort of sagacity in dealing with the Cyclops. Sagacity is the essential virtue for the hero of a comedy. It is the art of making the best of a bad job, the art of finding the practical rather than the ideal solution to a problem, the art of lucking out when things look hopeless.

Cherry-Garrard gives Scott his due. It was true, as Cherry-Garrard says, that Scott's life and death made a first-rate tragedy. First-rate in every sense, in the nobility of character of the hero, in the grandeur of the geographical setting, in the epic quality of Scott's prose, and in the tragic flaw of Scott's nature, the pride and stubbornness which led him to demand more of himself and of his companions than was humanly possible. A first-rate tragedy indeed, worthy of all the fine speeches and sermons that have been devoted to it. And yet, Cherry-Garrard, who lived through it, has the last word. Tragedy, he says, was not our business. When all is said and done, Amundsen knew his business as an explorer and Scott didn't. The business of an explorer is not tragedy but survival.

The main thing I am trying to say in this talk is that Cherry-Garrard's words apply to us too. Tragedy is not our business.

Too much preoccupation with tragedy is bad for our mental health. Tragedy is a real and important part of the human condition, but it is not the whole of it. Some people try to make a tragedy out of every aspect of modern life. In the end their mental state comes to resemble the attitude of another famous character of modern fiction:

> Eeyore, the old grey Donkey, stood by the side of the stream, and looked at himself in the water.
> "Pathetic," he said. "That's what it is. Pathetic."
> He turned and walked slowly down the stream for twenty yards, splashed across it, and walked slowly back on the other side. Then he looked at himself in the water again.
> "As I thought," he said. "No better from this side. But nobody minds. Nobody cares. Pathetic, that's what it is." *

The Eeyore syndrome is somewhere deep in the heart of each one of us, ready to take over if we give it a chance. Anyone who has to deal with mentally sick people will be familiar with the voice of Eeyore. Those of us who consider ourselves sane often feel like that too. The best antidote that we have against the Eeyore syndrome is comedy, comedy in the new-fashioned sense, making fun of ourselves, and also comedy in the old-fashioned sense, the drama of people like Odysseus and Amundsen who survive by using their wits. Survival is our business, and in that business it is the heroes of comedy who have the most to teach us.

Odysseus and his friends can teach us a trick or two which may come in handy when we are in a tight spot. But the tricks are not important. The important thing which comedy does for us is to show us meanings. Just as the central theme of the *Iliad* is death, the central theme of the *Odyssey* is homecoming. The homecoming of Odysseus gives meaning to his adventures and his sufferings. Homecoming is still in the modern world a powerful symbol and a source of meaning. Millions of Americans come home each year

---

* A. A. Milne, *Winnie-the-Pooh* (New York: E. P. Dutton and Co., 1926), p. 70.

for Thanksgiving. The homecoming of Jews to Jerusalem gave meaning to their two-thousand-year Odyssey.

Homecoming is the reward for survival, but it is not the end of the story. There is no end, because homecoming means a new beginning. Homecoming means renewal and rebirth, a new generation growing up with new hopes and new ideals. Their achievements will redeem our failures; their survival will give meaning to our bewilderment. This is the lesson of comedy. No matter how drastically the institution of the family is changed, no matter how authoritatively it is declared moribund, the family remains central to our social and mental health. The children find meaning by searching for their roots; the parents find meaning by watching their children grow.

Clara Park's book *The Siege* is a celebration of the remedial power of the family. It is family love and discipline which breaks through the isolation of a sick child and gives meaning to the suffering of the parents. William Bradford's book *Of Plymouth Plantation* is also, in the same classic tradition, a comedy, and it is altogether appropriate that it ends with a family chronicle, a list of the surviving Pilgrims and their descendants unto the third and fourth generations:

> Of these hundred persons which came first over in this first ship together, the greater half died in the general mortality, and most of them in two or three months' time. And for those which survived, though some were ancient and past procreation, and others left the place and country, yet of those few remaining are sprung up above 160 persons in this thirty years, and are now living in this present year 1650, besides many of their children which are dead and come not within this account. And of the old stock, of one and other, there are yet living this present year, 1650, near thirty persons. Let the Lord have the praise, who is the High Preserver of men.

Many of us do not share Bradford's religious belief, but we can all share his pride and his hope. Pride for what the old people have done, hope for what the young people will do. The most important lesson which comedy has to teach us is never to give up hope.

This lesson, not to give up hope, is the essential lesson for people to learn who are trying to save the world from nuclear destruction. There are no compelling technical or political reasons why we and the Russians, and even the French and the Chinese too, should not in time succeed in negotiating our nuclear weapons all the way down to zero. The obstacles are primarily institutional and psychological. Too few of us believe that negotiating down to zero is possible. To achieve this goal, we shall need a worldwide awakening of moral indignation pushing the governments and their military establishments to get rid of these weapons which in the long run endanger everybody and protect nobody. We shall not be finished with nuclear weapons in a year or in a decade. But we might, if we are lucky, be finished with them in a half-century, or in about the same length of time that it took the abolitionists to rid the world of slavery. We should not worry too much about the technical details of weapons and delivery systems. The basic issue before us is very simple. Are we, or are we not, ready to face the uncertainties of a world in which nuclear weapons have been negotiated all the way down to zero? If the answer to this question is yes, then there is hope for us and for our grandchildren. And here I will let Clara Park have the last word: "Hope is not the lucky gift of circumstance or disposition, but a virtue like faith and love, to be practiced whether or not we find it easy or even natural, because it is necessary to our survival as human beings."

Biological Determinism

R. C. LEWONTIN

THE TANNER LECTURES ON HUMAN VALUES

Delivered at
The University of Utah

March 31 and April 1, 1982

RICHARD LEWONTIN was born in New York and attended the public schools there. He was an undergraduate student in mathematical statistics and genetics at Columbia. He has taught at North Carolina State University, the University of Rochester, the University of Chicago, and at Harvard, where he is currently Alexander Agassiz Professor of Zoology, Professor of Biology, and Professor of Population Science. He has spent his professional life studying genetic variation in natural populations of insects and human beings, from both an experimental and a theoretical point of view. He has also written extensively on philosophical and historical issues in biology. In addition to about 100 papers in scholarly journals, he has written *The Genetic Basis of Evolutionary Change* and, most recently, *Human Diversity*.

Over the last fifteen years the English-speaking public has been made aware of a variety of theories and claims about human beings and their societies that, at first sight, seem unrelated and of independent origin. In 1969 A. R. Jensen published a now-famous article, "How much can we boost IQ and scholastic achievement?" in which he argued that black children, on the average, were genetically less able than white children to solve cognitive problems so that no attempts at compensatory education could erase the differences in social status between the races.[1] In 1975, the evolutionist E. O. Wilson wrote in the *New York Times Magazine* that all societies of the future, no matter how egalitarian, would always give a disproportionate share of power to men because of unchangeable genetic differences between men and women.[2] More recently, it has been suggested that men are biologically better able to do mathematics than women. During a period of great social unrest and uprisings of urban blacks, three neurologists, in the leading American medical journal and later in a popular book, advanced the theory that urban rioters suffered from irreversible brain disease that could be treated only by neurosurgery.[3] At the same time large numbers of inmates of state prisons were being subjected to neurosurgery in an attempt to make them more manageable.

These examples, which can be multiplied many times over, are the continuation of a long tradition of social explanation going back to the nineteenth century. They have in common that they attempt to deal with observed variation in human social conditions

---

[1] *Harvard Educational Review* 39 (1969), pp. 1–123.

[2] "Human Decency Is Animal," *New York Times Magazine*, October 12, 1975.

[3] V. H. Mark, W. H. Sweet, and F. R. Ervin, "Role of brain disease in riots and urban violence," *J. Am. Med. Assoc.* 201 (1967), p. 895. See also the book by V. H. Mark and F. R. Ervin, *Violence and the Brain* (New York: Harper and Row, 1970).

by an appeal to the determinative role of individual biology. Far from being isolated independent theories about particular phenomena arising from new scientific developments, they are manifestations of a general world view that has characterized social explanation for more than 150 years. Actual discoveries in biological science have had remarkably little influence on their major premises, but rather have simply changed the specific mechanisms to which appeal is made.

So, in the nineteenth century, in the heyday of anatomy, it was supposed that differences in brain *size* were responsible for differences in intelligence and social achievement. When biologists finally satisfied themselves that there was no relation, within the human species, between brain size and brain function, the emphasis changed to the pattern of neuronal connections and, with the increasing importance of genetics in biology, to the genes that supposedly governed those connections. So too with the explanation of the condition of women. It was widely believed among Victorian physicians that the uterus and brain were in competition for development, so that educated women would be barren and fertile women dull. Why does the anatomical theory appear so quaint to us, while the notion that women are genetically incapable of doing creative mathematics has such modern credence? Certainly it is not because of any scientific evidence, which is the same for both theories. It is just that the notion that anatomy is destiny seems rather old-fashioned when we all know that it is really DNA that makes the world go round. If we want to understand where these biological determinist theories of human life come from and what gives them their perpetual appeal, we must look not in the annals of biological science, but in the social and political realities that surround us, and in the social and political myths that constitute the ideology of our society.

One of the most obvious features of our social existence is the vast inequality that exists between individuals and groups in their status, wealth, and power. Some people have great wealth and

others live in the direst poverty; some have control over the conditions of their own lives and over the lives of others, while most
people feel themselves passive objects of social forces beyond their
own control. Some few, by their high status, are constantly reminded of their own worth and importance, while most perceive
their lives as unappreciated and essentially socially valueless. Just
as there is material wealth and poverty so, too, there is vast variation in the psychic rewards dealt out by society to its members.
Nor are the psychic and material inequalities simply an individual
matter. There are rich nations and poor, powerful countries and
their client states. Everyone knows that in America blacks as a
group are poorer, less employed, die earlier, and spend more time
in prison than whites. And virtually everywhere men, as a group,
are more socially powerful than women. What makes these various inequalities between individuals, races, nations, and the sexes
so problematic for us is the obvious contradiction between the fact
of inequality and the ideology of equality on which our society is
supposedly built. If we indeed live in a society of "liberty, equality, and fraternity," why are so many people unfree, why are there
such immense inequalities of wealth and power, why do relations
of domination so characterize our collective lives? The ideology of
biological determinism has been built over the last two hundred
years as a solution to this socio-political paradox.

Before the bourgeois revolutions of the seventeenth and eighteenth centuries in Europe and North America, inequality of station was regarded as natural and normal. The privileges of the
ancien régime were grounded ideologically in Divine Providence.
Charles I, before he had his head cut off, ruled *Dei gratia* and, in
general, the conferral or withdrawal of divine grace was the explanation offered for radical changes in fortune. The chief agent
of ideological control of society was thus the church. Social unrest arising from the great inequalities in material and political
power was opposed from the pulpit with the aid of the Doctrine
of Grace. Even that most seditious and revolutionary priest Martin

Luther preached that "peace is more important than all justice; and peace was not made for the sake of justice, but justice for the sake of peace." [4] The successful overturning of the old order by the seventeenth- and eighteenth-century revolutionaries demanded that this old legitimating ideology be destroyed and that a new view of a just society be put in its place, a view that would justify new political, social, and economic relations. Thus, it was discovered that God was not really on the side of the nobility after all and that grace was not the exclusive property of the nobility. On the contrary, "all men are created equal, and they are endowed by their Creator with certain inalienable rights." Of course the founding fathers did not mean literally "*all* men," since blacks were counted only as three-fifths of a person each, but they certainly did mean "all *men*," women having to wait nearly 150 years even for the right to vote. Revolutions are not made with the slogan "Liberty and equality for some," however, so the ideology of equality became universalized far beyond the ability or desire of the new ruling political forces to make it actual. Inequality has remained a prominent fact of social life, and with it a unique social dissonance has emerged. In the bad old days of the *ancien régime*, social unrest could be met with the argument that an unequal society was the way God meant it to be. Social theory and social practice were in conformity. After the democratic bourgeois revolutions, however, social practice was, for the first time, in direct contradiction to the stated political values of the society.

The solution to the contradiction between the value of equality and the fact of inequality has been to put a new gloss on the word "equality." It is not that democratic society provides equality of *station*, but rather equality of *opportunity*. Life is a race, as the psychologist E. L. Thorndike put it, "a race not to get ahead, but to get ahead of *somebody*." In the old days the privileged few had a headstart in the race, or perhaps were the only ones permitted to run, but now we all start together. Those who win are

---

[4] Martin Luther, *On Marriage*, 1530.

simply those who are intrinsically better runners. In this view democratic society is a meritocratic society. Social entropy has been maximized, or nearly so, and only a small amount of tinkering is necessary before inequalities become as small as they can be, given the intrinsic differences between individuals. The view of democratic society as removing all externally imposed inequalities and allowing the "natural" differences between people to determine their lives was expressed by Lester Frank Ward, a major figure in nineteenth-century American sociology, when he wrote that education "is destined to remove all artificial inequality and leave the natural inequalities to find their true level. The true value of a newborn infant lies . . . in its naked capacity for acquiring the ability to do." [5] It is this claim that natural and intrinsic inequalities between individual human beings at birth are determinative of eventual differences in their status, wealth, and power that is the defining property of biological determinism.

A second feature of biological determinist theories of society is their reductionism. Individuals are regarded as ontologically prior to groups, so that inequalities between races, classes, sexes, or nations are claimed to be the direct consequence of intrinsic differences between the individuals who make up the groups. If blacks are less successful than whites, it is not because blacks as a group suffer from racism, but because individual blacks have, in general, less ability than individual whites. Men dominate women because men as individuals are intrinsically more aggressive and more rational than individual women. In this way social classes become biological entities, groups whose individuals possess different inherent biological properties. The psychologist Richard Hernnstein, a prominent modern ideologue of biological determinism, explains that:

> The privileged classes of the past were probably not much superior biologically to the downtrodden, which is why revolution had a fair chance of success. By removing artificial barriers

[5] Lester Frank Ward, *Pure Sociology* (London: Macmillan, 1903).

between classes, society has encouraged the creation of biological barriers. When people can take their natural level in society, the upper classes will, by definition, have greater capacity than the lower.[6]

It follows from such a reductionist view that improvements in the general level of psychic and material welfare of society as a whole can come only by changing the mix of individuals that make it up. That is, general social amelioration can come only from eugenic measures.

> Oh could we do with this world of ours,
> As thou dost with thy garden bowers,
> Reject the weeds and keep the flowers,
> What a heaven on earth we'd make it.
>
>   Sir Thomas More, "Irish Melodies"

Of course, the possibility of "rejecting the weeds and keeping the flowers" depends on knowing one from the other. That is, it depends on having a society in which "true merit" will be allowed to manifest itself, a virtue claimed for democratic bourgeois society as opposed to the artificiality of a previous time. It is ironic that precisely the same argument was used by H. J. Muller in the early 1930's to claim that only after the socialist revolution would eugenic measures be worthwhile, since only under socialism would "true merit" appear, uninhibited by the artificial class structures of capitalist society!

The claim that inequalities in society are a consequence of intrinsic differences in ability between individual human beings is not sufficient to resolve the problem of inequality because there is a second disturbing observation that reminds us of aristocracy. Social power runs in families. The children of oil magnates own banks, while the children of oil workers borrow money from the banks. All studies of the social origins of higher professions show

---

[6] *IQ and the Meritocracy* (New York: Little Brown, 1973).

them to be virtually entirely recruited from middle and upper middle class families. The most quoted study of American social mobility by Blau and Duncan shows that 71 percent of the sons of white collar workers are themselves white collar and 62 percent of the sons of blue collar workers remain in that category. This study greatly underestimates the familiality of social class, however, since most passage from "blue collar" into "white collar" is a passage into jobs as sales clerks, typists, and service workers.

But if parents pass on social power and wealth to their children, what has happened to meritocracy? The answer offered is that the inheritance of social class is a consequence of *biological* inheritance and is not an arbitrary passing of privilege across generations. That is, success is not only a consequence of intrinsic biological properties, but those properties are coded in the genes. Thus, it is only natural and fair that wealth and poverty run in families because success is genetic. The Doctrine of Grace has thus been replaced by the Central Dogma of Molecular Genetics.

The specific claim that biological differences between individuals are the consequence of differences in their DNA is also a manifestation of the reductionist outlook of biological determinism. Society is nothing but the collection of individuals that make it up, and individuals are nothing but the collection of genes that are present in the fertilized egg. An interesting consequence of the belief that an organism is completely determined by its genes is that not only abortion, but any birth-control method that acts to prevent implantation of a fertilized egg is equivalent to the killing of a fully-formed infant or even of an adult since the adult is already completely contained in the fertilized egg.

Even the assertion that there are inherited differences in abilities does not complete the justificatory argument. I might claim, as did Thomas Dobzhansky in *Genetic Diversity and Human Equality*, that even though there are intrinsic inherited differences in abilities between people, there is no necessity to build a society that gives differential rewards. Why not a society in which in-

ternists and plumbers, artists and housepainters, dentists and ditch-
diggers all receive the same psychic and material rewards? To
handle this problem, biological determinism shifts its ground from
explaining the differences between individuals and groups to
claims about human universals and, in particular, about the biological determination of hierarchies. Biological determinism as a
total system of explanation then must include a human nature
theory. According to this theory, differences in ability between
individuals and groups will always be translated into hierarchical
social structures with dominant and subordinate groups because
the tendency to form such hierarchies is coded in the human genome. During the course of evolution, human nature has been
produced by natural selection — a human nature that guarantees
the domination of women by men, a drive to accumulate wealth
and social power, and a general self-interest that precludes real
cooperation or self-sacrifice except as means to a selfish end.

Sociobiology, the evolutionary theory of human nature, is both
determinist and reductionist in common with other aspects of biological determinist thought. The reductionism of sociobiology lies
in the ontological priority it gives to the individual over society
and over the species as a whole. If people behave in a certain
way, say they are entrepreneurial, it is because each person, individually, possesses an intrinsic property of entrepreneurship.
Individual entrepreneurs create an entrepreneurial society, not the
other way round. Moreover, the entrepreneurial tendency is coded
in the genes of which we are the ineluctable product. No matter
how hard we try we cannot escape the dictates of our genes. The
extreme determinism of biological human nature theory, together
with its mechanical reduction of social organization to the properties of the DNA molecules possessed by individual human beings,
is epitomized by Richard Dawkins' description of people in *The
Selfish Gene* as "lumbering robots" controlled by their genes "body
and mind." The political implications of this determinism are that
nothing significant in human society can be changed. So, in specu-

lating about the future of social relations between the sexes, E. O. Wilson predicts that "the genetic bias is intense enough to cause a substantial division of labor even in the most free and most egalitarian of future societies.... Even with identical education and equal access to all professions, men are likely to continue to play a disproportionate role in political life, business and sciences." [7]

Biological determinism has taken a number of specific forms as particular social problems have become the focus of attention:

1. Most basic, differences between *individual* human beings in manifest abilities and temperament are ascribed to unalterable genetic differences. In particular, differential social success is ascribed to differential innate intelligence, coded by the genes.

2. *Race* differences in social status and group behavior are ascribed to genetic differences between the different races. Blacks have lower social status than whites because, it is claimed, blacks on the average lack genes for cognitive function that are possessed by whites.

3. *Sex* differences in social status are ascribed to differences between the sexes in innate abilities and temperament that are a consequence of the chromosomal difference between males and females. Male anatomical and physiological development is claimed to cause greater aggressiveness, analytic ability, synthetic ability, leadership, and rationality in the face of danger or emergency.

4. *Class* differences are thought to be a consequence of the poorer genetic endowment of those who find themselves in the lower social classes. This is not simply a circular argument, defining the lower social classes as the collection of individuals of low social status, because social class is said to be biologically heritable. Poverty runs in the family for genetic reasons.

5. *Aberrant social behavior* is said to arise from biological predisposition. The criminally insane, especially violent men, are said to owe their behavior to their possession of an extra Y chromo-

---

[7] Wilson, "Human Decency Is Animal."

some that, so to speak, magnifies the male tendency to aggressiveness beyond the normal bounds. Social violence, like that shown in urban riots, is a consequence of anatomically and chemically disordered brains. An important difference from most biological determinist theories arises in this case, because the disorder is regarded as treatable — by surgery or psychoactive drugs. Similarly, behavior patterns in children labeled as "hyperactivity" or "minimal brain dysfunction" (MBD) are supposed to be the consequence of chemical imbalances that are to be treated with drugs. Indeed, the entire range of behavioral variation from severely debilitating schizophrenias and autism, to the mildest fidgeting of a bored school child, are laid at the door of disordered molecules.

6. *Human nature* theories, particularly sociobiology, universalize historically contingent social forms and postulate genes that produce them. So, warfare, territoriality, entrepreneurship, religion, incest taboos, male dominance, conformism, and spite, among many other traits, are said to be human universals that have been built into our genes by natural selection during the course of human evolution. These characteristics are then said to be unchangeable so that any society which consciously attempted to change or eliminate them would be bound to fail.

Biological determinism is, then, an articulated theory of human social existence that provides a complete explanation of the hierarchical structure of present human society as both natural and unavoidable. Differences in abilities between individual human beings are unchangeably coded in their genes. Races, classes, and sexes are biologically different in their abilities because the individuals that make them up are intrinsically different. So, group differences are also unchangeable except perhaps by eugenic measures. Finally, because of the genetically fixed and unchangeable properties of human nature, the differences in individual abilities that exist will always be translated into structures of social inequality and domination. Put so baldly, there seems little to choose between the justification offered in biological terms for the structures of privilege in modern democratic society and the justification offered by the *ancien régime* for its structure of unchangeable privilege. If the biological determinists are right, then the society we now live in will be with us until the extinction of the species. The question is, are they right?

It is not possible in a short space to examine in detail all the specific forms of biological determinism as they have appeared even in recent years. The conceptual and factual errors on which these theories are built, however, can be fairly well exposed by a close look at two of the manifestations of the theory: the theory of intelligence and social achievement and the sociobiological theory of human nature.

IQ AND SOCIAL STATUS

The theory that social status of individuals and groups is fixed by means of fixed genetic differences in intelligence has a straightforward logical form that makes its detailed analysis fairly easy. The argument of the biological determinists is:

1. There are differences between individual people in their status, wealth, and power.

2. The achievement of high status, wealth, and power is a consequence of the possession of intrinsic intellectual ability.

3. Such intellectual ability can be assessed even in childhood by a set of tests loosely called "IQ tests," which measure intelligence on a one-dimensional scale.

4. IQ test performance (and therefore intrinsic intelligence) is largely inherited genetically. The figure of 80 percent heritability is widely quoted.

It then is said to follow from (1) to (4) that,

5. Differences among individuals in status, wealth, and power are largely biologically inherited and therefore unchangeable.

6. Differences between groups (e.g., blacks and whites) in social status are largely genetic and are therefore only trivially changeable by environmental or social change arrangements.

What are we to make of this argument?

1. There are differences in status, wealth, and power. No one, of whatever political viewpoint, can quarrel with the first assertion. In the United States and Britain, about 20 percent of the total income accrues to the highest 5 percent of families, while only 5 percent goes to the lowest 20 percent of families. The distribution of wealth is much more unequal, with 60 percent of all corporate stock belonging to 1 percent, while 83 percent of stock belongs to only 5 percent of all families. Across racial and class lines the facts are equally clear. In the United States blacks have 1.8 times the infant mortality rate of whites and a 10 percent lower average expectation of life. In Britain, prenatal mortality of working class children is more than twice that for upper middle class children. Moreover, virtually no change has taken place in these racial and class differentials in the last fifty years. There is, indeed, vast social and material inequality.

2. Differences in status come from differences in intrinsic abilities. There are serious difficulties here at two different levels. First there is the problem of whether persons of high status and wealth do indeed manifest skills not possessed by the poorer members of society. What skills did, say, Nelson Rockefeller possess that were not also a property of, say, a shop foreman in a General Motors plant? Did the managers of the Chrysler Corporation, or Braniff Airways, have special skills that enabled them to draw immense salaries and stock benefits while driving their corporations into bankruptcy? Do internists, radiologists, and neurologists possess special abilities (as opposed to special *knowledge*) that is not in the possession of their nurses and aides? Several studies of the stock market have concluded that in the absence of inside information, no investor can do, on the average, better than the Dow Jones Index, and that especially successful speculators have been either especially lucky or in possession of special information. No one has ever succeeded in isolating the special skills and abilities, if any, needed to be a physician rather than a lower grade medical

worker. One form the abilities argument has taken is the assertion that success in modern technological industry favors the more skilled, more sophisticated worker, so that the intrinsically un-intelligent sink permanently into an under-class. Yet the close examination of productive work has shown a progressive deskill-ing of labor with greater and greater specialization into atomized tasks requiring less and less cognitive ability and manual skill from each worker.[8] Moreover, the prejudice that urbanization some-how requires greater mental ability can only come from an urban intellectual élite who have never tried to make a living in a rural setting, especially in farming.

The deeper problem that is raised is the difference between manifest abilities and intrinsic talents. A professional mathemati-cian has a much greater manifest ability to solve mathematical equations than I do. What would it mean to say that she had greater intrinsic or innate ability? It certainly cannot mean that irrespective of upbringing and education she would, at the age of fifty-two, have greater mathematical skill than I since, if she had been brought up in a highland peasant village in Guatemala, she would not have been able to solve equations at all. Nor can it mean that at birth she was better able to solve equations than I, since at the age of 52 hours neither of us could do mathematics. All it might mean is that, given identical and sufficient education and upbringing, she would have turned out a better mathematician than I am. But there is no way to check up on such an assertion since two people clearly do not have identical education and up-bringing. Claims about innate talents or abilities are claims about in principle unobservable forces that may or may not become mani-fest depending upon circumstances that are themselves unspecified, and unspecifiable. There is, in fact, no independent evidence for the existence of innate or intrinsic abilities as distinguished from manifest achievement.

[8] See, for example, Harry Braverman, *Labor and Monopoly Capital* (New York: Monthly Review Press, 1975).

3. Intelligence tests measure intrinsic cognitive ability. It is the claim of intelligence testers that, even if one cannot independently describe what intelligence is, IQ tests measure it. Indeed, the relative constancy of the IQ score of a person over his or her lifetime is regarded as a major evidence that there is something real and intrinsic that is being measured, although it cannot otherwise be isolated or seen. In E. G. Boring's famous dictum, "Intelligence is whatever IQ tests measure." But the ability to perform an operation that produces a numerical value is no evidence that some natural property is, in fact, being measured. If I multiply the length of my nose by the year of my birth and divide by my social security number, I will obtain a number that characterizes me as an individual, possibly uniquely so, and will remain stable over my lifetime. Yet no natural property with any causal efficacy has been measured. The reification of IQ scores, with no independent evidence for the existence of a real property or intrinsic force, is a major epistemological difficulty of the theory of innate intelligence. Moreover, the tests must do more than measure "something." They must measure something that itself is the cause of social and material power or else the entire exercise is irrelevant.

The chief support for the claim that IQ tests measure an intrinsic ability to succeed is the often-repeated assertion that IQ scores in childhood are highly correlated with eventual socioeconomic status. That is, it is claimed that if I know a child's IQ, I have a powerful prediction of his or her eventual success in life and that the prediction arises from a direct chain of causations. There are two problems, however. First, IQ score is not all that good a predictor of eventual success. It is certainly true that if one measures success by income, or by what sociologists call Socioeconomic status (SES), a combination of income, years of school, and occupation, then people with higher incomes or higher SES did better on IQ tests when they were children than did people with low incomes or low SES. Only about half the variation in SES among adults is related to variation in IQ scores, however, the other half arising from independent sources. More to the point, it is essential to distinguish between a factor A being a *statistical predictor* of a second factor, B, and A being a *cause* of B. A may be correlated with B if A is a cause of B, but also if A and B are both the result of a third cause, C. On a worldwide basis, protein consumption and fat consumption per capita are highly correlated. Rich countries consume a lot of both, and poor countries little. Yet protein consumption is neither the cause nor the effect of fat consumption. Both are a consequence of how much money people have to spend on food. This is precisely the case with IQ and socioeconomic status. For example, a child in the top 10 percent of IQ performance is fifty times more likely to wind up in the top 10 percent of income than is a child who is in the lowest 10 percent of IQ performance. If, however, we hold constant the number of years of schooling, and the socioeconomic status of the child's family, then a child in the top 10 percent of IQ has only twice, not fifty times, the chance of winding up in the top 10 percent of income. On the other hand, a child whose parents are in the top 10 percent of economic success has a twenty-five times greater chance of also being at the top of the economic scale than does a child whose parents are in the lowest 10 percent economically, *even when both children have only average IQ*. Thus, the leading underlying cause of socioeconomic success is family background, not IQ, which is a result, not a cause, of social status. Obviously, it is better to be born rich than smart.

An examination of IQ tests bears out these statistical results. Over and over such tests ask questions that reflect substantive knowledge, sophisticated vocabulary, and middle class social attitudes. ("Who was Wilkins Micawber?" "What is the meaning of *sudorific*?" "What is the right thing to do when you find you are late for school" are examples of test questions.) Most important, an acceptance of the necessity and eventual value of sitting attentively for several hours, answering meaningless questions, depends upon a general acceptance of the routine of formal schooling and a belief that, after all, it will lead to a useful result. Most working class children, and children from chronically depressed families, simply do not see the relevance of schooling to their future prospects.

4 and 5. IQ performance and social status are largely heritable and unchangeable. This is the heart of the biological determinist position and its greatest weakness. The notion of "heritable" is used in a way that implies a fixed and unchangeable character that is passed from parent to child. Determinists mix a technical meaning of heritability with this everyday sense of its popular usage and thus seem to be saying that intelligence is, essentially, determined by genes. We need to distinguish three forms of error about inheritance that are committed by biological determinists at various times. The most vulgar error is to say that a character is determined completely by genes and is therefore unchangeable. So, if I inherit the gene for blue eyes, I will have blue eyes. In fact, there is virtually no trait whose relation to genes is so simple and direct. An organism at every stage of its life is the result of a developmental process in which the internal genetic factors and the external environmental factors are in constant interplay. If the genes of the fertilized egg are specified, the eventual organism is not fixed, because development also depends upon the sequences of environments in which the embryo and juvenile finds itself. Size, shape, behavior, physiological activity all depend both on genes and on environment. A fruit fly with "normal" genes will develop an eye that has about 1000 cells if it is raised at 15°C, but at 30°C it will develop an eye with only 800 cells. Even the classical inherited diseases are not independent of environment. Wilson's disease results from a single recessive gene that codes for a defective enzyme. The consequence of the enzyme defect is an inability to detoxify copper which, consumed in the diet, continues to accumulate until the victim dies of copper poisoning. The disease can be prevented completely, however, by taking a drug, penicillamine, that removes the copper. So an inherited disease is both

dependent on the food taken in for its expression and, at the same time, curable by an environmental manipulation. The most fundamental rule of the relation between gene and organism is that genes are inherited, while traits are developed. This fundamental distinction is that between the *genotype*, the set of DNA molecules and cytoplasmic factors that is present in the fertilized egg, and the *phenotype*, the set of traits that characterizes the whole organism at each stage of its life. Between the genotype and the phenotype are complex developmental processes that occur not in a vacuum, but in an impinging world of environmental circumstances and developmental accidents.

Biological determinists sometimes recognize the contingent nature of development and substitute a slightly less vulgar error for the fixity of inherited phenotype. "Of course," they say, "we know that environment matters. It is not the phenotype that is inherited, it is a tendency that is in the genes." The introduction of predispositional language, the language of tendencies, however, does not come close to expressing the biological situation, although it has a great deal of common-sense appeal. What does it mean to say, "Diana tends to be fat, while Charles tends to be thin"? It must mean that under some circumstances Diana will be fat but that under other circumstances she will not. How then do we choose which circumstances are to be the background for the characterization of tendency? If she is sometimes fat and sometimes thin, the descriptions are symmetrical. Clearly, there is a set of environmental circumstances that is taken as normal or usual and which serves as the reference for characterizing tendency. And it is certainly true that under the usual conditions of social existence and education in America, blacks "tend" to do more poorly on IQ tests than whites. But this observation begs the entire question of what set of environments can or ought to be established for human existence. In some other circumstances blacks may "tend" to do better on IQ tests than whites, or there may be no difference at all. From the standpoint of biology, tendency statements are mislead-

ing. All that can be described is the set of phenotypes that will
develop from various combinations of gene and environment.

A third form of popular but misleading language about genes
and organisms is the statement that genes determine *capacity*. This
is the bucket metaphor. At birth we are empty buckets to be filled
by our life experiences, and by education in particular. Some of us
are born with large buckets and some with small. If we are edu-
cationally deprived, if little is poured into our buckets, then we
will all be deficient. If, however, a rich set of experiences is provided, then those with the large buckets will acquire great knowledge and mature abilities, while the small buckets will soon be
filled to overflowing and no matter how much more is added, they
will not exceed their inherited capacities. A corollary of this view
of gene action, one explicitly invoked by A. R. Jensen, is that
genetic differences between the races will only be exacerbated by
improvements in the general education, so that blacks will be
stimulated to expectations they cannot hope to have fulfilled. Far
better that the blacks be provided with an education more suited
to their limited genetic capacities. Like genes as tendencies, genes
as capacities are without any biological basis. It must be literally
true that there is some maximum height, say, to which I can grow
under the best of all possible environments for growth and that
my maximum height is different from that of someone with a
different genotype. It turns out, however, from experiments with
both domesticated animals and plants and laboratory organisms,
that the environment which produces maximum phenotype for one
genotype is, in general, different from the environment necessary
for maximum expression in another genotype. Moreover, the
order of the genotypes in one environment is no clue to the order
in another. So, if genotype A is taller than genotype B at 2,000
calories per day, it is not possible to say which will be taller at
1,500 calories, in the absence of direct observation, and it certainly
cannot be said that A has a greater "capacity" than B for growth.
For example, modern varieties of hybrid corn yield a good deal

more per acre than varieties used fifty years ago when the varieties are tested under poor-to-average conditions of cultivation with mechanical harvesting and high planting densities. At the best levels of cultivation, however, or with hand harvesting and low planting densities, the older hybrids outproduce the modern ones. Whatever the relative phenotypes of two genotypes may be in one environment, when the environment is changed, all bets are off.

If neither phenotype nor tendency nor capacity is inherited, what is? What is inherited *physically* is a set of molecules and subcellular structures in the nucleus of the cytoplasm of a fertilized egg. For brevity we may call these the genes, but they include other structures outside the DNA. What is inherited *potentially* is a vast set of alternative pathways of development, a set of alternatives specified by the physical genes, each alternative being contingent for its realization on the environmental history of the developing organism. That is, what is inherited in a set of correspondences between possible environmental sequences and organismic end products. Different genotypes have different sets of correspondences. The genes act as a kind of mapping function that converts environment into phenotype. This function, the *norm of reaction* of a genotype, is known in detail for only a few genotypes over a relatively small range of environments. It is important to note that genotypes map a *sequence* of environments into a *sequence* of phenotypes. Development is a process that is extended in time, and the order of environmental events is critical to the outcome at any future stage. There are sensitive moments in development, moments at which particular environmental events have a strong influence on future development, while at other times the same environmental variation will be without any effect. If fruit flies are given a brief treatment with ether vapor in early development, some will eventually develop an extra set of wings, but a later ether treatment will have no effect. Environments cannot be arbitrarily ordered with the expectation that the end product of development will be the same.

To characterize the norm of reaction of a genotype requires that individual organisms with the same genes be raised in a variety of different environmental sequences. But this requires the production of a large number of individuals all of the same genotype. In some experimental organisms that is possible, as for example in plants that can be cut into several pieces, each of which will form an entire new plant. To characterize human norms of reaction would require, first, that a group of identical decuplets or, better, centuplets be produced and, second, that each infant be subjected to carefully chosen alternative environmental sequences. Fortunately, such an experiment lies entirely in the realm of science fiction, but its impossibility means that we have no information about the norms of reaction for human genotypes. If these norms are anything like those measured for physical, physiological, and behavioral traits in laboratory organisms, they are nonlinear and cross each other in unpredictable ways over a range of environments. There is certainly no evidence that the phenotypic differences between individuals will increase as environment is "enriched." Jensen's argument is pure invention without the slightest evidence to support it and a good deal of evidence from experimental organisms contradicting it. If there is any genetic variation for IQ performance at all, and that is by no means certain, we simply cannot say how that variation will be altered by social manipulation, nor what will happen to the relative ordering of individuals under changed circumstances.

We come finally to the question of what is meant by numerical characterizations of heritability, such as the often repeated claim that IQ is 80 percent heritable. This sounds like it is saying that 80 percent of one's IQ is determined by genes and 20 percent by environment, but that is clearly absurd. Of my height of five feet, eleven inches, I can hardly say that five feet were produced by my genes and the remaining eleven inches by the food I ate. There is, nevertheless, the vague feeling that such a percentage must mean that genes are four times as important, in some sense, as environment in determining IQ. And indeed it is precisely the intention of giving such numbers that the unwary will draw the conclusion that environmental manipulation can only change people's IQ a little because the genes predominate. Yet the actual meaning of a heritability of 80 percent is quite different.

In any population there will be variation from individual to individual in a trait, say height. That variation arises from two interacting sources. First, there are many different genotypes in the population, each with a different average height. Second, the various individuals of the same genotype will nevertheless differ from each other because each has experienced a different environmental sequence. Thus, there will be variation around each genotypic average. The total variation in the population is a consequence of pooling all the genotypes, each different on the average and each with variation around its average. Of the total variation some proportion can be calculated among the genotypic means, the remainder being the variation between individuals within genotype. The *heritability* of a trait in a population is defined as the proportion of all the variation within a population that arises from the variation among the genotypic averages, as opposed to the so-called "environmental variation" among genotypically identical individuals. So defined, the heritability of a trait is not some universal constant for the trait, but is contingent on the population and the environment. So, a population made up mostly of one genotype, or of genotypes that had similar norms of reaction, would have a low heritability, while the very same trait would have a high heritability in a different population containing a greater variety of genotypes. More to the point, different sets of environment will produce different heritabilities, even when the environments are in some physical sense equally variable or equally constant. Among the readers of this essay are people with varying amounts of body fat, a trait that is known to be influenced by genes. Provided they are all fully clothed, the internal body temperature of all the readers will be 37°C, whether they are out in the hot sun, in the house at moderate temperature, or outside on a cold day. Thus there will be no variation in body temperature arising from the genetic differences in body fat. Suppose, however, that all my readers were stripped naked and then sent out into the snowy winter. The thin ones would soon lose enough heat to suffer a marked reduction in internal body temperature, while the plumper ones could maintain themselves at 37°C for much longer. Under these environmental circumstances, absence of clothing, the genetic difference between individuals would manifest itself as an observable variation.

In general, the amount of variation in phenotype among different genotypes depends on the environment. Thus, the heritability of a trait will be large or small, depending upon what specific environments are experienced. If it were really the case that IQ variation was 80 percent heritable in some circumstances, nothing could be predicted about its heritability in other circumstances. More to the point, a heritability of 80 percent does not mean that 80 percent of the variation among individuals would remain even if all the environmental variation disappeared, or that environmental manipulation could only change the trait by 20 percent. There is no relation at all between the percent heritability of a trait in a particular population in a particular environmental range and how much the trait can be changed by shifting the environments. Indeed, the heritability of a trait could be 100 percent in some environment, yet could be radically altered by a change to a different environment. Wilson's disease is 100 percent heritable with a normal diet and no medication, yet a relatively simple environmental intervention eliminates it. There is thus no foundation whatsoever for the biological determinist claim that IQ differences among individuals are virtually unchangeable because IQ is 80 percent heritable. Indeed, the most striking feature of IQ studies is the very large change in IQ that accompanies major changes in the circumstances of upbringing. Children from orphanages who are adopted, usually by middle class families, show average increases in IQ of about 20 points after adoption.

There remains the question of whether IQ is really 80 percent heritable or indeed heritable at all. The evaluation of the data on which heritability of IQ has been calculated has had a long and tortured history. The attempt to measure heritability has depended entirely on the similarity in IQ performance between persons of various degrees of genetic relationship. The most widely used data are those from reports of identical twins raised apart and together. When these studies have been examined, they have turned out to be deeply flawed methodologically and, in the infamous case of the reports by Sir Cyril Burt, they turned out to be a fraudulent fabrication of non-existent twins.[9] The scandal of the Burt frauds, which has destroyed the only "data" on separated twins which claimed to eliminate biases from similarity of environment, has cast a pall over studies of the heritability of IQ from which they are not likely to recover for a long time, if ever. The methodological difficulties of separating genetic from environmental similarities in human beings are virtually insuperable. But even if the heritability of IQ could be established with some confidence in some human population, it would have no significance for social policy because of the total lack of relationship between heritability and changeability.

6. Differences between races and classes in IQ performance are genetic and unchangeable. The last conceptual and factual error of the determinist position on IQ is the translation of the causes of differences between individuals within groups into the causes of the differences between groups. It has been explicitly claimed that the 15-point difference in average IQ performance between black and white American school children is probably "mostly genetic" (whatever that may mean) because the heritability of IQ is 80 percent.

[9] For a critical survey, see Leon Kamin, *The Science and Politics of IQ* (Potomac, Md.: Erlbaum, 1974).

The conceptual error is to suppose that the causes of differences between individuals are the same as the causes of differences between groups. In fact they are independent. Consider variation in skin color. Among New Yorkers classified as white, there is considerable variation in skin color, largely genetic, arising for the most part from the varied migrant populations into the United States. There are fair-skinned Swedes and Scots, darker central Europeans and even darker Mediterraneans. If we compare the difference in skin color between white New Yorkers and the richer members of their families who live in Miami and Fort Lauderdale, we will find a very considerable difference in average skin color between the two groups, but the difference is entirely environmental. The fact that group boundaries can be established is, in itself, evidence that there are likely to be causes acting to differentiate the groups that are different from the forces acting differentially within each group. Differences in locality, in diet, in social status, in self-image, in wealth, in employment, in language, in transmitted cultural identity, in every conceivable aspect of social life exist between groups defined by ethnicity, religion, and race. It is simply not possible to judge the importance of these intergroup variables by studying the heritability of a trait within groups where the variables are constants, or at least have a different range.

There are, in fact, some direct observations that are relevant to the existence of genetic differences in IQ between races. The results, and the way they have been reported, are revealing. There are just four sets of observations that are relevant to genetic differences in IQ performance between blacks and whites. Children of German mothers and black American soldiers who left the mothers and children behind after the Second World War have slightly higher IQ scores than the children of German mothers and white fathers. The difference is not statistically significant. Black children in Dr. Bernardo's Homes in Britain taken into the Homes before the age of six months do better than white children in the same Homes on three tests of IQ, although the difference is not statistically significant. There is no significant correlation between the degree of white ancestry as judged by blood groups and the performance of black children on IQ tests, although the more white ancestry they had, the more poorly the children did. Finally, there is no greater proportion of white ancestry in black children of exceptionally high IQ than in black children of average IQ. This is the totality of the evidence, and it points unambiguously to a lack of any genetic differentiation for IQ performance between blacks and whites. When the results are summarized, it is stated that there were small differences between black and white children, but these differences were not statistically significant. The summaries leave the impression, however, that it is the white children who did better than the blacks, if only slightly, whereas the results are in the contrary direction. If there are any genetic differences between blacks and whites in IQ performance, it is the blacks who are superior!

HUMAN NATURE

The second biological determinist doctrine that has been of powerful influence on popular and scientific thought has been sociobiology, developed over the last ten years. As applied to the human species, sociobiology has the two aims of ascribing human social universals to the action of genes possessed in common by all members of our species, acquired during the process of human adaptive evolution, and of explaining the differences between human cultures as the consequence of genetic differences that have arisen between local groups during evolution.[10] The social agenda, made quite explicit by human sociobiologists, is to provide a technological background for determining how societies may be constructed or reconstructed, based on the limitations imposed by the genetic determination of behavior. The political agenda, as I have

---

[10] The first of these two programs is laid out most specifically in E. O. Wilson, *On Human Nature* (Cambridge: Harvard University Press, 1978); and the second in W. Lumsden and E. O. Wilson, *Genes, Mind and Culture* (Cambridge: Harvard University Press, 1981).

already suggested, is to argue that no serious reconstruction of society is possible because our genes make us what we are and that no reconstruction is desirable since natural selection has optimized our behavior, or nearly so. The philosophical discrepancy between these two positions seems not to have bothered sociobiologists, who take sometimes one and sometimes the other position. They seem not to realize that if we live in the *only* possible world, we cannot, except in the most trivial sense, describe it as the *best* possible world. Where there is no choice, there are no oughts.

The argument of sociobiology is in three parts. First, a description of human nature is given. Sociobiologists look around the world, both in their own culture and in the ethnographic record (although never, apparently, in history books) and abstract from their perceptions of the human condition what they conceive to be human universals. These constitute their picture of human nature. It is not an accident that historiography provides no data for their inferences, since the assumption of a universal human nature cancels out history. To the extent that any changes in time are assumed, those changes are thought to lie far back in human evolution. Differences between cultures are accepted but regarded as variations on basic universal themes, alternative formulations of the same innate drives.

Second, it is postulated that the described elements of human nature have a genetic basis and, in the usual argument, are directly coded by the genes and are therefore unchangeable. Differences between cultures are said to result from genetic differences between groups.

Third, an evolutionary story is told for each element of human nature. The story is in each case an adaptive one showing why natural selection would favor the particular trait, say religiosity, over alternative phenotypes, say skepticism. What is required in each case is to show why the possessor of a trait will leave more living offspring and thus spread the genes determining the trait through the population.

When one contemplates the description of human nature offered by sociobiologists, the immediate impression is of extraordinary superficiality and ethnocentricity. Faced with the extraordinary richness and complexity of human social life in the past and the present, they have chosen the nineteenth-century path of describing the whole of humankind as a transformation of European bourgeois society. Wilson's description of human political economy, in a book purporting to be a technical work on evolutionary theory, is a fine example: "The members of human societies sometimes cooperate closely in insectan fashion, but more frequently they compete for the limited resources allocated to their role sector. The best and the most entrepreneurial of the role-actors usually gain a disproportionate share of the rewards, while the least successful are displaced to other, less desirable, positions." [11]

That this description of a possessive individualist entrepreneurial society would apply to the peasant economy of eleventh-century France or the serfs of Eastern Europe, or Mayan and Aztec peasants, seems patently wrong. One can only assume that the insectan hordes of cooperators are blue-clad Maoist Chinese "energized by goals of collective self-aggrandizement." [12] The list of universal human traits varies from author to author, but generally speaking, human beings are seen as selfish, self-aggrandizing, territorial organisms in which cooperation is a mask for reproductive advantage. Among the traits that are said to constitute human nature are religiosity, conformity, territoriality, male dominance, entrepreneurship, indoctrinability, blind faith, and xenophobia. Some of the "scientific" descriptions of human nature smack of barroom wisdom ("Men would rather believe than know"). [13]

There are a number of problems of the description of human nature that have not been considered in sociobiological theory, which lead to serious errors.

[11] E. O. Wilson, *Sociobiology: The New Synthesis* (Cambridge: Harvard University Press, 1975), p. 554.

[12] Wilson, *On Human Nature*, p. 3.

[13] Wilson, *Sociobiology*, p. 561.

1. *Confusion of proscription and proscribed.* In an attempt to explain the near-universality of incest taboos, sociobiologists refer to a genetic predisposition to avoid incest. But incest taboos and incest are two very different things. Both are common. Father-daughter incest in the United States is an everyday affair, and, although the data are understandably hard to obtain, it appears from psychiatric interviews that brother–sister incest is also common. Any theory that tries to explain incest taboos as a consequence of a genetic detestation for the act itself is in serious difficulties.

2. *Tautological universality.* By appropriately redefining each trait and providing enough latitude in its characteristics, any behavior can be claimed to be universal. A classic is Wilson's definition of territoriality:

> Anthropologists often discount territorial behavior as a general human attribute. This happens when the narrowest concept of the phenomenon is borrowed from zoology. . . . Each species is characterized by its own behavioral scale. In extreme cases the scale may run from open hostility . . . to oblique forms of advertisement or no territorial behavior at all. One seeks to characterize the behavioral scale of the species and to identify the parameters that move individual animals up and down it. If these qualifications are accepted, it is reasonable to conclude that territoriality is a general trait of hunter gatherer societies.[14]

Of course, if love is really hate and passivity really a form of hidden aggression, then hate and aggression are universals, but what is not?

3. *Conflation.* Different meanings of the same word are conflated into the same phenomenon, although they are utterly different. Thus, warfare is described as simply the group manifestation of individual aggressiveness because the word "aggression" is used for both. But warfare is an organized activity for political and

[14] Ibid., pp. 564–65.

social ends which does not begin because the contending parties want to punch each other in the nose. People go to war because they are forced to do so by state apparatuses that threaten them with dire punishment if they do not go out and kill for the common good. That is the basis of selective service.

4. *Reification.* Abstract constructs are given a material reality as causes and effects. Many of the mental constructs that are said by sociobiologists to evolve have only historical and cultural contingency. What could "religion" have meant to the Athenians, who had no word for it and for whom it did not exist as a separate social phenomenon? Is violence real, or a construct with no one-to-one correspondence in the physical world? What is meant by "verbal violence," or "a violent exception"? The possession of real property is a modern legal fiction unknown in thirteenth-century Europe, when the relationship was between persons rather than between a person and property that could be alienated. It is absurd to talk of property possession as an ahistorical real phenomenon that has evolved biologically.

5. *Arbitrary agglomeration.* Behavioral units are built up arbitrarily out of bits and pieces. But how are we to know what the natural units of behavior are that evolution has operated upon? In the case of physical parts, the issue is in doubt. We are not sure whether the hand, each finger, or each joint of each finger is an appropriate unit of heredity and natural selection. For social behavior, the choice of elements of behavior is entirely arbitrary.

6. *False metaphor.* Words that describe human behavior are taken over into animal behavior (slavery, aggression, warfare, cooperation, kinship, loyalty, coyness) and then, when these are described in animals, by a kind of back etymology they are rederived in humans as a special case of a general animal phenomenon. Slavery in ants is not the same as the economic property relation called slavery in humans. Ants know neither auction block, commodities, economic surplus, nor rates of interest, yet the two "slaveries" are described as the same institution.

If the problems of adequate description of human nature are severe, the problems of studying its inheritance are enormous. To put it briefly, there is not one jot or tittle of evidence that any of the traits described as human behavioral universals are coded in specific genes, nor that any of the differences between populations are a consequence of genetic differentiation between them. Nor is there any prospect of getting such information. The evidence offered by sociobiologists for the genetic basis of traits of human nature is either that the trait is universal, and on that basis alone must be presumed to have a genetic basis, or else that a heritability has been demonstrated in studies of relatives, in which case the trait is not universal. In fact, there are no studies which would pass even the minimal tests for adequacy that demonstrate heritability of human social traits. In nearly all cases, the resemblance of parents and offspring is the only evidence. But parents may resemble offspring for purely cultural reasons, and the chief problem of human genetics is to distinguish familial resemblance, the observation, from biological inheritance, a possible cause. The highest parent–offspring correlations for social traits known are for political party and religious affiliation, yet even the most sanguine biological determinist would not suggest that Republicanism or being a Seventh-Day Adventist is coded in the genes.

The other error committed by sociobiologists is one they have in common with all biological determinists, the belief that phenotypic traits are unalterably coded in the genes. E. O. Wilson's dictum that men would always dominate women, even in the most egalitarian society, was based, it will be remembered, on his supposition that the domination was genetically determined. Sometimes sociobiologists say that genes do not fix characters but only provide tendencies or possibilities. But, as we have shown, the language of tendencies is empty, and if all that sociobiology is saying about human behavior is that all known human behaviors are biologically possible, they have wasted a great deal of time and effort on a truism.

The deepest problem of genetic determination of behavior is the incorrect assumption that individual constraints translate into constraints on social function. The reductionism of sociobiology leads it to characterize social behavior as nothing but the collection of individual behaviors, and social limitations as individual limitations writ large. Yet this reductionism misses an essential truth about human social activity — that social organization can actually negate individual limitations. I mean this negation in much more than the sense that ten people can lift a weight ten times as great as can one person. None of us can fly by flapping our arms. That is a biological limitation. Yet we do fly as a consequence of the social organization that has given rise to airplanes, airfields, pilots, controllers, fuel, metallurgy, hydrodynamic theory, and organized economic activity. It is not society that flies, however, but individuals. Thus, the constraints on individual human beings have been negated by social activity, and they have become new individual human beings with new properties and abilities. (And constraints. I cannot bring myself to kill another human being, but I could, had I been raised differently.)

The third step in the process of sociobiological explanation is the invention of a suitable adaptive story to explain why the trait supposed to be universal, coded by the supposed genes, has been incorporated into the human genome by natural selection. A direct explanation can be invented for most traits. A xenophobic person will keep out strangers, and so have less competition for food in short supply and so successfully raise more offspring. As a result the genes for xenophobia will spread. The same story can be applied to territoriality and aggressiveness. Male domination is incorporated because dominant males control more females and so simultaneously produce more offspring and maintain a captive labor force to rear them. And so on. There is no end to the just-so stories that can be invented. A difficulty arises with some traits, however, that appear to be of reproductive cost to their possessor. Such so-called altruistic traits ought not to be established by natural selection. A triumph of sociobiological theory, regarded by most sociobiologists as the major theoretical contribution of the field to evolutionary studies, has been the invention of *extended fitness*. This notion is based on the realization that the gene for a trait will spread in a species even if its carriers do not directly benefit reproductively, provided that a group of organisms who also carry the gene are sufficiently benefited. In particular, if close relatives of the actor receive a sufficient reproductive benefit, the actor may sacrifice its own reproduction, yet its genes will still spread.

An example of an explanation involving this sort of kin selection is the just-so story for homosexuality. The problem posed is to explain the widespread occurrence of homosexuality when the genes for the behavior should have been selected out of the population because of the failure of homosexuals to reproduce. It should be noted, first, that there is no evidence that homosexuality does lead to lower reproductive fitness. Only a typological definition of homo- and heterosexuality which assumes that all people are exclusively one or the other would lead to such a conclusion. The evidence is clear, however, that people display a broad range of mixed homosexual and heterosexual behavior in their lives, and many persons who later declare themselves to be exclusively homosexual have been the fathers and mothers of children in their earlier lives. Second, there is not the slightest evidence that different degrees of homo- and heterosexuality are in any way genetically based. So the problem may be a pseudo-problem. Given that the assumptions of lower reproductive rate and heritability are correct, the following story has been invented. Since homosexuals do not have their own children, then in primitive societies they were free to help raise and feed the children of their brothers and sisters so that their genes actually increased by kin selection. Aside from the difficulty of checking up on the behavior of homosexuals in the Neolithic (if indeed there were any as a distinct group), what we know of modern hunters and gatherers lends no plausibility to this story. Nevertheless, it is a model for the kind or uncheckable story that can be invented ad hoc to explain observations. The sociobiologist Barash has, with unusual candor, called this kind of story-telling "Let's Pretend." [15] It seems a strange procedure for a modern biological science.

BIOLOGY, CAUSATION, AND FREEDOM

Biological determinist theories are easy targets. They combine elementary misconceptions about genes and organisms with philosophical naïveté, bad data, and an overtly political purpose. But they speak to a deep problem. How are we to understand the etiology of human differences and similarities, especially in social structures? Those who expose the fallacies of biological determinism are often accused of being radical environmentalists who view human individual and social behavior as determined in detail by the sequence of experiences that each of us undergoes, especially in early childhood. Vulgar economism, which explains all attitudes by social class and immediate economic pressure is an example. So is Skinnerian behaviorism. Radical environmentalism so described is as much a biological determinism as the genetic determinism of A. R. Jensen and E. O. Wilson. Both are positions taken because their proponents reject what seems to them the only alternative, a dualism that introduces free will. How are we to understand human freedom in a world of cause and effect? If we give up cause and effect, we fall into the pit of mysticism and antimaterialism. If we insist on cause and effect, we seem to be determinists of one sort or another who can, in principle, like Laplace's Demon, predict every last detail of every life from previous information. We are then not free.

There are two solutions offered to this dilemma that are current. One is Kant's dualistic solution, if it can be called that, which simply asserts that as physical beings we are determined,

[15] David Barash, *Sociobiology and Behavior* (Amsterdam: Elsevier, 1977), p. 277.

but as moral social beings we are free and must accept responsibility for our acts. Hume's solution was to change the terrain of the problem to a political one. We are free, he held, if we can act according to our wishes and desires. The prisoner is not free because, no matter how much he wishes to be at large, he is confined to his cell. But Hume does not deal directly with the determination of our wishes and desires. If *they* are determined, then in what sense is the free man freer than the prisoner?

At a political level, we must ally ourselves with Hume. A theory of human freedom that does not distinguish between a free person's liberty and a prisoner's confinement is a political weapon that can only enslave people. Slavery is not freedom, not even in 1984. Our problem is to accept material cause and to see how human freedom can be a consequence of cause and effect rather than its negation.

When we examine physical systems, we see that randomness and determination are not in contradiction, but arise one from the other as levels of organization are crossed. Random radioactive decay is the basis for the most exquisitely exact clocks, accurate to a millionth of a second. On the other hand, the completely determined forces acting on a molecule in a gas may nevertheless give it a movement that is random for all practical purposes. It is usually said that this latter randomness is only epistemic since, in principle, we could, if we knew enough, predict that path of the molecule. There is, however, an important difference between the determined molecule moving at "random" and, say, a railroad train moving on a track, although both are completely determined. The train is determined by a small number of causes and is strongly constrained by the track. The movement of the molecule, however, is the conjunction of a very large number of causal chains, no one of which strongly constrains it. Thus, the molecule is infinitesimally correlated with any one cause, while the train is strongly correlated with the direction of the track. On the other hand, the train *is* moving at random with respect, say, to people in houses near the railway, whose movements are, again, only infinitesimally correlated with it because of the weakness of gravitational forces.

We are then led to a definition of freedom within causality. A process is free from, or at random with respect to, some set of causes if it is extremely weakly correlated with any one cause or small subset of these causes, although its movement may be perfectly determined by the conjunction of all of them. Normal human beings are free to the extent that no single obsession rules their lives and no walls pen them in. The obsessive madman, like the prisoner, is controlled not by a conjunction of a vast number of infinitesimally small causes, but by one large one. The fox is free; the hedgehog is not. Our biologies, created in the course of evolution, make us foxes and not hedgehogs. We are forever re-creating our own psychic and material environments, and, as the result of the social organization produced by our material brains and hands, our individual lives are the consequences of a bewildering variety of intersecting causal pathways. In this way, our biology has freed us from the constraints of biology.

Psychiatry and Morality

ALAN A. STONE

THE TANNER LECTURES ON HUMAN VALUES

Delivered at
Stanford University

March 31 and April 5, 1982

ALAN A. STONE was educated at Harvard University and Yale Medical School. He trained in psychiatry at McLean Hospital and in psychoanalysis at the Boston Psychoanalytic Institute. He has been a member of the Harvard Medical School faculty since 1961 and of the Harvard Law School faculty since 1968. He is now Touroff-Glueck Professor of Law and Psychiatry in the Faculty of Law and the Faculty of Medicine, Harvard University. Professor Stone has been President of the American Psychiatric Association, a Guggenheim Fellow, and a Fellow of the Center for Advanced Study in the Behavioral Sciences, in Stanford. He is the author of a number of articles and books on law and psychiatry and has been awarded the Manfred Guttmacher Prize and the Isaac Ray Award for this work. He has served on the Editorial Board of the *American Journal of Psychiatry*, and he is a member of the Board of Trustees and Chair of the Council on Governmental Policy and Law of the American Psychiatric Association.

I want to express my appreciation to Roberto Mangabeira Unger and A. Douglas Stone for their helpful discussion of the ideas which found their way into these Lectures.

I

It is difficult, as Erik Erikson has suggested, not to approach the subject of psychiatry and morality with a chip on each shoulder.[1] The very conjunction of the terms is calculated to make blood boil. There are psychiatrists on the one hand who insist that psychiatry is a medical science having nothing to do with morality. And there are philosophers and theologians who are repelled by the thought that modern psychiatry, particularly as influenced by Freud, has anything good or worthwhile to contribute to the subject of morality. I am reminded of a distinguished Harvard philosophy professor who while attending a symposium on psychoanalysis and philosophy was so outraged at the very conjunction of these two disciplines that he allegedly exclaimed "psychoanalysis is a dirty dishpan in the great ocean of philosophy." I have no doubt that if he were here tonight he would express a similar opinion about the conjunction of psychiatry and morality. One can assume that his sentiments would run as follows:

The question of morality is the noblest question of mankind, involving the possibility of freedom, the grounding of morality in reason, or some ideal of an ordered society. Psychoanalysis and psychiatry, in contrast, are ignoble, small-minded, reductionistic, backward-looking, even somewhat prurient, and here I quote the Catholic theologian, Hans Küng, psychoanalysis has been "identified in public opinion with irreligiousness and sexuality, with the

[1] *Young Man Luther* (New York: Norton, 1958), p. 21.

[187]

breakdown of religion, order and morality." [2] Many other critics
have suggested that modern psychiatry as influenced by Freud is
to be blamed for all of the "decadence" of the "permissive society."

These are not just the prejudiced opinions of outsiders. The
same views have been echoed by voices within the field. Erik Erikson, for example, in his psychohistory *Young Man Luther*, writes,

> Neurotic patients and panicky people in general are so starved
> for beliefs that they will fanatically spread among the un-
> believers what are often as yet quite shaky convictions. Because
> we did not include this fact in our awareness, we were shocked
> at being called pansexualists. We were distressed at the spread
> of a compulsive attitude of mutual mental denuding. We were
> dismayed at a widespread fatalism according to which man is
> nothing but a multiplication of his parents' faults. We must
> grudgingly admit that even as we were trying to devise, with
> scientific determinism, a therapy for the few, we were led to
> promote an ethical disease among the many. [P. 19]

Although there are aspects of this indictment which I think
are true and which I shall rely on in my subsequent discussion, I
would like to sound a cautionary note. It seems to me that it is too
easy to blame too much on Freud. The American hunger for Freud
is an appetite which itself needs to be explained. And there has
been a similar loss of moral consensus, a similar cynicism about
traditional moral authority, and a similar phase of breakdown in
conventional religion, order, and morality in societies where Freud
and modern psychiatry have had little perceptible influence. But
whether or not Erikson is entirely correct about the etiology of the
ethical disease, he is certainly ingenuous in asserting that the goal
of psychoanalysis was to devise a therapy for the few. That has
certainly not been *his* goal for most of his life nor was it what
inspired Freud's work, from *The Interpretation of Dreams* to
Civilization and Its Discontents. As Hans Küng rightly observes in

---

[2] *Freud and the Problem of God* (New Haven: Yale University Press, 1980),
p. 55.

Freud and the Problem of God, "psychoanalysis was now applied to literature and aesthetics, to mythology, folklore and educational theory, to prehistory and the history of religion. It was no longer merely a therapeutic procedure but an instrument of universal enlightenment" (p. 27).

I would prefer to describe psychoanalysis as a descriptive developmental theory of human subjectivity, but "instrument of enlightenment" comes closer to the mark than Erikson's scientific therapy for the few. Modern psychiatry, though less enthusiastic about psychoanalysis than an earlier generation, has been no less ambitious in its general claims of offering universal enlightenment. Particularly has this been the case in psychiatry's contribution to contemporary problems of morality.

It is difficult to think of a pressing moral question on which my profession has not made "authoritative pronouncements." Abortion, capital punishment, racism, sexism, nuclear disarmament, gun control, apartheid, pornography, terrorism, the Vietnam war, euthanasia, poverty, love and marriage are only some of the subjects on which we have felt that our professional expertise qualified us to speak. In fact, I should admit to you that I myself have contributed to psychiatric pronouncements on all of these issues. These two lectures are therefore in some sense confessional — an examination of my own professional conscience. How did psychiatrists presume so much, and how is it that we were permitted so much? One president of the American Psychiatric Association, using the jargon associated with the community mental health movement, announced to his colleagues that "the world is our catchment area."[3] And he might have added, "man in the world is our subject matter." He received a standing ovation and went on to become president of the World Psychiatric Association.

The grandiosity of modern psychiatry may seem unjustified today, but I believe it can be understood from a certain point of

---

[3] Cited in Alan A. Stone, "Presidential Response," *American Journal of Psychiatry* 136:8 (August 1979), pp. 1020–22.

view. There is in Western thought a long tradition of understanding the human condition in terms of its abnormal manifestations.
This tradition is by no means confined to psychiatry. It can be
found in such unlikely places as Immanuel Kant; see for example
his *Anthropology from a Pragmatic Point of View*. (I shall be
making some comparative comments about Freud and Kant
throughout these two lectures.) The intellectual tradition which
Kant exemplifies attempts to isolate the abnormal, madness, at an
extreme of the human spectrum as "the most profound degradation of humanity which seems to originate from nature." [4] But
having put madness to one side and isolated it, as though it had
nothing to do with his understanding of the "normal," in his
analysis of the situation of the rest of humanity, Kant is somehow
haunted by the analogy to madness: "to be subject to emotions and
passions is probably always an illness of mind because both emotions and passions exclude the sovereignty of reason." [5] For Kant
emotion is akin to "apoplexy" and "passion is delusion." Although
Kant had important philosophical justifications for deriving morality from reason, his attempt to do this was set against this conception of passion as delusion. He also, in a way, anticipated
contemporary psychiatry's obsession with the problem of self-
deception: that we are unaware of our own motives. He wrote,
"the veil with which self love conceals our moral infirmity must
be torn away." Kant, I am sure, believed that the tearing away
would be done by a rational moral philosophy, but psychiatry's
attribution of self-deception to the unconscious suggested that the
veil must be lifted in some other manner.

One of psychiatry's most convincing claims that it has a right
to participate in moral discourse is bottomed on this assertion of
unconscious self-deception. For example, many psychiatrists believe we have a professional as well as a personal justification for

----

[4] With an introduction by F. P. Van Der Pitte (Carbondale, Ill.: Southern Illi-
nois University Press, 1978), p. 112.

[5] Ibid., p. 251.

becoming involved in the movement for nuclear disarmament. We argue that many people are denying, repressing, or suppressing the frightening possibility of an atomic holocaust. These psychological mechanisms, which in this instance lead to moral and political inertia, are, we assert, a classic example of pathological self-deception. I shall return to this theme. But here let me just emphasize that a claim that someone is practicing self-deception, if it is to be a powerful claim, must also mean that the psychiatrist sees through the self-deception to the truth of the matter — what lies concealed behind the veil of self-deception. To know that is to know something about the "meaning of life."

At any rate, it should be clear that the attempt to understand human nature in the metaphors of madness and self-deception did not begin with modern psychiatry. Freud would use language identical to Kant's: "the id is the place of passions" and the ego of "reason and sanity." [6] The tradition to which Kant and Freud belong sees the peril of humanity in the triumph of passion over judgment and reason. This tradition accepts the basic dichotomy of reason and passion as a given in human nature. Passion at war with reason remains even today one of the most compelling paradigms both of mental abnormality and of the human condition.

Modern biological psychiatry grounded in twentieth-century medical science has little professed interest in this rational humanist tradition. However, its practitioners share Kant's opinion that madness originates from nature and they agree with Kant's view that "the germ of derangement develops together with the germ of reproduction and is thus hereditary." [7] But if madness is biological and genetic, how shall we understand the rest of the disorders of consciousness that stretch from madness at one end of the scale to normal human suffering at the other.

---

[6] *The Ego and the Id and Other Works*, trans. by James Strachey, standard ed., vol. 19 (London: Hogarth Press, 1927).

[7] Kant, *Anthropology from a Pragmatic Point of View*, p. 115.

Some psychiatrists have argued that this is no longer our business, the old psychiatry, they say, is dead, madness is part of the neurosciences, the rest is the human condition.[8] But even as biological psychiatrists say this, they are busily engaged in studying the whole spectrum of the disorders of consciousness and charting the biological substrate of the human condition. Nor are they hesitant to extend the reach of biologically determined mental illness further and further from the extreme of madness. And if we look to practice rather than theory, we find everywhere the prescription of chemicals to ease the pain and suffering of the human condition. Through the prism of medical science, the passions of everyday life become symptoms to be treated chemically. In analogy to Kant, biological psychiatry, after having declared madness a biological disorder, is haunted by biology in its understanding of the rest of humanity. The problem is and always has been for psychiatry whether it provides only a theory of madness or a more general theory of human nature as well. Or is it even possible in principle to make such a distinction? Can one explain madness without explaining human nature?

What is important for my purposes tonight is that when psychiatry begins to gain popular acceptance as in fact providing a theory of human nature, it begins to establish the context of moral action and moral obligation. It does this in at least two obvious ways. First, most Western notions of morality require as a fundamental premise the existence of a unified and continuous self and a will. Philosophers who construct theories of morality recognize the need to ground these fundamental premises on some assumptions about mind and mental functioning — a psychology, no matter how limited, is required. One can demonstrate this need for a psychology not only in Kant, but also in such contrasting moralists as St. Augustine in his *Confessions* and Sartre in *Being and Nothingness*. If morality must be constructed on a psychology, as I believe, then profound changes in the accepted psychol-

---

[8] E[dwin] Fuller Torrey, *The Death of Psychiatry* (New York: Penguin, 1975).

ogy inescapably raise questions about the accepted morality. Modern psychiatry as influenced by Freud seems to many observers to have produced just that result. Sartre recognized this and went to great lengths to repudiate the central Freudian construct of unconscious self-deception and to replace it with the formidable moral notion of bad faith.[9]

A second way in which modern psychiatry established the context of moral action and obligation was by producing convincing stories about what it means to be a person. It did this by "uncovering" the "true history" of human drives and by revealing, in Ricoeur's phrase, "The archaeology of desire."[10]

Psychoanalysis not only challenged the unity of the self; it privileged a certain account of virtues and vices which made the will a minor actor in the moral drama of life. Though there was for academics much to criticize in these Freudian revelations, they had a compelling influence on popular psychology and mass culture. Freudianism could not be kept out of the dialogue on the "meaning of life."

From the moment American psychiatry embraced Freud, it had a unified theory of human nature from which its explanations of mental disorder and treatment could be derived. That, I believe, is what Freud intended, contrary to what Erikson suggests. If modern psychiatry, guided by Freud, started down the path that Kant and other theorists of human nature had taken, we reached a different destination. Modern psychiatry produced a vision of human nature in which morality was itself a passion at war with reason. Moral choices and decisions were based on unconscious determinants, all of which seemed incompatible with Kant's idea of free moral agents choosing between right and wrong. Erikson wants to write this off as a kind of misunderstanding, a premature

[9] Jean Paul Sartre, *Being and Nothingness: An Essay on Phenomenological Ontology*, trans. by Hazel E. Barnes (New York: Philosophical Library, 1956). See particularly part I, ch. 2, "Bad Faith," and part IV, ch. 2, "Doing and Having."

[10] Paul Ricoeur, *Freud and Philosophy: An Essay on Interpretation*, trans. by Dennis Savage (New Haven: Yale University Press, 1970).

acceptance of tentative conclusions. But Freud intended on the basis of his theory of human nature to throw down the gauntlet before the idea of man as a free moral agent. What else could he have meant when he embraced Groddeck's words, "we are lived by unknown and uncontrollable forces," [11] or when he placed Kant's categorical imperative in the id as the legacy of a phylogenetic past. The morality which had power over men came not from any higher authority, not from reason, but from an unknown moral passion, a stranger within. Immorality was equally mysterious and required deciphering.

Generations of American psychiatrists have tried to find ways around what more and more of them came to recognize as problematic and embarrassing. The best known and most beloved American popularizer of Freud's ideas, Karl Menninger, was moved to wonder, *Whatever Became of Sin?* [12] But it is not just psychoanalysis in modern psychiatry that called into question the ideal of a free moral agent. All of the dominant conceptual paradigms of modern psychiatry — biological, behavioral, psychodynamic, and social — conflict with traditional ideas about free moral agents. Although I am sure philosophers would say that this bald statement of conflict is wrong, I am equally sure that they would disagree on just how it is wrong. At least for psychiatrists who explain behavior in terms of biological transmethylation, reinforcement schedules, defective superegos, and demographic trends, there is still no convincing resolution of this problem.

Perhaps the most obvious practical implication of explaining morality and immorality in terms of the unconscious, the reinforcement schedule, or the DNA — and undermining the ideal conception of free moral agents choosing to do right or wrong — is that it undermines the theory of our criminal law. It makes it much more difficult to attribute moral blameworthiness to those

[11] Freud, *The Ego and the Id*, p. 23.
[12] New York: Hawthorn Books, 1973.

who break the law or who in some way offend. As Lord Devlin stated it, "Everywhere the concept of sickness expands at the expense of the concept of moral responsibility." [13] The concept of moral responsibility is of course what justifies punishment. Viewed from this perspective, modern psychiatry appeared as the antagonist of the principle of retributive punishment. It joined forces with Christian forgiveness in a secular version of "to understand is to forgive." Christopher Lasch makes Lord Devlin's point with more sweeping rhetoric: "But it is precisely this universal understanding, sympathy, and tolerance (which in any case does not conceal the persistence of intolerance at a deeper level) that reflect the collapse of moral consensus, the collapse of distinctions between right and wrong, the collapse of moral authority.[14]

But if psychiatry as influenced by Freud made people uncomfortable about punishing sinners, it soon became clear that in the alternative to punishment more was involved than simple forgiveness. Reviewing Karl Menninger's book *The Crime of Punishment*,[15] the late Professor Packer of Stanford Law School suggested that the impulse to treat and the impulse to punish originated in the same region of the psyche.[16] Foucault argues that at the end of the Middle Ages evil went out of the world and madness came in.[17] One might in that vein say about twentieth-century America that progressivism and psychiatry drove retribution out of our moral deliberations and replaced it with treatment.

Many critics began to find similar evidence that psychiatry, far from being a threat to conventional social morality, had become the very instrument of that morality. The criticism came from an

---

[13] P. Devlin, *The Enforcement of Morals* (London: Oxford University Press, 1959), p. 17.

[14] *Haven in a Heartless World: The Family Besieged* (New York: Basic Books, 1977), p. 221.

[15] New York: Viking Press, 1968.

[16] Review by Herbert Packer of Karl Menninger's *The Crime of Punishment* in *New York Review of Books*, October 23, 1969, p. 17.

[17] Michel Foucault, *Madness and Civilization: A History of Insanity in the Age of Reason*, trans. by Richard Howard (New York: Pantheon Books, 1965).

entirely different direction than Erikson anticipated. Indeed, Erikson was himself a target of this attack. Far from being a corrupter of conventional social morality (or a liberating influence), psychoanalysis and psychiatry were identified as the chief vehicles of conventional social morality of oppression and of passing judgment on people. Of course this partly can be explained away in historical terms, the vanguard of social change had passed Freud by. The Freudian revolution becomes, over time, a counter-revolution; what was liberating for one generation becomes oppressive for the next. Another way to think of this is that Freud's descriptive theory of human nature was seized on, particularly in the United States, as a prescriptive theory. This is one way to account for the grandiosity of Modern Psychiatry: all deviance, including crime and morality, became a disease, and the psychiatrist presides over both the diagnosis and the cure.

At any rate, we now have encountered three perspectives on the involvement of psychiatry in moral issues. First, there is the notion that psychiatry, particularly as influenced by Freud, undermined the consensus of conventional social morality and traditional moral authority. Second, that psychiatry embodied and enforced conventional social morality and authority. Finally, that psychiatry undercut our fundamental conception of free moral agents whom we can justly punish. I shall attempt tonight to offer you a partial account of how all this happened.

Thomas Szasz, himself a psychiatrist and psychoanalyst, has made all three of these arguments against psychiatry.[18]

1. In *The Myth of Mental Illness*, he argues that Freud transformed what was in essence a kind of cheating, malingering, and lying into an illness, hysteria.

[18] *The Myth of Mental Illness: Foundations of a Theory of Personal Conduct*, rev. ed. (New York: Harper and Row, 1974); *The Manufacture of Madness: A Comparative Study of the Inquisition and the Mental Health Movement* (New York: Harper and Row, 1970); *Law, Liberty and Psychiatry: An Inquiry into the Social Uses of Mental Health Practices* (New York: Macmillan, 1963).

2. In *The Manufacture of Madness*, he describes psychiatry as the continuation of the Inquisition — "the defense of the dominant ethic." Just as the Inquisition invented witches, psychiatry invented the holy myth of schizophrenia.

3. Throughout his writing Szasz repeatedly attacks every psychiatric paradigm that undercuts the traditional view of the free moral agent. He is particularly obdurate in his demand that the insanity defense be abolished. Even the most obviously deranged person intends the consequences of his acts, and to deny this is to deny that person's humanity. Although Szasz sometimes makes this claim as though it were an empirical fact, at other times it seems to be a normative or ideal view of human nature. In order to maintain this view, he has declared that even Kant is wrong about the extreme of madness. There is no mental illness, everything is the human condition. Perhaps the essence of Szasz's criticism is that psychiatry is nothing but ideology masquerading as scientific objectivity.

Although Foucault suggests in *Madness and Civilization* that these charges against psychiatry have been true since the Middle Ages, the psychiatrist was at the periphery of society until the twentieth century. It was Freud who turned the attention of psychiatry from the madhouses to the middle class. It is against Freud and his influence that the ideological arguments are made. Although Freud had very little experience with psychotics himself, in the course of his work he conceived a coherent unified psychological theory of mental illness. He broke through the dividing line between the most profound degradation of humanity at one end and between the normal and the neurotic at the other end. One can no longer think of a continuum from madness to sanity; normality is no longer on the continuum. Freud literally believed that neurosis was the price we pay for civilization. Although American Freudians sacrificed this idea on the altar of therapeutic optimism, Freud had declared normality a nearly unattainable ideal. In this respect I doubt that he differed very much from Kant or from certain other moral philosophers, if you allow me to analogize between Kant's assessment of the moral infirmity of mankind due to the veil of self-love and Freud's assessment of our neurotic infirmity due to the veil of unconscious repression.

There is another distinction in Freud's thought which is essential to my analysis. Freud believed that there were no qualitative differences between the mental processes of the psychotic and those of the rest of us. Ultimately, the only distinctions were quantitative. The only difference between a delusion and a fantasy was quantity. The only difference between a memory and a hallucination was quantity. Psychosis was dreaming while awake. Everyone had all variations of the Oedipus complex. The difference between heterosexual and homosexual was quantitative. I think it was Goethe who said no man ever had a fantasy that I have not had. Freud would have said the claim was believable.

But there is something deeply problematic about a theory which though it provides us an understanding of all mental processes, normal and abnormal, relies on unspecified quantities to explain all of the differences. This problem of quantity becomes more troubling when we recognize that the determinist conception of Freudian theory is grounded on these mysterious quantities which impel fantasy, emotion, thought, and behavior. In the end it is not clear whether Freud placed the categorical imperative in the id and rejected the notion of free moral agents based on empirical observations of how people actually behave — that is, on some empirical view of human nature or on some a priori assumption about human nature derived from the determinist theory of science. He often seems to be saying both at once. This, you will recognize, is the criticism I made of Szasz, only from the other direction. I believe that in both instances these are simply different intuitions about what it means to be a person. The way Freud imposed this intuition on his theory is by invoking the quantitative factor. In fact the quantitative factor can be used as a red flag, as one reads Freud, marking the places where descriptions of mental processes and subjective experiences are transformed into explanatory determinist theories. The quantitative factor is central to the hydraulic theory of emotions, to the catharsis theory of therapy, and to Freud's mean conception of the human possibilities of freedom and love. It is on the basis of the quantitative factor that Freud ridiculed the biblical injunction to love thy neighbor, and the more mysterious injunction to love thine enemy.[19]

If one deprives Freud of this quantitative factor, one can no longer claim for him that he offers either a coherent theoretical explanation of mental disorder or a compelling account of human nature. The strongest claim one can make is that it is a description of a kind of subjective experience, the history of desire in the individual rendered in a deterministic and selfless discourse.

Freud said neurotics suffer from reminiscences, and we might say that reminiscences were Freud's subject matter. *Not* man in the world but man and his reminiscences. Out of that subject matter one can not get a complete explanation of the human condition or perhaps even a correct understanding of one of Freud's most important subjects, *guilt*.

But having said all these things, and there are other critical things to say about Freud, I find it hard to reject his most basic contribution to Western thought, the dynamic unconscious. After Richard Nixon had lost the presidential election to John F. Kennedy, he came back to California and eventually ran for governor of the state. Everywhere Nixon went on his campaign trail, reporters would ask the obvious question, was he running for governor in order to run again for president? Finally, after having been asked this again and again, at one press conference Nixon drew himself up, looked the reporter in the eye, and said, "Listen, I would like to tell the press once and for all, please stop asking this question. I can assure you that I will be fully satisfied if I am elected governor of the United States." We all now understand

---

[19] *Civilization and Its Discontents*, standard ed. (London: Hogarth Press, 1961), p. 109.

this error in a Freudian perspective, namely that the conscious and the mental are not identical, and I think most of us have some feeling that we do not fully understand our selves and that we are all capable of similar revealing Freudian errors. The basis of the psychoanalyst's claim to special knowledge is that by his methods he has access to our unconscious and understands the processes by which our repressed desires become known. We are trapped in our self-deceptions, and the psychoanalyst can see through us to the truth of the matter. We must now examine this supposed truth because in it are the concealed human values and the moral postures which have had such a great influence on modern life. It is by contributing the dynamic unconscious to our understanding of what it means to be a person that psychoanalysis has had its greatest influence on morality.

Freud believed that the truth about the unconscious and the shaping of personality, conscience, and passion came from two major sources — infantile experiences which were repressed to comprise infantile amnesia and the phylogenetic unconscious including the core of the superego. This phylogenetic element was Freud's sociobiology, and in retrospect it seems entirely speculative. Modern Freudians have tried to read this sociobiology out of Freud, but it was a crucial aspect of his theory and it was pervasive. It could not be removed by clean theoretical surgery and it contained the hidden ideology of psychoanalysis. It is equally important to recognize that Freud's theory of infantile experiences was only dubiously empirical; it was also structured by sociobiological assumptions and by Freud's intuitions about what it meant to be a person.

It was Freud's sociobiological assumptions and his emphasis on early infantile experiences within the family that allowed him to construct a theory of what it meant to be a person which was transcultural and transhistorical.[20] The limitations of such a theory and the errors in Freud's sociobiology now seem obvious to us. We

[20] Herbert Marcuse, *Eros and Civilization: A Philosophical Inquiry into Freud* (Boston: Beacon Press, 1955); see especially Epilogue, "Critique of Neo-Freudian Revisionism."

recognize that what Freud understood to be the truth of the matter was to a large extent ideological, and nowhere is this more obvious than in his truth about women.

Before turning to that, let me summarize and reformulate my thoughts. I have been trying to think through with you some of the moral ramifications of modern psychiatry; at the same time I have a more basic question, is it possible to have a theory of mental illness which does not imply a theory of ·human nature that in turn contextualizes the problem of morality? Now it is possible to minimize the apparent moral implications of psychiatry by limiting mental illness to an extreme as Kant and some contemporary biological psychiatrists would do. Madness comes from nature and the rest of our disorders perhaps from living. But even those who draw such lines find it difficult to keep the domains of madness and the human condition separate. Now by examining Freud I am hoping to show you the most powerful example of psychiatry's attempt to give a coherent unified theory of mental disorder and human nature and to tell us what it means to be a person. If we accept and apply these theories as valid self-descriptions, we have accepted the values and moral postures concealed in them. The appeal of Freud's theories to twentieth-century men and women as revealing self-descriptions is ultimately the key to his influence on contemporary morality. Even Jean Paul Sartre, who made elaborate arguments against Freud's unconscious and who created his own existential psychoanalysis partly in reaction to Freud, when it came to writing his autobiography, took as a central theme a Freudian self-description. He reports that a psychoanalyst had told him that because his father had died when he was an infant, Sartre did not have a superego. This seems to have delighted Sartre. He wrote that other men went through life weighted down by their fathers "like Aeneas carrying Anchises from the walls of Troy" but he, the philosopher of radical freedom, had no such burden.[21]

[21] *The Words*, trans. by Bernard Frechtman (New York: G. Braziller, 1964).

If his theories were attractive as valid self-descriptions even for philosophers skeptical of Freud, they were enormously attractive to bourgeois American men and women. Or as Kate Millett, the radical feminist, suggests, they were the ideas with which American men and women were indoctrinated. She writes, "The new formulation of old attitudes [bourgeois, patriarchical, moralism] had to come from science and particularly from the emerging social sciences . . . the most useful and authoritative branches of social control and manipulation. . . . New prophets arrived on the scene . . . . The most influential of these was Sigmund Freud, beyond question the strongest individual counterrevolutionary force in the ideology of sexual politics." [22]

Freud summarized most of his theories about women in a brief lecture on "Femininity." He begins by demonstrating that it is impossible to define male and female, therefore, "Psychoanalysis does not try to describe what a woman is — that would be a task it could scarcely perform — but sets about inquiring how she comes into being, how a woman develops out of a child with bisexual disposition." [23] But Freud does not in fact begin his description of the course of a woman's development with a bisexual child. As his many critics have repeatedly pointed out, Freud's little girl is a bisexual defective boy. The supposed travails of this defective boy in reaching adult feminine sexuality are, I assume, well known to you. The ultimate achievement of mature female sexuality was a rare event in Freud's view. There were other consequences of Freud's theory of how woman "comes into being": her weak superego, her failures of sublimation, her envy, and her deficiencies in a sense of justice. The woman who did internalize these Freudian self-descriptions would assuredly think of herself as erotically and morally inferior to men. But despite the many criticisms of these theories, many women did internalize them as

---

[22] *Sexual Politics* (Garden City: Doubleday, 1970), p. 178.

[23] "Femininity," in *New Introductory Lectures on Psychoanalysis* (1933), trans. by James Strachey (New York: Norton, 1964), p. 116.

valid self-descriptions and particularly Freud's ideal of mature
female sexuality. This Freudian truth about female sexuality based
on a speculative sociobiology was widely accepted as a correct self-
description. It led millions of women to believe they were sexually
inadequate, a conclusion that millions of their husbands shared.
For decades women would be told that their sexual "problem"
was a manifestation of their masculine protest, as was their wish
to have careers.

As a psychiatrist and psychoanalyst who has lived through all
of the things I have been describing, you can perhaps imagine how
discomforting all this has been to me. Freud's theory of human
nature had been shown to be unnatural. Ironically, we were wrong
about sexuality. The subject is more complicated and the answers
still more elusive than Freud imagined. And if we were wrong
about that, what else was wrong? When we penetrated the patient's veil of self-love and self-deception, what we had found was
not the truth of the matter but our own ideology. And we had
been guilty of a certain kind of immorality ourselves. We had
treated our patients' self-descriptions as false. Indeed, the basic
therapeutic posture of the psychiatrist raised moral questions because it was grounded on the premise that we should treat much
of what the patient said about himself as self-deception.[24]

I shall have more to say about the moral aspects of the therapeutic relationship itself. The problems of domination, the under-
currents of love, the risks of vulnerability and attachment. But for
now we should be clear that the supposedly nonjudgmental psychoanalyst had as the framework of his understanding of illness
and treatment a prescriptive theory. That prescriptive theory was
in many respects an ideology which some critics argued was designed or applied for the purpose of rationalizing interpersonal
oppression of women by men, homosexuals by heterosexuals, and
rebels by conservatives.

[24] See Sissela Bok, "Address to American Psychiatric Association," New Or-
leans, May 1981.

These criticisms raised questions not only about the enterprise
of therapy but also about the whole conception of mental illness
in American psychiatry. As attempts were made to revise the psychodynamic conception of mental illness by removing what was
considered offensive, the explanatory power of Freud's theory of
mental illness was lost. Psychiatry has entered a period in which
there are no convincing connections between the diagnosis described in our Diagnostic Manual and our explanations of those
diagnoses.[25] Increasingly we agree that the extreme of madness
has a biological explanation, but as to the rest of the disorders
of consciousness there is a struggle of competing views. Simple
depression, for example, might be the result of an enzyme disturb-
ance, a cognitive disorder of self-image, an unconscious introject,
or a consequence of social isolation and alienation. The treatment
the patient receives depends to a large extent on the psychiatrist's
commitment to one of these approaches. Some psychiatrists seem
to think there are four kinds of simple depression, depending on
which of these etiological elements dominates. Others are eclectic,
and the patient will be met at the door by a team of clinicians each
applying a different approach. Each of these four paradigms —
biological, behavioral, psychodynamic, and social — has its own
problematic moral implications. But when they are all put together
there is no coherent vision of the human condition and there is
considerable confusion about what kinds of moral judgments are
being made or evaded. If this is true for all of these paradigms
put together, it is also particularly true for the psychodynamic
paradigm.

Without a unifying theory about the truth behind self-
deception, more and more psychodynamic psychiatrists are at-
tracted to the possibility of listening to their patients without any
theoretical preconceptions. Even if this is possible, and even if
the therapist avoids imposing his definition of what it means to be

---

[25] See Alan A. Stone, "Presidential Address: Conceptual Ambiguity and Morality
in Modern Psychiatry," *American Journal of Psychiatry* 137:8 (August 1980).

a person on the patient, there are still inescapable moral implications to this enterprise.

Many of our patients seek help in situations where they are struggling not just with depression, stress, or anxiety but also with moral problems. Should they get a divorce? Should they fight for custody of their children? Should they leave a job where they are needed and have made a commitment for one that pays more? Should they tell their spouse about their affair? Should they put their parents in a nursing home?

Psychiatrists tend to think that if we allow our patients to ventilate their feelings it will help them not only to understand themselves but also to attain greater clarity in making these moral decisions. The psychiatrist, without expressing his own potentially oppressive moral convictions or ideology, will help the patient get in touch with what seems right for him. But what seems right is often a conclusion reached as the result of exploring repressed desires, weighing competing inclinations. It is a kind of reflection in which the outside world shrinks and the self expands. This may be the correct way to get in touch with unconscious desires and to identify self-destructive impulses, but is it a sensible way to frame moral questions for oneself? Can moral questions be framed and resolved in a process where the self looms large and the world seems small?

I remember a patient, the wife of a scientist; they had several children. Her husband, she felt, was remote even in the rare instances when he was home. The patient came to me troubled about her unsatisfactory marriage; I encouraged her to explore her feelings and did little more than listen compassionately two hours a week. Within six weeks, this woman had met a wonderful new man, a real companion, was happily in love, and had decided to leave her husband and four children. Now whether this was good or bad, right or wrong, it seemed that I and the process of therapy were partly responsible both for her new-found great happiness and her moral decisions, all of which she ceremonialized by un-

expectedly bringing her new friend to the therapy hour for my
seal of approval. Human problems do not come packaged in psychiatric bits and moral bits. There may be a moral cost even in
nonjudgmental listening. Clearly cultural bias and concealed
moral assumptions played a part in the fallacies of the theory of
psychoanalysis. But is it possible that the introspective method of
free association is itself a major factor in painting the false picture of human nature? After all, it is on reminiscences — free
association — and not man in the world that the theoretical edifice
was built.

Freud asked his patient to give free rein to his thoughts and
report "everything that comes into his head, even if it is disagree-
able for him to say it, even if it seems to him unimportant or actually nonsensical." If the patient allows himself to free associate,
"he will present us with a mass of material . . . subject to the influence of the unconscious." That influence can then be examined
and deciphered so that the patient comes to understand himself.[26]

But more than a century before Freud discovered this fundamental rule of psychoanalysis Kant had considered and rejected it.
He writes in the *Anthropology*,

> To scrutinize the various acts of the imagination within me,
> when I call them forth, is indeed worth reflection, as well as
> necessary and useful for logic and metaphysics. But to wish to
> play the spy upon one's self, when those acts come to mind un-
> summoned and of their own accord (which happens through
> the play of the unpremeditatively creative imagination) is to
> reverse the natural order of the cognitive powers since then
> the rational elements do not take the lead (as they should)
> but instead follow behind. This desire for self investigation is
> either already a disease of the mind (hypochondria), or will
> lead to such a disease and ultimately to the madhouse. He
> who has a great deal to tell of inner experiences (for example
> of grace or temptations, etc.) may, in the course of his voyage to

[26] *Outline of Psychoanalysis*, standard ed., vol. 23 (London: Hogarth Press,
1964), p. 174.

self-discovery, have made his first landing only at Anticyra [the land of the insane].[27]

Although I do not entirely share Kant's opinion about "the natural order of the cognitive powers" or about the negative value of such "self-discovery," it may be that he is right as far as its value for framing moral questions. There is a tradition in moral philosophy of stepping back after you have attempted to explore and understand the facts of the situation, and then attempting to reexamine the case at hand in terms of some broader moral principle. But psychiatry has no such tradition of stepping back and no generally accepted moral principles if we did. Kant made these observations about free association in the *Anthropology*, where he argued that psychology generally would get nowhere so long as it relied on introspection. He advised psychologists to develop an anthropological method based on systematic observations of men and women in the world. He then offered the fruit of some of his own systematic observations. Although one can find evidence of Kant's uncontestable genius in this book, it is clear to any modern reader that Kant, this preeminent figure in Western moral philosophy, had nothing in his store of rational morality to protect his systematic observations against his personal biases and cultural prejudices — some of which he shared with Freud, particularly his attitudes toward women. The philosopher who introduces the English translation of Kant's *Anthropology* is "amazed at [Kant's] uncritical views" and asserts that "any failure on [Kant's] part to live up to the moral ideal must be ascribed to a lack of experience which permitted his prejudices to remain undetected."[28] But one might ask what then would correct Kant's "lack of experience."

Freud subjectively explored the unconscious and found his own biases. Kant objectively observed his fellow man and found his own biases. Is there no solution to this problem? If there is,

---

[27] Kant, *Anthropology from a Pragmatic Point of View*, p. 17.

[28] See pp. xix–xx of the Introduction by F. P. Van Der Pitte.

I am sure you do not expect to hear it from me. But I do have a sense of what has been missing from my own moral vision as a psychiatrist and psychoanalyst. First, I think we must recognize that even the most neutral and compassionate psychotherapy potentially misframes moral questions. We have to begin by acknowledging that to ourselves and to our patients. (Psycho-analysts in days gone by used to insist that their patients make no major life decisions during the process of psychoanalysis. The pace of life has quickened, and it is difficult to maintain this require-ment.) Next, we have to think of ways of stepping back or better helping our patients to step back so that moral questions can come into focus. Third, we must rethink our conception of guilt.

If the psychotherapeutic situation does not bring moral prob-lems into focus for the patient, it may also be true that the psycho-therapeutic situation prejudices the attempt to set out the context of morality. I want to argue that there is a crucial confusion in modern psychiatry which has arisen in this way that has to do with our understanding of depression, guilt, and what Freud called moral anxiety. What we see in our depressed patients (and who is not "depressed"?) has little or nothing to do with moral obliga-tions to others. This "superego" is not the inner voice of morality or the categorical imperative: it is the voice of self-loathing. The same patient who is tortured by what Freud called moral anxiety as he reflects on his life has little or no sense of his moral obliga-tions to anyone else; in fact his self-loathing typically stands in the way of his moral ambitions and obligations. The patient will say that he is tortured by compulsive ideas, that he is really a fraud and worthless even though he is a distinguished professor at a great university. His psychoanalyst will say about this man that he has a strict superego which has initiated a critical moral attack upon his ego. But this professor typically has the same view of everyone else. If he has a strict superego it is not an inner voice commanding moral obligations, duty, or kindness to others. This voice from the unconscious is not the voice of morality, it is the voice of self-loathing. Psychiatry influenced by Freud has confused self-loathing and moral conscience.

I once complained to a distinguished philosopher that he had failed to honor an obligation he had made to me. His immediate response was, "I thought you psychiatrists are supposed to help people *not* to feel guilty." He said this with a smile, but I think his humorous sally bespeaks the real confusion in ordinary language. Psychiatry needs to rethink the subject of guilt and we need to begin with a careful distinction between self-loathing arising because the self is not as perfect, as powerful, as lovable as the person believes it should be and guilt which arises because one has failed in one's moral obligations to others. Of course the enterprise of conceptualizing what it means to have moral obligations is not one that psychiatry can embark on alone. But we hope that in the future psychiatry will be one of a family of disciplines which knows that to study human nature is to study moral obligations. This enterprise will help us to remember what Kant learned from Rousseau—"What is truly permanent in human nature is not any condition in which it once existed and from which it has fallen, rather it is the goal for which and toward which it moves." [29]

II

In my first lecture I described how modern psychiatry has been criticized: first for undermining conventional morality, then for enforcing conventional morality, and more generally for undercutting what seems to be essential to moral theory — the idea of an autonomous person choosing between good and evil. I suggested that the reason these criticisms were tenable was that modern psychiatry presented itself as offering not just a theory of mental disorder, but also a theory of the human condition. This

---

[29] Ernst Cassirer, *Rousseau, Kant, Goethe: Two Essays*, trans. by James Gutmann, et al. (Princeton: Princeton University Press, 1970), p. 20.

theory of the human condition contained certain moral postures and established a context for moral ambition.

At the same time, I was working through my own critique of psychoanalysis as a dominant theory of the human condition in American psychiatry. My presentation of that critique might have been easier to follow if I had begun by considering the method of Freud's "discovery," the situation in which the patient is asked to free-associate. I argued that this method develops a certain kind of evidence which prejudices the attempt to construct a theory of the human condition. I suggested that Freud's theory based on that evidence is not an explanation of the person in the world but rather a developmental description of human subjectivity. Two other ideas were important to this critique. First, that the way Freud made his descriptive theory seem like an explanatory theory was by invoking mysterious quantities. For example, it may be true that when we reminisce and free-associate about our parents we do evoke sensual feelings about them and fearful, hostile memories as well. It may even be true, as I think it is, that everyone who reminisces will eventually come upon such memories. But the mystery of how those memories explain our personality, our lives, and our current behaviors remains a mystery because Freud invoked an unknown quantitative factor as the crucial explanatory element in the connection.

The other point I tried to make is that the psychotherapeutic setting in which the self looms large and the world small is not an appropriate setting *in which* to frame moral questions or *from which* to conceptualize the possibilities of human morality. Psychiatrists are called head shrinkers, but from this perspective it is the world and not the head they shrink. I suggested two ways for changing this predicament, one clinical and one theoretical. At the clinical level it is necessary to acknowledge the problem and to develop a method for stepping back and reexamining human problems in a moral perspective. At the level of theory it is necessary to reconceptualize the superego and the idea of guilt. I distinguished between self-loathing arising out of the failure of the self to be perfect, powerful, or lovable; and guilt because one has failed in one's moral obligations to others. The former is the theme of narcissism and the latter of moral obligation. At the most general level I wanted to suggest to you that psychiatry has contributed to the general acceptance of a kind of discourse about the moral adventure of life in which the veil of self-love has not been torn away. Self-love has instead been reinterpreted as self-fulfillment or self-actualization.

The problem with self-fulfillment and self-actualization, like the problem of narcissism, is that these can be lonely modes of existence. If Freud's neurotics suffered from reminiscences, today our patients suffer from loneliness.

There was another theme in my last talk that I want to re-emphasize. The basic premise of any psychiatry that posits an unconscious is that the patient's self-description is a self-deception. The power and significance of this premise depends on whether the psychiatrist truly knows what lies behind the self-deception. I gave the example of Freud's truth about women to demonstrate that we did not know the truth about self-deception. Nonetheless, I continue to believe that the dynamic unconscious is real, that self-deception is crucial, and that if psychiatry is to understand the human condition it must understand self-deception. The problem is that with this presumption of the patient's self-deception, psychiatry teeters on the threshold of paternalism and of disrespect for the person. The charge of paternalism today confounds the psychiatrist at every turn. Whether treatment is voluntary or involuntary, whether it is a matter of diagnosis or prescription, whether the treatment helps or not, every interaction between psychiatrist and patient has taken on this political and controversial dimension of paternalism. If you disagreed with Freud for telling his women patients that their striving in the world outside the home was a masculine protest based on penis envy, you may agree with Karen Horney. She, in refuting Freud's influence, told her women patients who wanted to be good mothers and homemakers to live lives more like men, because modern women invest too much of themselves in love and thus leave themselves too vulnerable to rejection and loss of self-esteem.[30]

But whatever your opinion of these two kinds of advice may be, you will acknowledge that both are implicitly a kind of paternalistic or maternalistic moral instruction implying that the patient has deceived herself about her goals in life and when the self-deception is stripped away the psychiatrist knows more than she about the true goals of women and the ideal relation between the sexes. If psychiatrists still practice moral instruction in the sense that they help patients to decide how to live their lives, from where do they get their vision of morality? Do they derive it from their psychological understanding of human nature? Do they import into psychiatry their own unexamined moral attitudes and beliefs? Or do they, as some claim, remain neutral and nonjudgmental, working entirely within the context of the patient, applying only the patient's values and moral convictions as they emerge in therapy? Philip Rieff, in his book *Freud: The Mind of the Moralist*, suggests that Freud did have a moral perspective which derived from his theory of therapy.[31] What this "penultimate morality" amounts to is the duty to examine the history and the development of one's moral convictions.

I think Rieff's underlying assumption about Freud's morality might be expressed as follows. Human beings typically cling to some childlike illusory ideal (the parent as god-like redeemer and moral authority). When they come into analysis they project that illusory ideal onto the analyst. This parental ideal is somehow tied up with a person's deepest moral convictions, which are typically unexamined. During analysis he will work through his attachment to this ideal, reconsider his moral convictions, face up to reality and necessity and relinquish his illusions, including the

[30] Karen Horney, *The Collected Works* (New York: Norton, 1963).
[31] New York: Viking Press, 1959.

illusion of moral authority as symbolized by the omnipotent father. Life without illusions is the goal of this penultimate morality. It is Freud's relentless pursuit of this vision which has led critics to say that Freud's inspiration lacked all of the religious virtues: faith, hope, and charity.

But if Freud offered only self-knowledge, there have been other psychotherapists willing to go beyond the analysis of illusions. They offer implicit moral instruction based on their psychological theories. Let me give you a published example from a well-known psychologist. His patient has reported her guilt about not doing enough for her parents — her father had a long history of alcoholism, her mother had had breast cancer surgery, there had been other long-drawn-out family problems. The patient feels she has no life of her own. She reportedly says, "I was brought up with that! You always have to give of yourself. If you think of yourself, you're wrong." To this the therapist responds, "Now, why do you have to keep believing that — at your age? You believed a lot of superstitions when you were younger. Why do you have to retain them? We can see why your parents would have to indoctrinate you with this kind of nonsense, because that's their belief. But why do you still have to believe this nonsense — that one should be devoted to others, self-sacrificial? Who needs that philosophy? All it's gotten you, so far, is guilt. And that's all it ever will get you!" [32]

Here is explicit, straightforward, shall we call it moral, instruction. The therapist in fact, later in this very first interview, goes on to deride the patient for attempting to be Jesus or Moses. This therapist is unique only in the sense that he is so clear about what he does. His theory is that people are sick because of their crazy beliefs, among which are nonsensical moral obligations. The therapist reports that this patient dramatically improved as a result of the victory of rational self-interest over her insane moral obligations.

[32] Albert Ellis, *Growth Through Reason: Verbatim Cases in Rational-Emotive Therapy* (Palo Alto, California: Science and Behavior Books, 1971), p. 228.

Now, I do not know whether this psychotherapist believes that there are any sane moral obligations which are counter to rational self-interest. But it is clear that the essence of his psychological theory is that sanity is rational self-interest and his therapy is directed toward that goal.

The second possibility, that we have imported into our theories and our therapy our own moral attitudes and beliefs disguised as health values, continues to be, as I discussed at length in my first lecture, a subject of enormous controversy in psychiatry today.

But the question is, what shall we do about it now that we recognize the problems? Psychiatry is very much divided on this difficult matter. There are those who believe that we must acknowledge the truth of this argument and that psychiatry should import some explicit vision of morality into its work. This, however, creates a struggle over what kind of morality it should be, and that has divided psychiatry into sects within schools. Do psychiatrists then have an obligation to reveal their moral values to patients in advance? This is not just a bizarre example of pushing an argument to an extreme; there are now, for example, radical psychiatrists, gay psychiatrists, Christian born-again psychiatrists, feminist psychiatrists, and other examples of an explicit conjunction of psychiatry and some specific value orientation, moral or ideological system. It cannot have escaped you that each of these conjunctions will generate not only different therapeutic objectives but also different conceptions of what mental disorder and its cure are.

There are other psychiatrists, however, who are attempting to identify and remove the moral values from psychiatric theory and therapy. This purging of hidden morality has led to intense debate over which of the "health values" are "moral values." This is what happened in the case of the diagnosis of homosexuality.

Let me briefly summarize the problem. Psychiatrists were told by the gay community that the diagnosis of homosexuality was nothing but a moral value disguised as a health value. Being called sick was damaging to their self-esteem; psychiatry was stigmatizing and harmful to their mental health. Now consider what happens when psychiatrists attempted to deal with a problem like this. There are, as I have already described, four major paradigms in modern psychiatry. The biological psychiatrist may believe that homosexuality is due to some enzyme imbalance. He may agree that the diagnosis of homosexuality is stigmatizing, but he will not agree that his scientific study of enzymes has anything to do with moral values. The behavioral psychiatrist may believe that homosexuality is the result of a certain kind of sexual reinforcement. He may also agree that the diagnosis of homosexuality is stigmatizing and harmful, but he will not therefore abandon his theory of how homosexual behaviors develop. The psychodynamic psychiatrist believes that homosexuality is the result of a negative Oedipus complex. He, too, may admit that the diagnosis of homosexuality is stigmatizing and harmful, but he is not about to give up his theory of the Oedipus complex. The social psychiatrist believes that homosexuality is associated with certain demographic, social, and cultural patterns. He is quite willing to agree that the diagnosis of homosexuality contributes to the unhappiness of homosexuals and that social change will alleviate this, but he is not going to forego his theories about the effect of demographics and social factors on the prevalence of homosexuality.

Each paradigm has a theory of homosexuality, and although eventually American psychiatry demonstrated its therapeutic good will and removed the diagnosis, very few psychiatrists changed their theories. What would be necessary to actually remove the moral value judgment about homosexuality from psychiatry is not just a change in nosology but a change in the basic underlying conception of the human condition and what salient aspects need to be explained.[33]

The third option of respecting the patient's own values and moral convictions and working within that framework is what

---

[33] Stone, "Presidential Address."

most psychiatrists would want to claim they do. The practical importance of this argument for the psychiatrist is that it implies that we are all able to treat patients whose values and moral convictions are antithetical to our own. I have been enormously impressed by the ability of some psychiatrists to do just this and to feel compassion not only for patients whose values and moral convictions are antithetical to their own, but also for patients who morally are terrible people by all conventional standards: drug pushers, rapists, child molesters, arsonists, etc. But one of the secrets of this therapeutic compassion is that the psychiatrist believes these patients are sick and that successful treatment will reduce their immoral behavior, and alter their values. Therapeutic compassion is not necessarily forgiving, but it is premised on the psychiatrist's ability to believe that immorality is psychopathological.

Many psychiatrists, I think, actually do believe this. There is a tendency for such psychiatrists to call every immoral act "acting out," implying that it is sick rather than bad. Many of these moral difficulties fade into the background when the psychiatrist stops being a concerned psychotherapist, ignores the patient's situation in life, and simply prescribes drugs. Then the psychiatrist need not even share the language of his patient. This situation has prevailed in many of our state hospitals.

This, I believe, is part of the great current attractiveness of biological psychiatry. Not only is there a claim of greater effectiveness, but also the hasty retreat toward explaining all psychopathology in terms of brain enzymes seems to promise an escape from the terrible moral dilemmas and entanglements which I have been rehearsing. "Scientific Psychiatry" wants to become the study of the organism, not of the person.

We have begun under this influence to reorder our conception of the categories of mental disorder so that they comport with our biological discoveries about the organism. It may well be that this is good and sensible; it is after all the way "normal" science progresses. It may be that psychosis should not be regarded as a life experience but rather as a dangerous medical illness of the organism for which there is a rapid, safe, and usually effective chemical treatment. But suppose the biological psychiatrist discovers that parents whose children have died produce identical chemical disturbances in their bloodstream to those produced by psychotically depressed persons. Will we then conclude that these grieving parents are experiencing a *dangerous medical illness?* Will we believe it is appropriate to give them rapid, safe, and usually effective chemical treatment so that we can eradicate their biological depression? Or will we want to assert our own non-biological ideas about what it means to be human? Does such science not begin to offend our most important intuitions about human nature?

If the descriptions I have given you are correct, if psychiatry is really so confused about moral questions, then how is it that society for so long allowed us to be the arbiters of difficult moral problems? The answer, I believe, is that our moral ambiguity and confusion, our inability to frame hard moral questions, has been our greatest asset as society's decision-makers.

Whenever there are hard moral conflicts to be resolved, it is socially and politically convenient to have a group of professionals who can redefine some of the toughest cases in a way that allows us to avoid paying the full price of our principles.

Consider the difficult moral questions attendant on abortion. Ten years ago the law in most states allowed abortion only when necessary to save the life of the pregnant woman or to preserve her health.[34] As public pressure began to mount against these strict legal restraints, the debate began which we now know as freedom of choice versus right to life. Early on, however, psychiatrists increasingly began to take advantage of the exception to the strict rule, that is, "necessary to preserve the health or save the life

[34] For review of state abortion laws at that time see report of the Task Force on Family Law and Policy to the Citizens' Advisory Council on the Status of Women (Washington, D.C.: Dept. of Labor, 1968), pp. 28–29, Government Publication No. Y3.IN8/21:2F21.

of the woman." They resolved the difficult moral question in individual cases by invoking the non-moral question — the mental health of the pregnant woman. The typical situation went like this: the woman who was desperate to have an abortion would be described by the sympathetic psychiatrist as "depressed and suicidal." The abortion therefore was necessary to keep the woman from putting her own life in danger. Since psychiatrists in effect controlled the only available access to safe legal abortions, you can imagine that many women who wanted abortions would have felt that their only option was to simulate or exaggerate these sorts of symptoms.

I was one of a group of psychiatrists who were called together to try and step back and look at what psychiatry was doing. Whatever therapeutic justification there may have been for psychiatric abortion, the data we assembled demonstrated that with psychiatrists controlling the abortion decision, middle and upper class women were twenty times more likely to receive therapeutic abortions than lower class women. And we found that women dying after illegal abortions tended to be poor, black, and Hispanic. We concluded, among other things, that having psychiatrists control the scarce resource of therapeutic abortions worked in a race- and class-biased fashion.[35]

An equally powerful example of this same unfairness occurred during the Vietnam war, when suddenly it seemed that contrary to all previous demographic evidence psychiatric illness was more prevalent among the middle and upper classes than among the lower class. At least this was the case among young males excused from military service because of psychiatric illness.

The abortion and Vietnam examples are in my experience typical. The psychiatrist in the privacy of his office in sympathy with his patient renders a therapeutic solution of a moral problem. These decisions, when aggregated, reveal a discriminatory distri-

---

[35] See Alan A. Stone, "Right to Abortion: A Psychiatric View," *Group for the Advancement of Psychiatry*, vol. VII, no. 75 (October 1969).

bution of psychiatric mercy. This happens even when psychiatrists are neither just plain dishonest nor partisan in their decisions. When we look closely we see that our notion of fairness is twice cheated: moral principles are bent and they are bent in an inequitable fashion.

After I had finished my first lecture, I was told that some members of the audience thought I had quite given up on psychiatry. I can assure you I have not. I cling to Hegel's aphorism that the owl of Minerva only spreads her wings at dusk. I admit, however, that it is well past nightfall. I want to end these Tanner Lectures with a description of a patient I have treated for twenty years. It will demonstrate at least that even a psychiatrist deeply influenced by Freud's vision has some faith, hope, and charity. But I also believe that this case will help me to explore with you how I think and feel about psychiatry and morality in the face of all the confusion I have described.

Immanuel Kant, at the conclusion of *Anthropology from a Pragmatic Point of View*, described a kind of thought experiment as follows, "It could well be that on another planet there might be rational beings who could not think in any other way but aloud. These beings would not be able to have thoughts without voicing them at the same time. . . . [U]nless they are all as pure as angels, we cannot conceive how [these beings] would be able to live at peace with each other, how anyone could have any respect for anyone else, and how they could get along with each other" (p. 250).

Now it turns out that Kant's imaginary beings of another planet exist in a certain way here on earth in the form of persons whom we psychiatrists describe as having schizophrenic disorder. It is not an uncommon symptom of such patients that they believe everyone else can read their minds. Thus, although there is no reciprocity in this mind reading, they suffer in some of the ways that Kant imagined. I have treated one such patient, as I said, for twenty years. She struggled to keep her mind as pure as an angel's but, being human, she often failed and she would experience terrible feelings of shame and humiliation when people read her mind. These experiences entirely disrupted her life. She felt vulnerable, intruded upon, and defenseless. As Kant correctly predicted, she felt no one could have any respect for her. She twice had made serious suicide attempts. She was thought to be a hopeless process schizophrenic. When she began treatment with me, she had constant auditory hallucinations, many complicated delusions, had twice been hospitalized in catatonic episodes, and had no sustained benefit from extensive electroconvulsive treatments. I cannot detail for you the many years of psychoanalytic therapy which spanned the era before and after the development of appropriate drug treatment. When I began treating her, she quickly formed the kind of intense attachment psychiatrists call a psychotic transference. She was obsessed with her great love for me, or as I repeatedly told her, her great love for her mother whom she had rediscovered in me. All of her hallucinations and delusions rapidly disappeared. The only loss of reality on her part was her conviction that I was equally in love with her, but temporarily unable to admit it. Five years of disordered schizophrenic thought cured by falling in love with her psychiatrist. During this honeymoon phase, she described the many complicated delusions she had had: my patient, however, was much more interested in the subject of love. I repeatedly assured her that I was happily married and she repeatedly gave me a knowing smile and told me that she was ready when I was. Finally I arranged to have a woman social worker meet with her and her husband to plan for *their* future. This "rejection" was followed by an exacerbation of delusions and hallucinations which terminated in a long suicidal depression. During this time we began the long process of exploring in great detail the story of her illness and her life. Out of this story we constructed a new self-description relevant to her one persistent delusion — it has lasted twenty years — that her mind was being read.

The patient's mother had intended her to be another Shirley Temple, and with the family's small income she had been given all of the necessary training to become a child star. The patient had been an only child and her mother totally dominated her life. But her mother died when the patient was a young teenager. Nothing came of her theatrical training; she drifted through adolescence trying to be beautiful and into a marriage. But, at some level of consciousness, she never abandoned her mother's project; unconsciously it was her desire to be a star in the spotlight. Measured against this project, her life was a failure and she struggled against feelings of total inadequacy. Every social encounter was for her, at some level, a failed public appearance in which the spotlight was meant to be on her. It was from this perspective that I interpreted her delusion that her mind was being read by everyone in a rather standard way as the pathological fulfillment of a fear and a wish, the fear that everyone would see her inadequacies and the wish that everyone would notice her. The delusion that her mind was being read served to place a kind of spotlight on her. This new self-description allowed my patient to cope with what was both a feeling and a belief that her mind was being read. During therapy she began to realize that this feeling/belief came on in two kinds of situations — at times of particularly low esteem, when she was isolated, lost, and ignored in a social group, or in situations when others were in the spotlight and she was part of an anonymous crowd, for example at the theater. When she became very disturbed she would have the feeling/belief that the famous people she watched on television were reading her mind. The nature of these situations, I suggested, was confirming evidence for the fear/wish interpretation I had given her.

There are many aspects of this highly condensed example that one might discuss. Did we discover the truth about her life or did I merely indoctrinate her with one set of self-descriptions which have little or nothing to do with either her actual life or her delusion? And, even if these were in some sense correct self-descriptions, are they an example of the logical fallacy of assuming that *understanding* her memories about the history of her life and her desires is the same as *explaining* her delusion, as though psychosis could be explained at the level of experience. Many psychiatrists today would consider this lengthy treatment process an absurd relic of a misguided era in psychiatry. They would attribute the relief of her symptoms to the drugs she was eventually given—a chemical imbalance in her brain no doubt explains her illness, and the drugs corrected that imbalance — and explain the cure. Understanding her life, they would argue, is a different enterprise from explaining her psychotic disorder.

I have no hard scientific rejoinder to these biological claims, but if her schizophrenia was only a biochemical imbalance, how is it that falling in love with me was sufficient to cure all of her psychotic symptoms but one. Falling in love had in fact temporarily transformed this disordered, distracted, hallucinating woman. I want to consider this question of my patient's love and her mind-reading delusion. Although my patient said she believed and understood the fear/wish self-description she had worked out with me, periodically her faith would weaken. She would come back to me for — what shall we call it — love, reassurance, reinforcement, or reindoctrination.

At these sessions I would ask her, how after all these years, two decades, could she still believe that her mind was being read. She never has been able to explain either to her own satisfaction or to mine why she periodically relives Kant's thought experiment, but one thing is clear to both of us: that she gets something from the human relationship when she sees me which is temporarily sufficient to overcome the delusional belief and renew her faith in the therapeutic self-descriptions sometimes for as long as three months. Now some of you may feel this therapy is merely a form of conditioning, a positive reinforcement, and it may be. My own understanding is that her mind-reading delusion is a passionate conviction about her vulnerable situation in the world. Her delu-

sion begins when she feels her self disappearing from other people's awareness. It requires both her understanding of what is
happening and her sense of attachment to me to control this disappearance of self. In her case, at least, it is not enough to keep
the interpretation of all this vividly in the forefront of her consciousness. She must also have a continuing sense of a loving connection with me, a sense that she exists in my awareness and I
in hers.

Some of the description I have given is, I think, a commonplace experience for psychiatrists; it is the frustrating recognition that insight in the form of a new self-understanding is for
many of our patients insufficient: they internalize the new self-
understanding only as they idealize the therapist. The supposed
goal of orthodox psychoanalysis was to work through this idealization of the analyst, but this goal is seldom fully attained, in my
opinion. What studies there have been of patients who have been
analyzed suggest that their failure to work through the idealized
transference is a common occurrence. Enjoying this idealized
transference is the secret vice of psychoanalysts. Even psychoanalysts themselves talk about their own psychoanalysts with a tone
of reverence, or at least appreciation, which they rarely accord to
mere mortals. But it may well be, as the example of my patient
suggests, that these reverential feelings are in some way essential
to the "cure" and to the stability of their new self-understanding.

We have reached the classic question: does psychotherapy cure
by love or by insight? I would claim that there is an analogous
question: does moral conviction come from loving the moral in-
structor or from the wisdom of his teachings? The answer seems
to me clear: both are involved in both cases.

I shall talk only about psychotherapy. I will leave it to the
moral philosophers to decide if there is, in fact, any parallel.

Psychiatrists are accustomed to think of disorders of consciousness in terms of the traditional distinction between thoughts and
feelings. There are thought disorders and mood disorders. There

are irrational ideas and unnatural impulses. This dualism between cognition and affect is reflected in the notion of the struggle between reason and passion. Even our legal test of insanity reflects this dualism. There is on the one hand insanity manifested by the inability to *know* right from wrong, and there is insanity manifested by an irresistible *impulse.* But delusion is not just a false belief about the world; it is a passionate conviction. A phobia is not just a feeling of anxiety; it is also a false belief. Depression is not just a disorder of mood; self-loathing expresses a set of deep convictions about the self.

What I want to suggest to you is that all mental disorders are in some sense passionate convictions about the situation of the self in the world. They are not just false beliefs; they are not just peculiar feelings. Mental disorder is a passion in the different sense that Roberto Unger has given it. Passion exists at the point "where distinctions between desire (wanting something from the other person) and knowledge (viewing him and myself in a certain way) collapse." [36]

Our patients, and I do not mean just our psychotic patients, seem reluctant or perhaps even unable to give up their passions. Passion is not so easily routed even by making the unconscious conscious. What I am trying to say by way of these arguments is that our most important convictions about ourselves and our situation in the world are passionate convictions, convictions which will change only when passion finds a new configuration. How does that happen in psychotherapy? Let us first consider therapy not performed by psychiatrists. My profession has for a long time recognized that alcoholics are better treated by Alcoholics Anonymous than by psychotherapy. Furthermore, it is clear that AA affords both powerful attachments to a new group and moral instruction about one's situation in the world. The dramatically cured alcoholic is often a fanatic. The same is often the case with cured drug addicts. And, of course, similar things happen in cults.

---

[36] R. M. Unger, "A Program for Late Twentieth Century Psychiatry," *American Journal of Psychiatry* 139:2 (February 1982), p. 159.

There is a powerful attachment to a new group and a profound change in one's convictions about oneself and one's situation in the world. Many of these "cures" are achieved with some better understanding of one's past, at least there is a confessional element, but a new and passionate conviction about the situation of the self in the world seems to be a crucial element of change.

You will recognize that in the view I am suggesting there is a considerable overlap between religious conversion and what goes on in the psychotherapist's office. The transference involves both a kind of love and the acceptance of the therapist as an authority about the subject of the situation of the self in the world. At the same time, the kind of intense transference of love that I described in my patient constituted in itself a new and passionate conviction about her situation in the world. Love, after all, is a profound change in one's experience of the self and its situation in the world. Love is perhaps the most powerful example we know of an experience at the point where the distinction between desiring and knowing collapses. It is love—which, after all, is a passion— that suggests there is something wrong with the notion that life is a struggle between reason and passion. Love is such a powerful counter-example that it demands that we reconsider the traditional dichotomy. If delusions like love are, in fact, located at this point where the distinction between knowing and desiring collapses, perhaps that is why patients are not fully persuaded by psychological interpretations of how they come by their delusions and are not easily deprived of their idealized transference. This is not to say that psychological accounts like those I gave to my patient are without power. I believe that ideas have power to change people's lives, not just because reason can overcome inclination but also because ideas can sometimes rally the passions.

If it is true, as it seems to be, for many patients that they rarely succeed in the task orthodox psychoanalysis sets for them of working through their idealization of their psychiatrists, then the enterprise of psychotherapy takes on a different aspect.

The crucial consideration is the psychiatrist as a person, his moral character, the kind of ideal he presents to his patient. In the end, the most important thing about a psychiatrist is probably the kind of person he is and the kinds of relationships he establishes. The psychoanalyst goes to great lengths to conceal the kind of person he is and to deny the reality of the relationship. But at some point he must speak and respond, and what he reveals about himself in those moments is more important than he has been taught to believe.

The goal of self-fulfillment, the feeling of self-loathing, and the experience of loneliness: this is the neurotic syndrome of our time. Love and moral ambition seem to be the cure, but to many this sounds like a prescription to embrace vulnerability. They are trapped by the subjective experience that hostility and contempt seem to be what hold the self together. This inner toughness is the only security they know, and love and moral ambition threaten that security.

Here on the inner stage of the psyche is played out the same drama we see in the world. Perhaps this is only rhetorical analogy, but in both cases it seems that the fear of vulnerability becomes the enemy of life. In saying this, I risk making the error that Freud made of claiming to know the truth behind self-deception, of offering a prescriptive theory of the human condition. But you will have realized by now that I believe there is no alternative; the risk cannot be avoided. The therapist who has no vision of what it means to be human forfeits his own humanity and has none to offer the patient.

The Death of Utopia Reconsidered

LESZEK KOLAKOWSKI

THE TANNER LECTURES ON HUMAN VALUES

Delivered at
The Australian National University

June 22, 1982

LESZEK KOLAKOWSKI was born in Poland. He received his Ph.D. at Warsaw University in 1953 and was Professor of the History of Philosophy in that university until March 1968, when he was expelled from his post by the government for political reasons. He was then visiting professor at McGill University, Montreal, and the University of California at Berkeley. Since 1970 he has been Senior Research Fellow of All Souls College, Oxford University; since 1975, Professor at Yale University, and since 1981, Professor for the Committee on Social Thought at the University of Chicago. He is author of about thirty books on the philosophy of culture, the history of philosophy and of religious ideas, and especially the seventeenth century and political matters; *Chrétiens sans église* (1964 in Polish, 1968 in French), *Die gegenwärtigkeit des Mythos* (1972), *Main Currents of Marxism* (3 vols., 1978), *Husserl and the Search for Certitude* (1975), *Religion* (1982).

When I am asked where I would like to live, my standard answer is: deep in the virgin mountain forest on a lake shore at the corner of Madison Avenue in Manhattan and Champs Elysées, in a small tidy town. Thus I am a utopian, and not because a place of my dream happens not to exist but because it is self-contradictory.

Are all utopias self-contradictory? This depends, of course, on the way we define the word; and there is no compelling reason why we should narrow its meaning down to those ideas of which either logical inconsistency or empirical impossibility are patent. In talking about utopia, we ought to stay reasonably close to the current usage of the word, even though we realize that this usage is to a certain extent shaky and imprecise. It is an interesting cultural process whereby a word of which the history is well known and which emerged as an artificially concocted proper name has acquired, in the last two centuries, a sense so extended that it refers not only to a literary genre but to a way of thinking, to a mentality, to a philosophical attitude, and is being employed in depicting cultural phenomena going back into Antiquity, far beyond the historical moment of its invention. This fact suggested to some historians and philosophers that we had to do with an everlasting form of human sensitivity, with a permanent anthropological datum for which an English thinker in the sixteenth century simply invented an apt name. This may sound plausible on the assumption that we inflate the concept to such a size as to pack into it (as Ernst Bloch did) all human projections of something better than what is and, on the other hand, all the religious images of paradisical happiness. Thus enlarged, however, the notion is of little use, since everything people have ever done in improving their collective or even individual life, as well as all their eschatological expectations, would have to be counted among "utopian" projections, whereby the concept would not be applicable any longer as a tool in any historical or philosophical inquiry. On the other hand, the adjective "utopian" has been given a pejorative sense in everyday speech and is applied to all projects, however trivial, which for any reason are impracticable ("it is utopian to expect that we shall be on time for dinner tonight"), and such a concept, again, is of no value in studying human culture.

Considering, therefore, that an amount of arbitrariness is unavoidable in trying to restrict the concept and that it is commendable to remain roughly within its current use, rather than to employ an existing word for entirely foreign purposes, I suggest that we proceed with a double limitation. First, we shall talk about utopias having in mind not ideas of making any side of human life better but only beliefs that a definitive and unsurpassable condition is attainable, one where there is nothing to correct any more. Second, we shall apply the word to projections which are supposed to be implemented by human effort, thus excluding both images of an other-worldly paradise and apocalyptic hopes for an earthly paradise to be arranged by sheer divine decree. Consequently, conforming to the second criterion, the revolutionary anabaptism of the sixteenth century may be included in the history of utopias so conceived, but not various chiliastic or adventist movements and ideas which expect the Kingdom on Earth as a result of Parousia. On the other hand, according to the first criterion, I would not describe as utopian various futuristic technological fantasies if they do not suggest the idea of an ultimate solution of mankind's predicament, a perfect satisfaction of human needs, a final state.

Being thus restricted on two sides, the concept is widened insofar as it may be applied not only to global visions of a definitively saved society but to some specific areas of human creativity as well. We may speak, for example, of epistemological utopias, meaning the search for either a perfect certainty or an ultimate source of cognitive values: neither can anything prevent us from labeling as "scientific utopia" a hope for a definitive foundation of any science — in particular of physics or mathematics — or of all empirical sciences, a hope which, once fulfilled, would close the path to future progress except for applications of the ultimate equation in specific cases. It would be difficult instead to look for architectural or artistic utopias, as one may hardly find in the history of human thought — much as it teems with wild expectations of an Eschaton — the idea of an ultimate building or an ultimate poem.

Descartes may be called the founder of the modern epistemological utopia. He did believe — and perhaps rightly so — that if no source of an absolute unshakable certitude can be found, no certitude at all is conceivable and therefore no truth except in a pragmatic sense. And he believed that this ultimate cognitive assurance can indeed be discovered and that he had revealed it. He did not reveal it in the Cogito alone: had he been satisfied with the Cogito as the only truth resisting all possible doubts, he would not have been capable of going beyond this discovery and the latter would have remained a self-contained, empty tautology leading nowhere. To proceed from this initial illumination to a trustworthy reconstruction of the universe, he had to be possessed of universally valid criteria of truth which he was unable to legitimize without the omniscient divine mind. A vicious circle which the first critics noticed in his reasoning (the criterion of clarity and distinctiveness of ideas is employed in proving God's existence, whereupon God appears as a guarantor of the reliability of clear and distinct ideas) and which would be subsequently discussed by philosophers to our day need not bother us now. Whether or not his proposal was logically sound, he asked (or revived) the formidable utopian question which has kept philosophy busy for centuries: is perfect certainty attainable at all; and if so, can it be reached without an appeal to absolute divine wisdom? If not — are we bound to give up, together with the ultimate foundation of knowledge, the very concept of truth in the usual, that is, transcendental sense and to be satisfied with practical criteria of acceptability, renouncing forever the dream of episteme? Whatever the answer might be, the question was not trivial, and the crucial moments in the vicissitudes of modern philosophy are marked by clashes between empiricists and skeptics on the one side and the defenders of sundry forms of transcendentalist approach on the other. The epistemological utopia has never died away in our culture, and its most stubborn and bravest defender at the beginning of our century was no doubt Edmund Husserl. Untiringly and unceasingly he kept improving, correcting, and rebuilding the Cartesian project, drilling deeper and deeper into the layers of transcendental consciousness in the quest for the ultimate ground of all grounds, a ground we can reach without appealing to the divine veracity. He was driven not only by a philosophical gambler's curiosity but also by a conviction that the skeptical or empiricist renouncement of the idea of certainty, and thereby of truth, would spell the ruin of European culture.

The philosophical movement did not go, though, along the grooves he had started to furrow. Even among those who were ready to take up his ideas, the most important thinkers — Heidegger and Merleau-Ponty above all — abandoned the hope for a radical phenomenological reduction. They did not believe that we might ever set ourselves in the position of pure subjects of cognition who have gotten rid of all the historically relative, socially assimilated sedimentations of our consciousness and start afresh, as it were, from a zero point. No matter at what moment we begin our reflection, we are already thrown into the world, we are moulded by experience and compelled to express ourselves in a language we have not invented. However far we might go, or imagine to have gone, in hunting the perfectly unprejudiced, "presuppositionless" beginning of knowledge, we will always be in the middle of the road. There is no absolutely transparent distance (let alone abolition of distance) between us and the world, no cognitive void whereby the world, in its undistorted shape, could reach and enter our inner space. The division into the external and the inner world which the Cartesian tradition established and which was a condition of the quest for the ultimate epistemological foundation was, of course, repeatedly attacked in the nineteenth century, by Avenarius and Mach among others, in fact by all post-Darwinian philosophers who believed that cognitive acts could be properly interpreted within a biological framework as defensive reactions and who thus dismissed the traditional search for truth as a result of metaphysical prejudices. It was against those anti-Cartesians that Husserl undertook his arduous journey into the Unknown of transcendental consciousness and tried to reverse the trend of relativistic naturalism. He failed to discover or to rediscover the paradisical island of unshakable knowledge, yet he did open various new paths for thinking and he left the entire philosophical landscape of Europe utterly transmuted; not unlike Descartes, Rousseau, or Kant before him, he compelled the next generations of philosophers, including those who refused to share his hopes, to define themselves in relation or in opposition to him.

A hidden nostalgia for epistemological utopia was still active in some empiricist trends of the first decades of our century: not in the sense of transcendentalist expectations, to be sure, but in the form of the long-lasting quest for the ultimate data of knowledge or ultimately irreducible propositions. And this, too, has gone. Transcendental phenomenology has come to a dead stop in chasing the perfect transparency; logical positivism got stuck in its unsuccessful attempts to devise satisfactory definitions of verifiability and analyticity. A lot has survived from both, no doubt, but not the hope for an epistemological Ultimum. Transcendental research retreated in favor of existential ontology which, in a variety of forms, expressed its refusal to believe that we might ever grasp either the subject or the object severally in their uncontaminated freshness, that either the Being or human existence could be conceptually dominated. Logical empiricism has been replaced by the late Wittgenstein, by the ordinary language philosophy. Philosophical utopia seems to have died off. Whether it

is truly and definitively dead or just temporarily asleep, we cannot
say with any certainty; but even though we do not detect in this
very moment any distinct signs of its resurrection, we may have
reasons not to believe in its final extinction. I am strongly reluctant to admit that a philosophical life left entirely as prey to prag-
matists and relativists is either likely or desirable, and my reluctance is grounded on a certain understanding of what philosophy
is as a cultural phenomenon, and this understanding in its turn is
based, of course, on an interpretation of its historical vicissitudes.

My general attitude may be thus expressed. What philosophy
is about is not Truth. Philosophy can never discover any universally admissible truths; and if a philosopher happened to have
made a genuine contribution to science (one thinks, say, of mathematical works of Descartes, Leibniz, or Pascal), his discovery,
perhaps by the very fact of being admitted as an ingredient of the
established science, immediately ceased being a part of philosophy,
no matter what kind of metaphysical or theological motivations
might have been at work in producing it. The cultural role of
philosophy is not to deliver truth but to build the *spirit of truth*,
and this means: never to let the inquisitive energy of mind go to
sleep, never to stop questioning what appears to be obvious and
definitive, always to defy the seemingly intact resources of common sense, always to suspect that there might be "another side"
in what we take for granted, and never to allow us to forget that
there are questions that lie beyond the legitimate horizon of science and are nonetheless crucially important to the survival of
humanity as we know it. All the most traditional worries of philosophers — how to tell good from evil, true from false, real from
unreal, being from nothingness, just from unjust, necessary from
contingent, myself from others, man from animal, mind from
body, or how to find order in chaos, providence in absurdity, timelessness in time, laws in facts, God in the world, world in language — all of them boil down to the quest for meaning; and they
presuppose that in dissecting such questions we may employ the

instruments of Reason, even if the ultimate outcome is the dismissal of Reason or its defeat. Philosophers neither sow nor harvest, they only move the soil. They do not discover truth; but they are needed to keep the energy of mind alive, to confront various possibilities of answering our questions. To do that they — or at least some of them — must trust that the answers are within our reach. Those who keep trusting that are real diggers; and although I can not share their contention that by digging more and more deeply they will eventually reach the Urgrund, the foundation of all foundations, I do believe that their presence in the continuation of our culture is vital and indispensable. They are utopians and we need them. Next to diggers, however, we need the healers who apply skeptical medicine in order to clean our minds from prejudices, to unmask hidden premises of our beliefs, to keep us vigilant, to improve our logical skills, not to let us be carried away by wishful thinking. Philosophy to survive needs both diggers and healers, both reckless adventurers and cautious insurance brokers. They even seem to prop each other amidst their never-ending squabbles. The trouble is that whoever says so while being himself interested in philosophical riddles and thus involved in the conflict in one way or another cannot avoid the risk of antinomy or of contradiction: he is not capable of not taking sides in the conflict, and he asserts something that would ultimately compel him to be on both extremes simultaneously. We can escape the contradiction only by trying to place ourselves outside the philosophy, to suspend our interest in the issues and to climb up to a vantage point from which philosophy itself appears as a part of the history of civilization. The trouble is, however, that to reach this point we almost certainly need some premises and some conceptual instruments that have been elaborated in the ambiguous realm of philosophy.

Still, it may be fairly said that today's life of mind is anti-utopian, that more often than not we are ready either to admit inescapable borders limiting the expansion of our cognitive passions or to argue, more consistently and more in keeping with the tradition of skepticism and empiricism, that the very notion of cognitive value or of "truth" metaphysically conceived is nothing but an aberration of mind which seeks to assert its illusory autonomy and self-reliance instead of seeing itself as what it is, namely, a useful defense device of our organism. It is possible that from a historical perspective some important achievements of twentieth-century science—Heisenberg's principle and Gödel's theorem—will be seen as contributions to the same anti-utopian spirit of our age; they pointed out fundamental barriers which were imposed—by the nature of Mind, by the great Nature, or by God—on our knowledge.

And when I say that the final extinction of the utopian drive in philosophy is neither likely nor desirable, I do not want to forget its intrinsic and apparently unremovable dangers. Whoever says that it is possible to discover a source of perfect certainty or an ultimate ground of knowledge says in effect not that it is possible but rather that he *has* found it. The expectations of an epistemological last judgment can certainly breed intolerance and self-righteous blindness. And they cannot escape the most traditional skeptical question about the infinite regression: *qui custodiet ipsos custodes?* Whatever criteria we establish, we may always ask what are the criteria of *their* validity.

The danger can be avoided, perhaps, if those ultimate criteria are considered — to use the Kantian idiom — as regulative, rather than constitutive, ideas; they serve us better if they are signposts which show the direction towards an unattainable goal, instead of asserting that the goal has been, or is about to be, reached. In other words, the spirit of utopia has two versions: one of them corresponds to the Kantian maxim of pure reason and consists in actually building the ultimate ground, or at least in the belief that the premise of all premises is going to be discovered; the other is the search for a ground of any ground which we believe to have already unravelled, and it corresponds to what Hegel stigmatized as the "bad infinity." The former includes a hope for finding and intellectually grasping the Unconditioned in its very quality of Unconditionedness, and thereby a hope for a kind of philosophical theosis, for a finite mind which has acquired God-like properties. The latter includes both the acceptance of the finitude of mind and the will to expand its potentialities without any definable limit being assigned to this expansion.

Analogous remarks may be made about social utopias. It might seem implausible to maintain that we witness the decline of utopian mentality when we observe so many movements promising us a secular or theocratic millennium around the corner and applying all kinds of instruments of oppression and violence to bring it about. I would argue, however, that the decline is going on, that the utopian dreams have virtually lost both the intellectual support and their previous self-confidence and vigor. The great works of our century are anti-utopias or kakotopias, visions of a world in which all the values the authors identified themselves with have been mercilessly crushed (Zamiatin, Huxley, Orwell). There are some works praising utopian thinking, to be sure, yet one can hardly quote an important utopia written in our epoch.

Apart from this matter-of-fact question, I would advocate an approach to the social utopias similar to the approach I tried to justify in discussing the philosophical ones. We know, of course, countless utopian fantasies, some revolutionary, some peaceful, some of socialist, others of anarchist character; and I am not going to make their inventory or to classify them. I want to point out those general characteristics which are relevant to my subject.

First of all, the idea of the perfect and everlasting human fraternity. This is the common and permanent core of utopian thinking, and it has been criticized on various grounds. The strictures boil down to this: first, a universal fraternity is unconceivable; second, any attempt to implement it is bound to produce a highly despotic society which, to simulate the impossibile perfection, will stifle the expression of conflict, and thus destroy the life of culture, by a totalitarian coercion.

This criticism is sound, but we should reflect upon the conclusions to which it leads. It is arguable indeed that, by the very fact of being creative and free, people are bound to strive after goals which collide with each other and to be driven by conflicting desires; by this very fact that they can never achieve a perfect satisfaction, human needs can increase and expand indefinitely, and thereby the clashes between them are inevitable. This seems to be a constitutional framework of human existence; it was known to St. Augustine and, for that matter, to all the authors of Christian theodicies. We can imagine the universal brotherhood of wolves but not of humans, since the needs of wolves are limited and definable and therefore conceivably satisfied, whereas human needs have no boundaries we could delineate; consequently, total satisfaction is incompatible with the variety and indefiniteness of human needs.

This is what the utopian mentality refuses to admit and what makes the utopias fundamentally and incurably "utopian" (in the everyday sense). A feasible utopian world must presuppose that people have lost their creativity and freedom, that the variety of human life forms and thus the personal life have been destroyed, and that all of mankind has achieved the perfect satisfaction of needs and accepted a perpetual deadly stagnation as its normal condition. Such a world would mark the end of the human race as we know it and as we define it. Stagnation is an inescapable condition of the utopian happiness; those changes which we used to call progress or enrichment in whatever area of life — in technology, science, art, institutionalized forms of social communication — are all responses to dissatisfaction, to suffering, to a challenge.

Those utopias which — like Campanella's or Marx's — promise us a world that combines satisfaction, happiness, and brotherhood with progress can survive only thanks to their inconsistency. Those which are consistent accept and praise a stagnant world in which all the variety has been done away with and human beings have been reduced to a universal, immobile mediocrity. The most consistent utopia was probably devised by Dôm Deschamps. This is a perfect society in which all people are completely exchangeable and entirely identical with each other; all the life forms which might differentiate human beings have been eradicated, and mankind has become a collection of absolutely uniform specimens, not unlike coins forged in the same mint. Social perfection has irreversibly killed human personality. The denizens of this paradise could as well be stones and would be equally happy.

The ideal of equality — conceived of as identity, the absence of differences — is self-contradictory, to be sure, on the assumption that people are what they have been throughout the history known to us. The utopians, nevertheless, keep promising us that they are going to educate the human race to fraternity, whereupon the unfortunate passions which tear societies asunder — greed, aggressiveness, power lust — will vanish. However, since Christianity has been trying to carry out this educational task for two millennia and the results are not quite encouraging, the utopians, once they attempt to convert their visions into practical proposals, come up with the most malignant project ever devised: they want to institutionalize fraternity, which is the surest way to totalitarian despotism. They believe that the evil resulted from faulty social institutions which run counter to the genuine impulses of human nature, without asking themselves how these institutions were created and established. In the famous fragment on the origin of inequality, Rousseau seems to believe that private property was simply invented by a madman; yet we do not know how this diabolical contrivance, opposed as it was to innate human drives, was taken up by other people and spread all over the human societies.

That, as a result of the institutional coercive abrogation of private property, human conflicts, the struggle for power and domination, greed and aggressiveness will remain where they have been or perhaps increase, this was a prediction fairly frequently made long before the prescription for everlasting brotherhood —

worked out on Marxist-utopian principles — was actually applied. This prediction was based on common experience, and it was to be infallibly borne out in the entire history of socialist societies.

An attempt to implement a conflictless order by institutional means can be indeed successful in the sense that it can, by applying totalitarian coercion, prevent conflicts from being expressed. Being incapable, however, of eradicating the sources of conflict, the utopian technology necessarily involves a huge machinery of lie to present its inevitable failure as a victory. A utopian vision, once it is translated into political idiom, becomes mendacious or self-contradictory; it provides new names for old injustice or hides the contradictions under ad hoc invented labels. This is especially true of revolutionary utopias, whether elaborated in the actual revolutionary process or simply applied in its course. The Orwellian language had been known, though not codified, long before modern totalitarian despotism. Rousseau's famous slogan, "One has to compel people to freedom," is a good example. So is the announcement of the Paris Commune stating simultaneously that the compulsory military service has been abolished and that all citizens are members of the National Guard. So is the egalitarian-revolutionary utopia of Tkachev (an important source of the Leninist doctrine) which asserts that the main goal of the revolution is to abolish all the elites and that this task is to be carried out by a revolutionary elite.

In other words the two most common tenets of utopian projections — fraternity by coercion and equality imposed by an enlightened vanguard — are, each of them, self-contradictory. They are, however, compatible with each other, and more often than not they appear jointly in utopian dreams. One can notice nonetheless a difference in the distribution of emphasis in the utopian phraseology. To some utopians a conflictless community is the ultimate goal, whereas others depict equality as the highest value in itself. In the latter case the assumption is thus made that it is not human individuals, their suffering or their welfare that matter, but only the fact that suffering and welfare are evenly distributed, so that we ought to aim at a perfect equality even if it is likely that all people, including the most underprivileged, will suffer more as a result of the egalitarian order being established. Apart from being obviously self-contradictory (the perfect equality could be conceivably implemented only by a totalitarian despotism, and an order that is both despotic and egalitarian is a square circle), this ideal is a curious phenomenon in the history of civilization; the psychological forces which have sustained and stimulated it can be only a matter of speculation. The dream of a consistently egalitarian utopia is to abolish everything that could distinguish one person from another; a world in which people live in identical houses, identical towns, identical geographical conditions, wearing identical clothes and sharing, of course, identical ideas, is a familiar utopian picture. To preach this ideal amounts to implying that there is an intrinsic evil in the very act of asserting one's own personality, even without harming other people — in other words, that there is something essentially wrong in being human.

Radical and consistent egalitarian utopias are thus anti-human. Based on the aesthetics of impeccable symmetry and ultimate identity, they desperately search for an order in which all variety, all distinction, all dissatisfaction and therefore all development have been done away with forever; even the word "order" is perhaps inappropriate as there is nothing to be ordered in a perfectly homogeneous mass. We recognize in the utopian temptation a vague echo of those oriental and Neoplatonic theologies to which the separation of man from the source of being, from the undifferentiated Whole — and this means individuality itself — was a sort of ontological curse that could be abrogated only once individuality has been destroyed. The perfect egalitarian utopia is thus a secular caricature of Buddhist metaphysics. It may be seen perhaps as a peculiar expression of the suicidal impulse of human society, a drive we detect in many historically relative versions all over the history of religious and philosophical ideas. Ultimately it amounts to this: life necessarily involves tension and suffering; consequently if we wish to abolish tension and suffering, life is to be extinguished. And there is nothing illogical in this last reasoning.

I am talking about perfectly consistent utopias, of which we have only a few examples. In the inconsistent ones we often discover the same temptation mixed up with ideas which are incompatible with utopian perfection: the praise of creativity, the glory of progress, etc. Few utopians (Fourier was no doubt the most notable example) were aware that the need for variety, for personal self-assertion and distinctiveness were forces that it was impracticable to cancel or to suppress in specifically human life; and they tried to design their blueprints for universal happiness accordingly. They believed that those needs could be met without stirring up hostilities and struggles among people, that competitiveness might be preserved and aggressiveness channeled in harmless directions, thus producing a society which would happily combine satisfaction with creativity and the drive for distinction with universal friendship.

What made utopias look malignant in our century was clearly not the very dream of perfection; whether self-contradictory or not, descriptions of a celestial felicity on earth were in themselves no more than harmless literary exercises. They have become ideologically poisonous to the extent that their advocates managed to convince themselves that they had discovered a genuine technology of apocalypse, a technical device to force the door of paradise. This belief has been the distinctive characteristic of revolutionary utopias, and it was eminently embodied in various ramifications of Marxist doctrine. Having become, as a result of many historical accidents, the main ideological self-justifying and self-glorifying support of the totalitarian cancer devouring the social fabric of our world, the Marxist or quasi-Marxist utopia naturally called our attention to the apocalyptic-revolutionary literature of old which had displayed similar features.

The second important characteristic of this utopia was the belief that the glorious future is not simply predetermined by the course of history hitherto, but that the future was already there, not empirically noticeable and yet more real than the empirical present about to crumble. This belief in a "higher" reality which, albeit invisible, was already embedded in the actual world could be traced back, to be sure, to its Hegelian sources; more exactly, it was an extension into the future—illegitimate in strictly Hegelian terms — of the Hegelian way of investigating the past. This enviable ability to detect in what appears to be something that appears not to be but that in fact *is* in a more eminent sense than what is "merely" empirical was itself in Hegel a secularized version of the Christian concept of salvation which, though not perceptible directly, is not just inscribed in God's plan but has already occurred, since in the divine timelessness whatever is going to happen did happen. It justifies the illimited self-righteousness of those who not only are capable of predicting the future but in fact are already its blessed owners, and it gives them the right to treat the actual world as essentially non-existent. The imminent, ultimate revolution being not simply a fortunate step in the succession of historical events but a rupture in continuity, a total beginning, a new time, the past — including everything that might yet happen before the great breakthrough — is not, properly speaking, a progress. The latter means cumulation, gradual improvement, growth; whereas the Ultimate Event, ushering in the new time, does not add more wealth to the existing stock mankind has already capitalized but marks a leap from the infernal abyss to the kingdom of supreme excellence.

These three characteristics of revolutionary-utopian mentality supply justification for three less innocent political attitudes. A hope for the brotherhood into which an illuminated elite can coerce people by decree provides a natural basis for totalitarian tyranny. Believing in a higher-order reality that is set into the present and, though undiscernible to the naked eye, is the genuine reality, justifies the utter contempt for actually existing people, who scarcely deserve attention when contrasted with the seemingly non-existent but much more important generations of the future. The idea of a new time gives legitimacy to all kinds of cultural vandalism.

In this sense the strictures of utopia are well substantiated. We may even say more: considering that the most perfect specimen of the genre was written in the eighteenth century by the just-mentioned Dôm Deschamps, it is arguable that the socialist utopia had killed itself by its own consistency before it was born.

The same, for that matter, may be said of the individualist quasi-utopia. Probably the most consistent individualist-anarchist utopia was devised by Max Stirner in 1844. Starting with a fairly reasonable premise that social life as such — and not any particular form of social order — necessarily imposes limits on the individual's aspirations and his exclusive concern about himself, it suggested a "liberation" which everyone could separately achieve by abandoning all the norms, restrictions, and requirements that the "society" dictates to him, including logical and moral rules and presumably the language as well. I am talking about "quasi-utopia" because the point is less to invent a perfect society and more to abolish the society for the sake of the highest value, which each human person is to himself.

And yet there is another side of the story which we may not lightly dismiss. The utopian mentality, I should repeat, is withering away. Its intellectual status sank to the level of a pathetic adolescent gibberish surviving in leftist sects; in the established Communist ideologies the utopian language and utopian imagery have been less and less noticeable throughout the last decades.

It is legitimate to ask whether this demise of utopia, however justifiable in terms of the gruesome history of utopian politics, may be seen as a net gain. My argument on this point is analogous to what I have just said about the epistemological utopias. I do believe, indeed, that the dream of an everlasting universal brotherhood of humankind is not only unfeasible but that it would cause the collapse of our civilization if we took it seriously as a plan to be materialized by technical means. On the other hand, it is too easy to use all the well-founded anti-utopian arguments as a device whereby we may accept or even sanctify any kind of oppression and of blatant injustice if only they are not supported by utopian phraseology. This, again, is not a matter of an abstract possibility but of a well-recorded historical experience. For centuries the intrinsic evil of human nature not only has been invoked as an argument against the attempts to restore the paradisical conditions on earth but has justified resistance to all social reforms and democratic institutions as well. Therefore, the anti-utopian critique requires important differentiations. The utopian dogma stating that the evil in us has resulted from defective social institutions and will vanish with them is indeed not only puerile but dangerous; it amounts to the hope, just mentioned, for an institutionally guaranteed friendship, a hope on which totalitarian ideologies were founded. Yet it might be no less pernicious to replace this optimistic fantasy with the opposite one, implying that in all human relationships there is nothing but hostility, greed, the lust for domination, and that all expressions of love, friendship, fraternity, and sacrifice are no more than deceptive appearances concealing the "real," invariably selfish, motivations. Whether based on the anthropology of Hobbes, Freud, or early Sartre, this creed makes us naturally prone to accept all man-made monstrosities of social life as inevitable forever. It may be reasonably argued that the fallacy of those who view human nature as hopelessly and utterly corrupted is safer and less sinister than the self-defeating confidence of the utopians: a society in which greed is the dominant motivation is much preferable, after all, to a society based on compulsory solidarity. The total corruption theory may be nevertheless employed as well to support a totalitarian or a highly oppressive order: examples abound starting with the theocratic doctrines and practices of early Calvinism. And the grounds for this theory are speculative, and not empirical; there is no evidence to refute the common-sense platitude that the potential for disinterested friendship and solidarity is in us as well as the seeds of hatred, envy, and greed. To state that whatever is good in us is but a mask of evil, far from being a report of experience, is a metaphysical axiom; it even makes social life unintelligible: if there is nothing in us but evil, what might the mask be for?

It might be true that the most notable examples of fraternity known to us have often had a negative background and could be found most easily when they were forced on people by a common danger, wars, or disasters. It is true that the experience of all voluntary communist associations — not to speak of compulsory ones — is not very encouraging; nothing of value has survived from the communities established in America by early socialists — Cabet, Weitling, Considérant — or by the hippies. The most lasting and most successful communes are perhaps Jewish kibbutzim, brought to life by joint socialist and Zionist ideals. Some monastic or quasi-monastic communities as well as many informal groups may serve as positive examples. Undeniably, however, people are able to create conditions in which aggressiveness, hostility, and selfishness, if not eradicated, are really minimized.

The general conclusion of these remarks might sound somewhat banal but, not unlike many banalities, worth pondering. It says that the idea of human fraternity is disastrous as a political program but is indispensable as a guiding sign. We need it, to use the same Kantian idiom again, as a regulative, rather than a constitutive, idea.

In other words, both Kant's theory of the radical evil and his belief in the indefinite progression of rationality — a progression which can go on amid the unremitting tension between our love of freedom and our sociability, between individual aspirations and societal order, between passions and reason — are useful to us. In the standard sense of the word "utopia," Kant was clearly an anti-utopian as he had never expected an ingenious technical contrivance that would bring about the actual state of perfection and bliss. He did believe, though, in the calling of the human race, in a teleologically propelled movement, the end of which we can never achieve or locate in time — an asymptotic growth, as it were — and which we nonetheless always have to keep in mind if we want to remain human. These two complementary sides of his "as-if" philosophy — a belief in a perpetual motion, loaded with struggles and contradictions, toward a goal, and a disbelief that the goal might ever be effectively reached — are certainly reconcilable in philosophical terms. It is unlikely, however, that mankind as a whole could ever be converted to Kantian philosophy. Therefore it is likely that two kinds of mentality — the skeptical and the utopian — will survive separately, in unavoidable conflict. And we need their shaky coexistence; both of them are important to our cultural survival. The victory of utopian dreams would lead us to a totalitarian nightmare and the utter downfall of civilization, whereas the unchallenged domination of the skeptical spirit would condemn us to a hopeless stagnation, to an immobility which a slight accident could easily convert into catastrophic chaos. Ultimately we have to live between two irreconcilable claims, each of them having its cultural justification.

THE TANNER LECTURERS

1976–77

Brasenose College, Oxford	Bernard Williams, Cambridge University
University of Michigan	Joel Feinberg, Brandeis University
Stanford University	Joel Feinberg, Brandeis University

1977–78

Brasenose College, Oxford	John Rawls, Harvard University
University of Michigan	Sir Karl Popper, University of London
Stanford University	Thomas Nagel, Princeton University

1978–79

Brasenose College, Oxford	Thomas Nagel, Princeton University
Clare Hall, Cambridge	C. C. O'Brien, London
University of Michigan	Edward O. Wilson, Harvard University
Stanford University	Amartya Sen, Oxford University
University of Utah	Lord Ashby, Cambridge University
Utah State University	R. M. Hare, Oxford University

1979–80

Brasenose College, Oxford	Jonathan Bennett, Syracuse University
Clare Hall, Cambridge	Raymond Aron, Collège de France
Harvard University	George J. Stigler, University of Chicago
University of Michigan	Robert Coles, Harvard University
Stanford University	Michel Foucault, Collège de France
University of Utah	Wallace Stegner, Los Altos Hills, California

1980–81

Brasenose, College, Oxford	Saul Bellow, University of Chicago
Clare Hall, Cambridge	John Passmore, Australian National University
Harvard University	Brian Barry, University of Chicago
Hebrew University of Jerusalem	Solomon H. Snyder, Johns Hopkins University
University of Michigan	John Rawls, Harvard University
Stanford University	Charles Fried, Harvard University
University of Utah	Joan Robinson, Cambridge University

INDEX OF NAMES

Ainslie, George, 49n
Amundsen, Roald, 139, 141, 143
Arrow, Kenneth, 57
Ashby, Lord, 4, 4n
Augustine, Saint, 20, 192, 238
Avenarius, Richard, 233

Barash, David, 181
Becker, Gary S., 50n
Bellow, Saul, 135
Benton, William, 11
Blake, William, 130
Bloch, Ernst, 227
Bok, Sissela, 203n
Bosanquet, Bernard, 22
Braverman, Harry, 161n
Brennan, Donald, 115–16
Bradford, William, 128–31, 144
Brewster, Kingman, 15n, 25n, 26n,
   28n, 29n
Brooke, Rupert, 87, 94
Brown, Harold, 108
Burt, Sir Cyril, 170

Cabet, Etienne, 246
Campanella, Tommaso, 238
Campbell, Angus, 39
Carter, Jimmy, 108
Carver, Lord, 103
Cassirer, Ernst, 209n
Charles I, 151
Chaucer, Geoffrey, 138
Cherry-Garrard, Apsley, 139–42
Clark, Elly, 131–33, 135
Considérant, Victor Prosper, 246

Dahrendorf, Ralf, 6
Dallet, Joe, 88–90, 94, 103
Dawkins, Richard, 156
Descartes, René, 231, 233–34
Deschamps, Dôm, 239, 244
Dicey, A. V., 14
Dobzhansky, Thomas, 155
Dresser, Rebecca S., 68n

Eisenhower, General, 95, 104
Ellis, Albert, 213n
Elster, Jon, 49n, 58n, 65n
Erikson, Erik, 187–89, 193, 196
Ervin, F. R., 149n

Fried, Charles, 64n
Friedman, Milton, 10, 25
Foucault, Michel, 195n, 197
Fourier, François, 242
Frechtman, Bernard, 201n
Freud, Sigmund, 188, 190–91,
   193–94, 196–204, 206–9,
   211–13, 219, 245

Gandhi, Mahatma, 112
Gödel, Kurt, 236
Grechko, Marshal, 110, 123
Groddeck, Georg, 194
Groves, General Leslie Richard,
   90–91

Haldane, J. B. S., 84–86, 89, 94,
   102
Handlin, Oscar, 9, 38
Hallie, Philip, 113
Hayek, Friedrich, 9–10

Hegel, G. W. F., 236, 243
Heidegger, Martin, 232
Heims, Steve J., 84
Heisenberg, Werner, 236
Hirsch, Fred, 12, 18, 37
Hitler, Adolf, 91, 112–13
Hobbes, Thomas, 245
Homer, 138
Hoover, Herbert, 24
Horney, Karen, 211, 212n
Hume, David, 182
Husserl, Edmund, 232–33

Jefferson, Thomas, 31
Jensen, A. R., 149, 166, 181

Kamin, Leon, 171n
Kant, Immanuel, 181, 190–94,
    197–98, 201, 206–7, 209,
    219–20, 233, 236, 246–47
Kennan, George, 104–5, 116, 119,
    123–24
Kennedy, John F., 199
King, Martin Luther, 115
Kipling, Rudyard, 142
Küng, Hans, 188

Lasch, Christopher, 195
Lawrence, T. E., 87–88
LeForestier, Doctor, 114
Leibniz, G. W., 234
Lenin, V. I., 240
Lewis, Cecil Day, 92–94
Luce, Henry, 11
Lukacs, Georg, 54
Lumsden, W., 173n
Luther, Martin, 152

McCain, Roger A., 50n
McGovern, George, 23
McMullin, Ernan, 79

McNamara, Robert, 106–8, 110,
    115, 119
McPhee, John, 141
Mach, Ernst, 233
Mann, Horace, 31
Marcuse, Herbert, 200n
Margolis, Howard, 50n
Mark, V. H., 149n
Marx, Karl, 238, 242
Mead, Margaret, 10
Menninger, Karl, 194–95
Merleau-Ponty, Maurice, 232
Metzger, Colonel, 113–14
Meyer, Alfred, 72n
Millett, Kate, 202
More, Sir Thomas, 154
Mountbatten, Lord, 103
Moynihan, Daniel P., 23
Muirhead, J. H., 23n
Muller, H. J., 154

Napoleon, 126
Nixon, Richard, 23, 199

Oppenheimer, Frank, 86–87
Oppenheimer, Kitty, 88, 90
Oppenheimer, Robert, 86–92,
    94–96, 101, 103–4
Orwell, George, 89
Osborne, John, 93, 126
Owen, Wilfred, 85, 87, 89, 94, 102

Packer, Herbert, 195
Park, Clara, 131–36, 138, 144–45
Park, David, 134
Park, Jessica, 135
Pascal, Blaise, 234
Perry, Lord, 33
Polenberg, Richard, 89
Popper, Karl, 5

Rabi, I. I., 90
Ricoeur, Paul, 193
Rieff, Philip, 212
Rockefeller, Nelson, 160
Roosevelt, Franklin D., 27
Rotblat, Joseph, 91
Rousseau, Jean Jacques, 209, 233, 239–40
Russell, Bertrand, 91

Sartre, Jean Paul, 192–93, 201, 245
Schelling, Thomas C., 47n
Schmehling, Major, 114
Scitovsky, Tibor, 50n
Scott, Robert F., 139–42
Sen, Amartya K., 50n
Shakespeare, William, 138
Shaw, Bernard, 115
Smith, Alice, 86
Steiner, George, 54
Stigler, George J., 49n
Stirner, Max, 244
Stone, A. Douglas, 187
Stone, Alan A., 189n, 204n, 215n, 218n
Strotz, Robert H., 49n
Sweet, W. H., 149n
Szasz, Thomas, 196–98

Tanner, Obert C., 4, 125
Temple, Shirley, 221
Thorndike, E. L., 152
Tolstoy, Count Leo, 110
Tocqueville, Alexis de, 11
Torrey, E. Fuller, 192n
Trocmé, André, 113–15
Truman, Harry, 101

Unger, R. M., 187, 224n

Van Der Pitte, F. P., 190n
Von Neumann, John, 84

Ward, Lester F., 153
Washington, George, 11
Wavell, Sir Archibald, 106
Weiner, Charles, 86
Weizsacker, C. C. von, 50n
West, Rebecca, 20
Whitman, Walt, 94
Wiener, Norbert, 84
Wilson, E. O., 149, 157, 173n, 175n, 176, 178, 181
Wilson, Woodrow, 27
Winston, Gordon C., 50n
Wittgenstein, Ludwig, 233

Yankelovich, Daniel, 37, 38n
Youderian, Philip, 134